Financial Engineering in Islamic Finance the Way Forward

Financial Engineering in Islamic Finance the Way Forward

A Case for Shariah Compliant Derivatives

Hussain Kureshi, Septia Irani Mukhsia
and Mohsin Hayat

PARTRIDGE
A Penguin Random House Company

To order additional copies of this book, contact
Toll Free 800 101 2657 (Singapore)
Toll Free 1 800 81 7340 (Malaysia)
orders.singapore@partridgepublishing.com

www.partridgepublishing.com/singapore

Contents

LIST OF FIGURES

DEDICATION

Dedicated to the multitude of talented individuals within the Muslim world who have not found a voice. This book is dedicated to the possibilities of self actualization that many within the Muslim world are not yet able to experience.

EPIGRAPH

**If one can live with imperfections, we realize we live in a perfect world.
Luqman Zuhdi – Islamic Banker.**

FOREWORD

I know Hussein because we grew up together in the same town and knew the same people; but we never 'hung-out' with each other. Today I am proudly contributing to Hussein's book which brings us together as more than friends- we are contemporaries in creating Islamic financial history. An author of Islamic finance, at this nascent juncture, is no less than a pioneer. The ideas and thought that a writer evokes without abundant references certainly is worthy of acclaim. This book is a masterpiece of originality and academic stimulation and an essential tool for augmenting Islamic financial insight. Hussein has made a courageous effort in taking on the challenge to discuss and vividly illustrate the ever-complex subject of derivatives and that, too, from the Islamic perspective. I have yet to come across a more exhaustive narration of the principles and dynamics of Islamic derivatives. I feel honored to introduce this book to the financial world. I think Hussein and I will now be spending a lot of time together.

Bilal Rasul

Head of Department/ Registrar (Modarabas), Specialized Companies Division
Securities & Exchange Commission of Pakistan

PREFACE

Islamic banking to date has come a long way to engineer financial products that facilitate trade, which we feel is the main goal of financial intermediation. Financial intermediation cannot be an end in itself, it must serve to fulfil the needs of trade and commerce. It is when financial products move away from any real function, and returns on financial products are no longer linked to returns on actual economic activity, do we witness a world of synthetic banking, bubbles and crises.

Yet products like derivatives, trading techniques like short selling, margin purchases and contracts where the consideration or price is fluid, can and do mirror real trade transactions and therefore need to be explored by the *shariah* community and the community of Islamic bankers. Another area of deficit is the domain of agriculture financing, which requires the focus of Islamic banks, and this is not possible without the development of commodity exchanges, the presence of speculators and futures trading. Unless farmers are not able to lock in the prices for their goods, banks will be reluctant to finance them. The participants or counterparties to such transactions are not always end users / buyers, but often enough include an array of market makers, speculators, brokers and traders that have no interest in actually taking delivery of any goods, but resell their purchases to other buyers before taking delivery and earning spreads between buying and selling prices thereof.

The commodities industry in the developed world is ripe with exchanges, futures contracts and speculators, and they play an important role in determining the actual price of things from coffee beans to grain to crude palm oil. Restricting the behaviour of speculators so that prices are not artificially increased is the role of regulators or the *muhtasib,* in the context of the Muslim world, and they should execute this role with diligence and regard for public interest. Much of the Muslim world lives in an environment where one or two agricultural goods are subsidized, be it rice, wheat, or grains. These subsidies are extended to a rural poor, and financed by tax revenues from the urban middle class, the rich or the IMF. Ironically many leaders harp about the choking hold of the IMF and the World Bank, and launch political campaign based upon pointing fingers at cruel lenders, but do not realize (or disclose) that these loans are being used to fund subsidies on electricity tariffs, or flour or wheat prices or purchases of crude oil. Subsidies do not offer a long term solution in as much as exorbitant borrowing is for funding public expenditure.

Nevertheless, this book looks at some structures that allow a seller and a buyer to hedge their prices and looks at the critical problem of hedging and why it has become necessary in today's world of commerce and trade. We shall draw heavily upon references to our first work title, Contracts and Deals in Islamic Finance as many of the basic contracts in Islamic Finance are covered in this piece. We shall also explore certain tradition contracts of *bai,* that have some features of derivatives such as options in them and also look at certain conventional trades that can be easily replicated by the Islamic financial services industry provided the necessary market framework and infrastructure is made available.

Finance is not the domain of bankers anymore but pertains to the everyday life of ordinary citizens whose deposits, pension contributions, tax payments, insurance premiums are channelled through various institutions and used to finance assets, projects, governments and companies that affect our everyday lives.

Financial intermediation has made us all part and parcel of a system whether we want to or not, and I believe that 21st century citizens are if nothing else *homi economicus* and they must realize their role in the global marketplace.

ACKNOWLEDGEMENTS

Hussain Kureshi's Acknowledgements

It is part of the traditions of Islam to acknowledge one's teachers. To honour this tradition I have to recognize the team at International Centre for Education in Islamic Finance in Kuala Lumpur, Malaysia. Professor Yusuf Saleem for encouraging me to write my first paper on *salaam,* which was published in the ISRA Journal of 2014. Professor Ezamshah for his eloquent explanation of risk and how to price risk. Professor Rosly who painstakingly answered every question I had. Professor Azam who is as elegant as he is knowledgeable. Professor Razak for dropping the one pearl of wisdom that the rate of zakat should be the minimum profit rate applied to a credit financing contract. Professor Pisal for his humorous anecdotes, and last but not least, Professor Yusuf. I must also thank Ghaith Mahaini for urging me to write in the first place.

Finally I must acknowledge the warmth and hospitality of the peoples of Malaysia that gave me and my family a home and an environment conducive for me to finish my program.

A warm acknowledgment to the support of my mother, Mrs. Bilquise Azam Kureshi who patiently mentored me through the challenges of going back to school at the age of 42. Finally I must acknowledge "team oomi zoomi", which consists of Inaya, Azam and Sophiya who were forced to be separated from their homeland and loving grandparents, Mamajaani, Mamo and Dado, to keep me company while I finished my studies and the book. Finally, I cannot thank Hannah my wife enough for putting up with missing out on her career and my mood swings. I am indebted to you for that.

Moraad Chodhry, who is possibly the most prolific writers on banking and finance, to him I owe a word of thanks for the encouragement. Sydney Felicio and Jade Bailey at Penguin, thank you for patiently taking all my calls, and then again where will you find a writer who submits material weeks before deadlines.

Septya's Acknowledgements

In the name of God, the most Merciful, the most Beneficent.

I would like to extend my utmost gratitude to my father, Andi Mukhsia, who created our surnames as a mark of the beginning of a new legacy; and my mother, Endang Ratnawati, who has been my best personal critique and friend throughout my whole life. Without them I would not be where I am right now and I am forever grateful for their support and patience towards my every single antics and whim. I would like to also give my words of acknowledgements for Andre and Sheila, my dearest younger siblings who in their own ways always remind me to relax a little bit more and enjoy what life will bring to my plate.

I am indebted to all my lecturers in INCEIF for opening my eyes towards Islamic Banking and Finance. This is for Dr Sheikh Hamzah, Dr Eskandar, Dr Magda, Prof Zainal, Dr Yusuf Saleem, Dr Pisal, Madam Kartini, Prof Syed, and Prof Saiful, who were always ready with answers and enthusiasm in guiding us with their teachings. Not to forget, is my acknowledgements to my classmates and friends in INCEIF. My special thanks to Hidayah, Amalina, Anis Farhana, Muhammad Aminuddin, Hazazi, Asyhar, Shahrul Izzat, Najib Rosli, Aslam Iqbal, Muhammad Zulfadhlee, Ghaniat, Alladeenn, Salman, Imran, Ahmad Safiq, and many more I could not fit into this short passage, for always reminding and correcting my wrongs and keeping me entertained throughout my whole course in INCEIF.

I would like to extend yet another big acknowledgement towards Hussain Kureshi on the opportunity for being a part of this team since his first book together with Mohsin Hayat, *Contracts and Deals in Islamic Finance*. I would not be here writing this page without his push and encouragement on contribution for this book. I wish to also dedicate my endless thanks towards

Arfah, Ericka Leigh, Iqbal Karmana, Adinda Medina, Bismo Sulharyadi, and Nimas Sitorini for always being there, putting up with my stubbornness and constant criticism, and just simply being my friends over all these years.

Last but not least, I would like to acknowledge my best friend and partner in crime Adam for being the greatest support from day one, listening to all my ramblings and what not with a smile, giving me the pat on my back for every smallest things I do, and providing me the shoulder to lean on to whenever I need it for. And above all, I am eternally grateful to my Creator to have blessed me with such beautiful and contended life, filled with all the people whom I love and find joy from; a life which I would not trade for anything or anyone else in this whole world.

Mohsin Hayat Acknowledgements
I acknowledge my family, which has always been supportive of my projects. Even though my two boys Zidaan and Araz would rather play with me, they understand the value of work. I also acknowledge my colleague and office manager, Nasir Rabbani, who for many years has organized, documented, researched, MS "Excel-ed," and made available anything and everything upon request. His work has always been invaluable.

My thoughts and ideas have evolved through people I've met along the way; ranging from colleagues, friends, restaurant owners, entrepreneurs, emerging market CEOs, financiers, investors from New York, Hong Kong, Kuala Lumpur, Islamabad, Karachi, London, Singapore—people such as Glen Taylor, Yee Hui Wong, Punit Khanna, Kaman Leung, Iqbal Latif, and many more.

And at last but not the least, I acknowledge my coauthor, who did the heavy lifting for this project. Hussain is passionate, thoughtful, and driven by what he believes.

INTRODUCTION

How do we convert real hard assets into financial products? Banks by definition do not trade in real hard assets, they trade in financial products that are linked to real assets. Normal bank loans are linked to either one of the two, future income streams of a borrower, or future revenue generated from an asset that is financed. Bank loans are therefore linked directly to a stream of income, which may be linked to an intangible asset like a borrower's skill, or may be linked to a tangible asset, like a factory machine, which produces goods and services. Bank loans are rarely disbursed merely on the value of the collateral provided by a borrower. The same holds for Islamic Banking, which to date is still a credit sale based financing system as is much of the global banking system.

How can financial products, or paper products be engineered such that the parties to the product benefit in a manner that "mirrors" the behaviour of a real good or product or asset. For instance, banks are not in the business of buying inventories of aluminium at a cost price and then selling it onward for a profit to a 3rd party. But banks are in the business of trading in aluminium futures contracts which allows them (the banks) to benefit from movements in the real prices of the real asset.

What if a product was devised between Bank A and Party B, where B agrees (for a consideration of $.10 paid by the bank), to pay the bank $2, if the price of copper goes up by 5% within a specific time frame, in a specific market, such as the London Mercantile Exchange. If this product looks rather vague, have a closer look at investing in commodities indexes. Needless to say, B charges a fee for this contract or promise. If the price of copper does go up by 5%, B pays the Bank $2, if the price of copper does not go up by 5%, B retains the $.10 fees. These products closely resemble the end result of options trades, and cash settled futures transactions. There is no desire, will, or intent to hold any asset, but just to benefit from the movements in prices of an underlying asset, which in this case is aluminium..

Banks may not be able to buy houses directly, but benefit indirectly from the real estate market by the interest income earned from financing the purchase of houses. The higher the prices of houses go, the more $ amount of loans banks will extend and therefore earn higher interest. Real estate brokers earn higher commissions, sellers earn higher profits, buyers get squeezed and banks earn higher interest income. However, banks participate in the real estate market not as purchasers of homes but financiers of homes. The value of the loans extended are obviously linked to the values of the homes financed, but banks do not make income from the differences between cost prices and selling prices of real estate assets, they enjoy a fixed or floating income from interest payments made by borrowers. However, is it possible to structure financial products in which banks are allowed to make investments in that offer returns much alike capital returns on buying and selling houses? Banks are always on the lookout for additional sources of income, and in an environment of decreasing interest rates, banks in the developed world have been hard pressed to find ways of benefiting from an array of economic activity, to which traditionally they have not had direct involvement in. Can banks benefit from the price appreciation of houses on Edgeware Road in London for instance? Only if banks take depositors money and buy houses with it. This is not permissible by regulators. Imagine a bank that extends a loan to a customer for $1,000,000 to buy a house in London at an interest rate of just 3% for 20 years. Keeping the math very simple, the bank will earn only $30,000 in interest income per year, hardly enough to pay the mortgage officer's salary. If this very same home sells for $1,500,000 in 2 years, the owner of the home will make a profit of $500,000, probably pre-pay the loan and make a tidy profit at the end of the day. The bank would not have benefitted from the price appreciation of the asset, and suffers from a pre-paid loan. Unless the new buyer also finances the purchase of the house from the same bank, the bank in fact stands to lose more than benefit from the appreciation in price of the underlying house.

The question arises, as to how banks can hedge against such risks, and if possible benefit from such events? Can banks develop products that offer returns linked to the appreciation in the price of an underlying asset such as homes? The answer is yes? These products are called synthetic products that mirror returns on real assets. If a counterparty is willing to offer the bank $400,000 in cash, if the prices of homes in a specific street appreciate by 50%, the bank has found a way of investing in a financial product that offers returns linked to price increases. The question is why would any counterparty offer such a product?

The whole concept behind derivatives is to structure, develop, engineer, some form of paper contracts or promises that allow parties to the contract or the promise to benefit from movements in the prices of an underlying asset. Critics have called this gambling, the author disagrees. Gambling allows one party to earn monies or profits based upon random events of no economic value. Derivatives trading allows parties to benefit from movements in real prices, of real assets which are caused by movements in levels of demand and supply of a good, in their natural markets. There is no random event involved, and the changes in prices are caused by changes in market forces, not by the spinning of a wheel or the racing of a horse.

The Islamic Finance community has been averse to the idea of forward sales, margin purchases and derivatives, and have often confused traditional concepts such as *salaam* with futures, or *khiyar ul shart* or *urbun* with options. We have addressed these matters in our work titled "Contracts and Deals in Islamic Finance a User's Guide To *Shariah* Compliant Financial Transactions", published by Wiley and Sons.

The *shariah* community at large is afraid that endorsing the usage of options will create circumstance similar to what the developed world has seen in the Global Financial Crises of 2008. This fear is rooted as much in a lack of understanding of derivatives products as it does in a lack of the understanding of the causes behind the crises. Products like Credit Default Swaps, Collaterised Debt Obligations, Asset Backed Securities and such have complex structures and can have pay outs linked to the performance of residential mortgages, commercial mortgages, credit card portfolios, and automobile loan portfolios. The same products linked to non-residential mortgages and other kinds of loans did not go into default, only those products that were linked to residential mortgages went into default. This indicates that it is not the inherent product itself which is at fault, but the underlying economic activity or asset to which the product is linked to which created the damage. In the case of the US, this underlying exposure on residential mortgages created the crises as prices for houses plummeted by nearly 30% in a short span of time.

Derivatives contracts can be adopted by Islamic Finance using the concept of enforceable *wa'ds,* instead of the concepts of contracts of *bai* or sale, which have been the underlying pillars of *shariah* compliant products. We shall discuss the concept of *wa'd* in greater detail in our book, but in its simplest form a *wa'd* is a promise. A promise given by one party (the promisor) to another party (the promisee) to perform a specific act at some time in the future. A promisee can also make a counter promise and be a promisor with respect to the same party who then becomes a promisee and thus a beneficiary of a second promise. The universe of *wa'd* is free from many of the restrictions that apply to to Islamic contracts, such as 2 contracts cannot be conditional upon each other, there must be absence of uncertainty and elements of speculation, a seller can promise to sell something not in the sellers ownership in the future. These restrictions along with those that are placed on *rabbawi* items do not in essence apply to promises, even if they are financial promises. One party can promise a counter party any permissible act, and can be legally bound to that promise if the legal jurisdiction within that environment requires it to be so. Thus, I can promise to buy US dollars at a specific rate in the future from you, or exchange them for euros, or I can promise to buy commodities in the future from another party by only making a down payment, and if the counterparty agrees, I can settle the purchase in cash instead of with actual delivery.

All economic theories have some underlying assumptions, and are affective within certain parameters. A 30% change in any parameter in any model is likely to cause disturbances, and cause the model to collapse, as it may lead to averse changes in other parameters within the model which are difficult to predict. This does not mean the model is at fault, it means it has certain limitations, and fair enough, banks, hedge funds, pension funds, insurance companies and their Islamic counterparts should have these limitations of these models in mind before investing other people's monies.

We shall begin our work with a chapter on *bai istijrar;* a traditional contract of *bai* within the Islamic sphere, and explore features that resemble conventional options. In the chapter titled "No Name", the authors wish to propose structures that are modifications of existing contracts or have no precedence and therefore have no name as such. Yet these structures allow for flexibility in trading contracts. We shall also explore Islamic Profit Rate Swaps and Islamic Currency Swaps, as these are already in the market and then discuss contracts based on *wa'ds* or promises, financial promises be it at that.

The subsequent section will cover such hybrid instruments as Credit Default Swaps and Credit Linked Notes and look at Islamic Structured Products. Islamic Repurchase Agreements are already in the market and are employed by Treasuries of various Islamic Banks in managing liquidity. The remainder of the book will look at how options are structured, how they offer rights to various parties to the contract and how the "behave". We also explore the possibilities of futures and how changes to certain legal maxims would be required if futures and forwards trading can be executed on margin by Islamic Financial Institutions or not.

Last but not least, we look at the world of commodity trading, which should be close to the heart of Islamic Bankers as it deals directly in real, hard assets. We close our work, with a brief look at the concept of risk, value at risk, and attempt to explain VAR in everyday terms.

On the issue of commodities trading, the first level attack from many within the *shariah* community has been that much of commodities trading is speculative in nature and causes inflation. We disagree, prices increase when there is a surge in demand with limited supply or a lag in supply. Speculative buy orders are usually quickly accompanied by sell orders of equal amounts, usually within the span of a few seconds. With each buy order accompanied by a sale order, there is no net increase felt by the markets in aggregate demand. The act of hoarding which is justifiably criticised in Islam creates inflationary pressures as demand is created artificially, and inventories are hoarded such that supply begins to lag. Speculative trading does not have the same net impact, in fact, speculative trading allows for markets of commodities to remain liquid, and efficient, allowing for price discovery.

We hope this book will be useful to beginners and bankers alike, and we also hope that it will help to take the discourse of Islamic Finance to another level altogether.

CHAPTER 1

BAI ISTIJRAR

Bai Istijrar [1] is a contract of sale between a buyer and a seller, where the subject matter for the sale is in existence, delivery is made on the spot, payment is made on a deferred basis, but price is not determined at the time of contracting, rather a pricing mechanism is determined.

We shall examine this concept by looking at a simple trade transaction to understand what a pricing mechanism may look like.

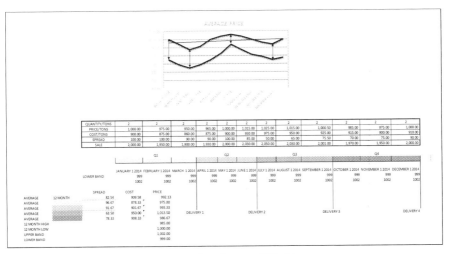

Figure 1.1 *Bai Istijrar* Workings

---

[1]   Securities Commission Malaysia, Guidelines-Islamic Securities_appendix 1, www.sc.com.my/wp-content/uploads/eng/html/icm/Guidelines-IslamicSecurities_apdx1.pdf8rc.

Party A contracts to sell wheat to Party B. Party B will purchase wheat as per a specific time table, at the end of each quarter (beginning from January 1st). The quantity specified will be 2 tons of wheat at each delivery. However, B offers to pay A on the 31st of December for all 4 deliveries taken during the course of the year of a total of 24 tons.

The subject matter is clear, the delivery date is clear, the time pf payment is also clear, but A and B are yet to agree on a price. Let us explore the options available to both parties at determining a price.

i)   Spot Price of Wheat at the time of contract (assuming January 1st) for all deliveries.
ii) Spot Price of Wheat at the time of contract for first delivery, then 30 days futures price, 60 days futures price, 90 days futures price etc as available on January 1st of the year.
iii) Average price between January 1st and December 31st.
iv) Spot Price of wheat on delivery date.
v)   Average price for 3 month interval prior to delivery date.
vi) Whatever the price will be on October 1st 2014, with an upper limit of $1002, and a lower limit of $999.

The price of wheat will fluctuate over this 12 month period depending on demand and supply for wheat in the markets. The seller would like to charge the highest price possible and the buyer would like to pay the lowest price possible. The buyer takes delivery every 90 days, which means the seller has the flexibility to source or grow the wheat at intervals of 90 days and would wish to ensure that costs are as low as possible during each 90 day interval. However, it is likely for any interval that wheat prices the cost of inputs will also increase as their will be greater demand for inputs. The seller must be able to anticipate costs correctly to earn a certain threshold return. Similarly, when prices for wheat fall, the costs of inputs also fall accordingly. One can see from the chart above that the Seller A actually enjoys higher spreads when prices are declining than when prices are increasing. This seems to be the case in industries where it is easy for suppliers to respond to increasing demand, by increasing production and therefore demand for raw materials.

Theoretically, the seller would prefer to sell in quarters where higher spreads can be earned, but this would require a complex contract where prices are not matched for the term of the delivery. If the buyer takes delivery in Quarter 2 and gives the seller the option to price the goods at the average price of Quarter 1, it would essentially be up to the buyer and seller what pricing mechanism to arrive at.

An average price arrangement over 12 months maybe agreeable, or the average price of the 3 months prior to each delivery may be agreeable, or the spot price on each delivery date may be agreeable, or a fixed price for all 4 deliveries may be agreeable to the parties. As long as the mechanism of the pricing is understood by both parties the options granted to both buyer and seller are bereft of any element of *gharar* or uncertainty.

Another right that can be granted by A to B, is that B does not pay the spot price of the underlying asset itself, which is wheat in this case, but instead pays on each payment a certain price for another asset say grain or rice. This application makes no sense in a normal sale transaction, but when takes into consideration how the prices of commodities are affected by prices of other commodities this factor does not come across as being ridiculous.

Furthermore, if the transaction is one between a bank customer and a bank, and the underlying sale is that of a specific commodity on an exchange such as *suq a sila* of Malaysia, then the sale price could be linked in fact to KLIBOR, LIBOR or any other benchmark rate for money, or it could be even benchmarked to the KLCI *Shariah* Compliant Index, S&P *Shariah* 500, or any other benchmark. In fact the price of the asset may be linked to the price of another asset. The price of wheat may be formulated as "price of potatoes + 2%" for instance. However, we are not discussing the benchmark asset only but also when the price is agreed upon between the two parties. Whether, it is the spot price of the asset on the day the contract is agreed upon, or some other price of the same asset (or another asset or benchmark), during the course of the validity of the contract.

Thus, if a buyer agrees to pay a price for wheat on March 31st 2015, on the spot price on that given day, as long as both parties agree to this, the transaction is deemed valid.

The contract of *istijrar* can behave like an options contract in that it allows the party to agree to a pricing mechanism for a particular asset over a specific period of time. Options differ in that they carry their own price as a standalone contract, and they allow a holder to exercise an option to buy or not, whereas in *istijrar* all rights are extended once a sale contract has been executed. The option is only on the right to buy at a certain price from a given range of prices.

Pricing Mechanism vs Price

Sales contracts with pricing mechanisms are already in place in Islamic Banks. *Murabaha and BBA* with floating rates offer a contract where a buyer is not sure what price will be paid at each instalment, but is aware of a pricing mechanism. We have explained this pricing mechanism in great detail in our previously cited work, in the chapter on *ibra*. The concept is rather simple, where a buyer and seller agree to a cap price, a maximum price the seller can charge. As payments are made by the buyer on a deferred basis the seller offers the buyer a discount from the capped price threshold based on market movements in benchmark interest rates. The amount of *ibra* is not predetermined but is linked to movements in interbank rates which are clearly disclosed to buyers or customers. *Istijrar* utilizes a similar concept of a pricing mechanism which is agreed upon between buyers and sellers alike.

Conclusion

We feel the contract of *bai istijrar* is rather unexplored and offers considerable potential. We invite the *shariah* community to deliberate in whether sales contracts with pre-agreed pricing mechanisms are valid just as contracts with pre-agreed prices, payments methods and delivery options are valid.

CHAPTER 2

PRODUCTS WITH NO NAMES

Product development in Islamic Finance has been linked to the following contracts:-

1) Murabahah
2) Bai Bithman Ajil
3) Wadiah
4) Qard
5) Mudharabah
6) Musharikah
7) Salaam
8) Istisna
9) Ibra
10) Hibah
11) Hawalah
12) Bai Ul Sarf
13) Bai Ul Urbun
14) Bai Ul Wafa
15) Wakalah
16) Kafalah
17) And Ijara

We propose departing from these structures and explore either variants or new structures that may not be linked to these 17 contracts in any shape or form.

MODIFICATIONS TO *SALAAM*

CONTRACT	ASSET IN EXISTENCE	PRICE AGREED	DELIVERY	PAYMENT
SALAAM	NO	YES	DEFERRED	IN FULL ON SPOT
ISTISNA	NO	YES	DEFERRED	IN STAGES
MURABAHAH	YES	YES	SPOT	DEFERRED

Figure 2.1 Sales Contracts

The contracts of *salaam, istisna* and *murabahah* are sale based contracts where either the delivery of the subject matter of the sale is deferred or the payment of the purchase price is deferred. We have written extensively on the applications of the contract of *salaam,* in the June edition of the ISRA Journal for 2014, but invite the reader to consider other modifications of the contract.

The *salaam* contract requires the buyer and seller to agree to a purchase price at the time of contracting. This price is typically discounted from the spot price of the underlying, as in essence, the buyer is financing the manufacture or cultivation of the underlying asset. The buyer is fully exposed to performance risk on the seller. As per the rules of the *shariah*[2], where a seller cannot sell an asset not in his ownership, the buyer cannot even secure another buyer for the underlying until the seller makes good on delivery. This places a lot of risk on the buyer.

1st Modification

We propose the following modification to the *salaam* contract. The buyer and seller agree to a purchase price, but the buyer does not pay the purchase price in full. The buyer pays a percentage of the purchase price to the seller. The seller is allowed to use this partial payment to finance securing the underlying asset in the required quantity. In this manner, the exposure of the buyer to the seller is limited.

---

[2]   "Bargain not about that which is not with you. Sahih Muslim, Kitab Al-Buyu, (The Book Pertaining to Business Transaction).

2nd Modification

This modification, follows the same steps as Modification 1, with a slight difference. The buyer is allowed to secure delivery from the seller with only payment of a partial purchase price. The seller is not allowed to use the purchase price to finance securing delivery of the underlying asset. In fact, the down payment is kept in a neutral account known as a margin account.

The buyer and seller agree that the buyer and seller both must always maintain 10% of the floating market price of the asset in the margin account at all times. In this manner neither seller nor buyer is able to default on payment or performance.

With these modifications, the *salaam* contract resembles a futures or forward contract, where a buyer and seller agree to sale/purchase in the future at a pre-determined price, but the buyer only pays for the goods on margin.

3rd Enhancement

We also propose the buyer in this case, if he or she is an intermediary be allowed to sell the asset to a 3rd party before taking delivery. These enhancement would certainly increase activity in futures contracts within the sphere of Islamic Finance.

4th Enhancement

The fourth enhancement we propose looks at the issue of price. We propose the buyer and seller be allowed greater flexibility in the settlement of the price. The actual price need not be agreed upon at the time of contracting, nor be paid in full or in margin. Rather, the calculation of the final price and payment thereof may be deferred till the time of delivery. The final price may be the spot price on the delivery date, or the average price between the contracting date and the delivery date. This enhancement would not sit well with many *shariah* scholars who feel that either payment or delivery of asset can be deferred in a contract of *bai,* both cannot.

We therefore propose, the above contract need not be under the concept of *bai* and *salaam,* but be drafted under the concept of *wa'd,* where the buyer promises to buy a certain asset in the future at a price to be determined by some pre-agreed mechanism. The seller promises to deliver the subject matter of the sale at a future date and agrees to the terms of the buyer.

5th Enhancement

The concept of *salaam* applied to financial assets can be looked at more closely. A buyer may pay a discount price in full or on margin for equities or *sukuks*, to be delivered in future. Another proposed concept to consider is that the payment for the asset, whether in full or on margin, be not in cash but also in the shape of financial assets.

A buyer in this case, offers a seller 10,000 shares in a *shariah* compliant company as down payment for purchase of 30,000 *sukuk*, of similar rating for future delivery. At final delivery of the *sukuk* instruments, the purchase price may be paid in cash, or partially in cash and the remainder with the equities held by the buyer.

A Liability Contract

LIABILITY CONTRACT	PRINCIPAL GUARANTEED	PROFIT GUARANTEED	PAYMENT OF *HIBAH*
WADIAH	YES	NONE	APPLICABLE
QARD	YES	NONE	APPLCABLE
MUDHARABAH	NO	NONE	APPLICABLE

Figure 2.2 Liability Contracts

The contracts above are typically found in the liability side of an Islamic Bank's balance sheet. The contracts of *wadiah* and *qard* allow Islamic Banks to mobilise deposits without guaranteeing any returns other than the principal amount. Funds are typically rewarded using the contract of *hibah*, the mechanics of this is fully illustrated in our work Contracts and Deals in Islamic Finance. These contracts place the burden of risk entirely upon the bank that mobilises the funds.

The contract of *mudharabah* is also utilised to mobilise funds whereby the recipient of the funds need not guarantee any profits but must agree on a Profit Sharing Ratio, by virtue of which any earned profits can be distributed by the capital provider and the capital recipient. All losses are borne by the capital provider, unless it can be proven that the recipient was negligent or guilty of misconduct. If the recipient in this case is an Islamic Bank, then the contract of *mudharabah,* in its pure sense places the burden of risk entirely on the shoulders of the capital provider or the depositors.

We propose a very simple structure. One party seeking to mobilise funds from a capital provider contracts to utilise the raised capital in certain investments, whereby returns generated will be shared as per a floating Profit Sharing Ratio and Losses shared on the basis of a Floating Loss Sharing Ratio. In this manner an Islamic Bank that mobilises funds is not absolved from losses, nor is the depositor absolved from any risk sharing mechanism. The ratios at which both the Islamic Bank and the depositors share losses and profits are changed at regular intervals to maintain an incentive structure that may greatly benefit one party at one time and the counterparty at another time.

Ijara with deferred payment.

The structure we propose is not entirely unique as certain Islamic Banks have employed it in various structured products. The contract of *ijara* is rather simple, and we have referred to it in other works. A contract between 2 parties, A and B, whereby an asset owned by A is leased to B for a specific period of time. The asset remains in the ownership of A for the period of the contract, but B is granted the right to enjoy the *manfaat,* or the usufruct of the asset. B pays A a rental fee for this privilege. We focus here on the rental terms. In typical contracts of *ijara,* the rental payments match the period of enjoying the usufruct to a certain degree. For instance A leases a car to B from January 1st 2014 to June 1st 2014, and B agrees to pay the rent for the car on the 31st of January, or the last day if the month in which the usufruct was enjoyed. Such structures are the norm in car leasing arrangements and most readers would be familiar with them.

We offer a structure, where the rental payments are deferred and may commence even after the asset has been returned by the lessee to the lessor. The cash flows in this case would not match the duration during which the lessee enjoys the usufruct of the asset. However, an important point to note is that the rent only becomes due when the usufruct of the asset has been enjoyed.

Lease (*ijara*) and lease *(ijara)* back

Lease and lease back is a structure we have encountered in certain Islamic Banks. In this structure an asset is owned by Party A and leased to Party B for a specific rent for a specific time. At the same time Party B leases the same asset back to A for another $ amount of rent for a specific time. If the first rent from B to A is paid in lump sum on the spot (prior to enjoying full usufruct), and the second rent from A to B is paid on a deferred basis, and the deferred repayment is greater than the spot rent, the net ash flows replicate a loan secured by A (from B) equivalent to the spot rent, repaid in instalments to B to the amount of the deferred rent. The difference between the 2 rental rates would be the profit for B and the cost for A.

Contracts of *rahn*

Rahn is a contract which allows one party to place a certain asset with another party as collateral to ensure fulfilment of certain debt obligations. These debt obligations may be to perform a certain task as in *salaam,* or to pay a deferred purchase price as in cases of *murabaha* and *BBA,* or in extending a loan as in *qard. Rahn* may also be obtained by a lessor when a certain asset is leased out to a lessee to ensure timely payments of rent. Typically, the asset placed under *rahn* is typically thought to be a fixed asset, be it a property, a vehicle, gold, stock of inventory or such. In a typical corporate loan in conventional finance, one finds the language of placing a "charge on fixed and current assets of a company". Current assets include accounts receivables. At this juncture we therefore look at the possibility of placing financial assets under *rahn,* such as accounts receivables. Can receivables due to a manufacturing or services company, be assigned to an Islamic Bank, and if they can, can an Islamic Bank use revenues from home mortgages to place as collateral to obtain funding from a 3rd party? Furthermore, can financial assets like receivables be used to pay margin on futures contracts or kept as collateral in repurchase agreements. Can a seller in a deferred delivery contract provide the buyer with financial assets such as *shariah compliant* stocks, or receivables owed by another client as collateral? This dialogue ultimately converges to the notion of using receivables against one loan to collaterize another loan and raises the issue of how far Islamic Banks can go to leverage their balance sheets.

Conclusion

We draw the attention of scholars and practitioners alike to revisit the current usage of all contracts employed in Islamic Finance and reflect if certain variations can evolve without infringing on the spirit of the Law. We do not wish to promote any practices that violate the letter and the form of the Law, but feel quite confident that there is room for adaptation and interpretation.

CHAPTER 3

ISLAMIC CONTRACTS OF SWAPS OR *MUBADLAH*

Swaps are transactions that allow one party to swap their position in an asset with that of another counterparty. The counterparty may hold a position in the same asset or it may hold a position in another asset. The Arabic word for swap is merely *mubadalah*.

Swaps can be executed for currencies, where Party A holds $ and wants to swap them for Party B's Euros. Swaps can be executed for cash flows, where A receives fixed interest payments and B receives interest payments which are revised every quarter and are floating in nature.

Essentially parties to a swap contract can swap any asset thy wish. For instance a real estate owner may sway a property in UK for a property of similar value in Paris for instance. What is essential to understand is what the motivation of such a swap maybe and what consideration is paid to make the swap. For instance our real estate owner may feel that prices will increase in Paris faster than in comparison to UK, and may also feel that the Euro to GBP levels will remain stable so that the appreciation in property prices in Paris can be actualized.

A bank may want to swap its holdings of equities and bonds with that of another bank, for a limited time. A bank may want to swap its receivables in $ with receivables in GBP. Both parties to the swap have opposing expectations of the returns on their portfolios; that is why they are willing to make the swap.

We shall illustrate this point with a simple example using interest rates.

Bank A has a loan portfolio that earns a fixed interest rate of 4%. Bank B has a similar portfolio but with a floating interest rate mechanism in place that earns LIBOR + 2%. For the first scenario we assume that LIBOR increases every quarter and the second scenario we assume LIBOR decreases.

	LOAN AMOUNT	COST OF FUND	FIXED RATE LOAN		SPREAD		VARIABLE RATE LOAN		SPREAD			FIXED RATES	FLOATING
				CASH FLOWS A			CASH FLOWS B					CF A	CF B
							INTEREST RATES INCREASE						RATES INC.
			LIBOR 4%			LIBOR	4.00%					6%	LIBOR + 200 BPS
			SPREAD 2%			SPREAD	2.00%						
1	100,000.00	4.00%	4,000.00	6.00%	6,000.00	2,000.00	6.00%	6,000.00	2,000.00	1	6,000.00	6,000.00
2	100,000.00	4.00%	4,000.00	6.00%	6,000.00	2,000.00	6.00%	6,000.00	2,000.00	2	6,000.00	6,000.00
3	100,000.00	4.00%	4,000.00	6.00%	6,000.00	2,000.00	6.00%	6,000.00	2,000.00	3	6,000.00	6,000.00
			LIBOR 4%			LIBOR	5.00%						
			SPREAD 2%			SPREAD	2.00%						
4	100,000.00	4.00%	4,000.00	6.00%	6,000.00	2,000.00	7.00%	7,000.00	3,000.00	4	6,000.00	7,000.00
5	100,000.00	4.00%	4,000.00	6.00%	6,000.00	2,000.00	7.00%	7,000.00	3,000.00	5	6,000.00	7,000.00
6	100,000.00	4.00%	4,000.00	6.00%	6,000.00	2,000.00	7.00%	7,000.00	3,000.00	6	6,000.00	7,000.00
			LIBOR 4%			LIBOR	6.00%						
			SPREAD 2%			SPREAD	2.00%						
7	100,000.00	4.00%	4,000.00	6.00%	6,000.00	2,000.00	8.00%	8,000.00	4,000.00	7	6,000.00	8,000.00
8	100,000.00	4.00%	4,000.00	6.00%	6,000.00	2,000.00	8.00%	8,000.00	4,000.00	8	6,000.00	8,000.00
9	100,000.00	4.00%	4,000.00	6.00%	6,000.00	2,000.00	8.00%	8,000.00	4,000.00	9	6,000.00	8,000.00
			LIBOR 4%			LIBOR	7.00%						
			SPREAD 2%			SPREAD	2.00%						
10	100,000.00	4.00%	4,000.00	6.00%	6,000.00	2,000.00	9.00%	9,000.00	5,000.00	10	6,000.00	9,000.00
11	100,000.00	4.00%	4,000.00	6.00%	6,000.00	2,000.00	9.00%	9,000.00	5,000.00	11	6,000.00	9,000.00
12	100,000.00	4.00%	4,000.00	6.00%	6,000.00	2,000.00	9.00%	9,000.00	5,000.00	12	6,000.00	9,000.00
										TOTAL	72,000.00	90,000.00

Figure 3.1 Interest Rate Swaps – Increasing Rates.

We see from the above table that Bank A stands to earn $72,000 from its loan portfolio. If interest rates increase i.e. LIBOR increases by 1% every quarter, or A expects rates to increase, B would earn $90,000 in the same period, on a similar loan portfolio with a similar credit rating but a different pricing mechanism.

A can offer to swap its cash flows with those of B. B may consider the offer if its expectations are not as robust on increases in LIBOR. B agrees to swap for a consideration of $5,000.

The effect of the swap is as follows:-

Cash Flows of A	=	-$5,000 paid to swap cash flows with B
	=	-$72,000 swapped
	=	+ $90,000 received in exchange for $70,000
Net Cash Flows for A	=	$13,000

A earns $13,000 extra from the swap. A surrenders $70,000 of cash flows, to B, in exchange for $90,000 for a consideration of $5,000. A pays $77,000 to earn expected cash flows of $90,000.

(-$72,000 – $5,000 + $90,000 = $13,000). Cash flows for B are as follows:-

Cash Flows of B	=	-$90,000 surrender cash flows to A.
	=	+ 5,000 income for agreeing to swap
	=	+ $72,000 cash flows of B.
Net Cash Flows for B	=	-$13,000 from the swap.

Although B accrues $72,000 from the cash flows of B and takes in $5,000 for the swap arrangement, this is still $13,000 less than what B would have earned by retaining its portfolio. B made a wrong guess on movements in interest rates whereas A made a correct guess. B would receive the $5,000 cash up front and would reinvest it at the Risk Free Rate to earn extra income. If $5,000 is invested in LIBOR, B would earn an additional $200.

The transaction can be interpreted as a sale of fixed cash flows for floating cash flows between A and B at a mutually agreed price of $5,000.

We can examine another scenario where interest rates decline. This sequence of cash flows is represented by the column B".

	LOAN AMOUNT	COST OF FUND	CASH FLOWS A			CASH FLOWS B"					CF A	CF B"
			FIXED RATE LOAN		SPREAD	VARIABLE RATE LOAN		SPREAD				
						LIBOR	4.00%					
						SPREAD	2.00%					
1	100,000.00	4.00%	4,000.00	6.00%	6,000.00	2,000.00	6.00%	6,000.00	2,000.00	1	6,000.00	6,000.00
2	100,000.00	4.00%	4,000.00	6.00%	6,000.00	2,000.00	6.00%	6,000.00	2,000.00	2	6,000.00	6,000.00
3	100,000.00	4.00%	4,000.00	6.00%	6,000.00	2,000.00	6.00%	6,000.00	2,000.00	3	6,000.00	6,000.00
						LIBOR	3.50%					
						SPREAD	2.00%					
4	100,000.00	4.00%	4,000.00	6.00%	6,000.00	2,000.00	5.50%	5,500.00	1,500.00	4	6,000.00	5,500.00
5	100,000.00	4.00%	4,000.00	6.00%	6,000.00	2,000.00	5.50%	5,500.00	1,500.00	5	6,000.00	5,500.00
6	100,000.00	4.00%	4,000.00	6.00%	6,000.00	2,000.00	5.50%	5,500.00	1,500.00	6	6,000.00	5,500.00
						LIBOR	3.00%					
						SPREAD	2.00%					
7	100,000.00	4.00%	4,000.00	6.00%	6,000.00	2,000.00	5.00%	5,000.00	1,000.00	7	6,000.00	5,000.00
8	100,000.00	4.00%	4,000.00	6.00%	6,000.00	2,000.00	5.00%	5,000.00	1,000.00	8	6,000.00	5,000.00
9	100,000.00	4.00%	4,000.00	6.00%	6,000.00	2,000.00	5.00%	5,000.00	1,000.00	9	6,000.00	5,000.00
						LIBOR	2.50%					
						SPREAD	2.00%					
10	100,000.00	4.00%	4,000.00	6.00%	6,000.00	2,000.00	4.50%	4,500.00	500.00	10	6,000.00	4,500.00
11	100,000.00	4.00%	4,000.00	6.00%	6,000.00	2,000.00	4.50%	4,500.00	500.00	11	6,000.00	4,500.00
12	100,000.00	4.00%	4,000.00	6.00%	6,000.00	2,000.00	4.50%	4,500.00	500.00	12	6,000.00	4,500.00
										TOTAL	72,000.00	63,000.00

Figure 3.2 Interest Rate Swaps - Decreasing Rates.

A still feels that LIBOR will increase and is willing to pay $5,000 to swap its cash flows with those of B". However, as the conclusion of the contract A loses out as follows:-

Cash Flows of A	=	- $72,000 in swap arrangement
	=	- $5,000 to pay for swap
	=	+ $63,000 in actual receipts from B
Net Cash Flow	=	- $14,000.

Cash flows for B are however:-

Cash Flows of B	=	+ $5,000 as price for swap
	=	+ $72,000 as cash flows of A
	=	- $63,000 as cash flows swapped with A
Net Cash Flow	=	+$ 14,000.

The net gain of one party is the exact net loss of the counterparty, this is a consequence of both parties have exactly opposite views or expectations of whether interest rates will increase or decrease in the future.

The scenario becomes a little more complicated if the two cash flows are in different currencies.

Interest Rate Swap in US $ and Yen

For illustration purposes we assume an American company based in America can borrow $100,000 at 6%, whereas a Japanese firm in Japan can borrow the equivalent amount in Yen which at an exchange rate of $1 = yen 1.039 comes 10,139,0000 at 4%. The American firm needs to borrow in Yen, to expand its operations in Japan, and the Japanese firm needs to borrow in US$ expand its operations in Japan. Assuming further that an American firm cannot borrow in Japan at lower rates than 4%, and the Japanese firm cannot borrow in the US for less than 6%, each company borrows in its own domestic market and an intermediary swaps the cash flows, such that the US firm pays off the loan in Japan, and the Japanese firm pays off the loan in the US.

| | AMERICAN FIRM - AMERICAN BORROWING | | | | | JAPANESE FIRM - JAPANESE BORROWING | | | | | | BANK'S |
| | BORROWING IN $ | | | | | BORROWING IN YEN | | | | | SWAP SPREAD | COMMISSION |
	LOAN AMOUNT	RATE	EMI $	YEN RATE	in Y		LOAN AMOUNT	RATE	EMI Y	$ RATE	in $		10%
1	100,000.00	6.00%	6,000.00	101.39	608,340.00	1	10,139,000.00	4.00%	405,560.00	0.009863	4,000.00	2,000.00	200.00
2	100,000.00	6.00%	6,000.00	101.39	608,340.00	2	10,139,000.00	4.00%	405,560.00	0.009863	4,000.00	2,000.00	200.00
3	100,000.00	6.00%	6,000.00	101.39	608,340.00	3	10,139,000.00	4.00%	405,560.00	0.009863	4,000.00	2,000.00	200.00
4	100,000.00	6.00%	6,000.00	101.39	608,340.00	4	10,139,000.00	4.00%	405,560.00	0.009863	4,000.00	2,000.00	200.00
5	100,000.00	6.00%	6,000.00	101.39	608,340.00	5	10,139,000.00	4.00%	405,560.00	0.009863	4,000.00	2,000.00	200.00
6	100,000.00	6.00%	6,000.00	101.39	608,340.00	6	10,139,000.00	4.00%	405,560.00	0.009863	4,000.00	2,000.00	200.00
7	100,000.00	6.00%	6,000.00	101.39	608,340.00	7	10,139,000.00	4.00%	405,560.00	0.009863	4,000.00	2,000.00	200.00
8	100,000.00	6.00%	6,000.00	101.39	608,340.00	8	10,139,000.00	4.00%	405,560.00	0.009863	4,000.00	2,000.00	200.00
9	100,000.00	6.00%	6,000.00	101.39	608,340.00	9	10,139,000.00	4.00%	405,560.00	0.009863	4,000.00	2,000.00	200.00
10	100,000.00	6.00%	6,000.00	101.39	608,340.00	10	10,139,000.00	4.00%	405,560.00	0.009863	4,000.00	2,000.00	200.00
11	100,000.00	6.00%	6,000.00	101.39	608,340.00	11	10,139,000.00	4.00%	405,560.00	0.009863	4,000.00	2,000.00	200.00
12	100,000.00	6.00%	6,000.00	101.39	608,340.00	12	10,139,000.00	4.00%	405,560.00	0.009863	4,000.00	2,000.00	200.00
			72,000.00		7,300,080.00				4,866,720.00		48,000.00	24,000.00	2,400.00

Figure 3.3 FCY interest payment swaps

The table above illustrates this point. The Japanese firm borrows Yen 10,139,000 in Japan at 4% and lends it to the US firm for 4%. The US firm borrows $100,000 in the US at 6% and lends it to the Japanese firm at 6%. A commercial bank facilitates this arrangement and charges a 10% commission on the spread. The US firm makes total interest payments of just Yen 4,866,720 or $48,000 on the loan in Japan and saves $24,000 in interest expense. If the cost of borrowing for the Japanese firm in Japan would have been 8%, the firm saves 2% or $20,000 on its borrowing costs. In reality each party has swapped their loan obligations. The US firm would pay 6% to borrow $100,000 in the US, less than what a Japanese firm may be able to borrow at. Similarly, the Japanese firm borrows at 4% in Japan, a rate a US firm could not avail from Japanese banks. As each company needs to raise funds in another country, in another currency, where they do not enjoy a competitive advantage in terms of borrowing costs, each company simply borrows in its domestic market and swaps the loan payments with its international counterpart.

The swap arrangement only makes sense if the Japanese firm to borrow in the US at rates above 6%, and the US firm in Japan at rates above 4%.

Islamic Profit Rate Swap

In this scenario both parties will merely generate cash flows in their respective currencies with a deferred payment sale. Subsequently, each party will exchange cash flows on the basis of the contract of *mubadlah*. These cash flows are constructed by sale and buy agreements for commodity executed by each firm in their respective currencies. These processes will be illustrated in detail in the next chapters.

Impact of changes in currency exchange rate.

To understand the impact of changes in exchange rates we simply change the US$ to Yen exchange rate to observe the impact on the net spreads. We shall make the changes slightly robust so that the reader may easily observe the impact on our swap arrangement.

Scenario 1. US $ increases to the Yen.

	AMERICAN FIRM - AMERICAN BORROWING						JAPANESE FIRM BORROWING							SWAP SPREAD	BANK'S COMMISSION
	BORROWING IN $						BORROWING IN YEN								10%
	LOAN AMOUNT	RATE	EMI $	YEN RATE	in Y		LOAN AMOUNT	RATE	EMI Y	$ RATE	in $				
1	100,000.00	6.00%	6,000.00	105.00	630,000.00	1	10,139,000.00	4.00%	405,560.00	0.009524	3,862.48			2,137.52	213.75
2	100,000.00	6.00%	6,000.00	105.00	630,000.00	2	10,139,000.00	4.00%	405,560.00	0.009524	3,862.48			2,137.52	213.75
3	100,000.00	6.00%	6,000.00	105.00	630,000.00	3	10,139,000.00	4.00%	405,560.00	0.009524	3,862.48			2,137.52	213.75
4	100,000.00	6.00%	6,000.00	105.00	630,000.00	4	10,139,000.00	4.00%	405,560.00	0.009524	3,862.48			2,137.52	213.75
5	100,000.00	6.00%	6,000.00	105.00	630,000.00	5	10,139,000.00	4.00%	405,560.00	0.009524	3,862.48			2,137.52	213.75
6	100,000.00	6.00%	6,000.00	105.00	630,000.00	6	10,139,000.00	4.00%	405,560.00	0.009524	3,862.48			2,137.52	213.75
7	100,000.00	6.00%	6,000.00	105.00	630,000.00	7	10,139,000.00	4.00%	405,560.00	0.009524	3,862.48			2,137.52	213.75
8	100,000.00	6.00%	6,000.00	105.00	630,000.00	8	10,139,000.00	4.00%	405,560.00	0.009524	3,862.48			2,137.52	213.75
9	100,000.00	6.00%	6,000.00	105.00	630,000.00	9	10,139,000.00	4.00%	405,560.00	0.009524	3,862.48			2,137.52	213.75
10	100,000.00	6.00%	6,000.00	105.00	630,000.00	10	10,139,000.00	4.00%	405,560.00	0.009524	3,862.48			2,137.52	213.75
11	100,000.00	6.00%	6,000.00	105.00	630,000.00	11	10,139,000.00	4.00%	405,560.00	0.009524	3,862.48			2,137.52	213.75
12	100,000.00	6.00%	6,000.00	105.00	630,000.00	12	10,139,000.00	4.00%	405,560.00	0.009524	3,862.48			2,137.52	213.75
	TOTALS		72,000.00		7,560,000.00				4,866,720.00		46,349.71			25,650.29	2,565.03

Figure 3.4 US $ strengthens wrt Yen

If the $ strengthens with respect to the Yen, and $1 converts to Yen 105, the savings to the US based firm would increase from $24,000 to $26,650.29. However, this converse weakening of the yen will result in making $ interest payments more expensive. The same loan will require Yen 7,560,000 to service up from Yen 7,300,080.

Scenario 2. US $ weakens to the Yen

| | AMERICAN FIRM - AMERICAN BORROWING | | | | | JAPANESE FIRM BORROWING | | | | | | SWAP SPREAD | BANK'S COMMISSION |
| | BORROWING IN $ | | | | | BORROWING IN YEN | | | | | | | |
	LOAN AMOUNT	RATE	EMI $	YEN RATE	in Y		LOAN AMOUNT	RATE	EMI Y	$ RATE	in $		10%
1	100,000.00	6.00%	6,000.00	100.00	600,000.00	1	10,139,000.00	4.00%	405,560.00	0.010000	4,055.60	1,944.40	194.44
2	100,000.00	6.00%	6,000.00	100.00	600,000.00	2	10,139,000.00	4.00%	405,560.00	0.010000	4,055.60	1,944.40	194.44
3	100,000.00	6.00%	6,000.00	100.00	600,000.00	3	10,139,000.00	4.00%	405,560.00	0.010000	4,055.60	1,944.40	194.44
4	100,000.00	6.00%	6,000.00	100.00	600,000.00	4	10,139,000.00	4.00%	405,560.00	0.010000	4,055.60	1,944.40	194.44
5	100,000.00	6.00%	6,000.00	100.00	600,000.00	5	10,139,000.00	4.00%	405,560.00	0.010000	4,055.60	1,944.40	194.44
6	100,000.00	6.00%	6,000.00	100.00	600,000.00	6	10,139,000.00	4.00%	405,560.00	0.010000	4,055.60	1,944.40	194.44
7	100,000.00	6.00%	6,000.00	100.00	600,000.00	7	10,139,000.00	4.00%	405,560.00	0.010000	4,055.60	1,944.40	194.44
8	100,000.00	6.00%	6,000.00	100.00	600,000.00	8	10,139,000.00	4.00%	405,560.00	0.010000	4,055.60	1,944.40	194.44
9	100,000.00	6.00%	6,000.00	100.00	600,000.00	9	10,139,000.00	4.00%	405,560.00	0.010000	4,055.60	1,944.40	194.44
10	100,000.00	6.00%	6,000.00	100.00	600,000.00	10	10,139,000.00	4.00%	405,560.00	0.010000	4,055.60	1,944.40	194.44
11	100,000.00	6.00%	6,000.00	100.00	600,000.00	11	10,139,000.00	4.00%	405,560.00	0.010000	4,055.60	1,944.40	194.44
12	100,000.00	6.00%	6,000.00	100.00	600,000.00	12	10,139,000.00	4.00%	405,560.00	0.010000	4,055.60	1,944.40	194.44
	TOTALS		72,000.00		7,200,000.00				4,866,720.00		48,667.20	23,332.80	2,333.28

Figure 3.5 US $ weakens to the Yen

However, if the US $ weakens to the Yen, such that $1 = 100 Yen instead of 101.39 Yen, savings pass onto the Japanese firm and the US firm ends up paying $667.20 more.

Scenario 3. Interest Rates in US increase.

| | AMERICAN FIRM - AMERICAN BORROWING | | | | | JAPANESE FIRM BORROWING | | | | | | SWAP SPREAD | BANK'S COMMISSION |
| | BORROWING IN $ | | | | | BORROWING IN YEN | | | | | | | |
	LOAN AMOUNT	RATE	EMI $	YEN RATE	in Y		LOAN AMOUNT	RATE	EMI Y	$ RATE	in $		10%
1	100,000.00	7.00%	7,000.00	101.39	709,730.00	1	10,139,000.00	4.00%	405,560.00	0.009863	4,000.00	3,000.00	300.00
2	100,000.00	7.00%	7,000.00	101.39	709,730.00	2	10,139,000.00	4.00%	405,560.00	0.009863	4,000.00	3,000.00	300.00
3	100,000.00	7.00%	7,000.00	101.39	709,730.00	3	10,139,000.00	4.00%	405,560.00	0.009863	4,000.00	3,000.00	300.00
4	100,000.00	7.00%	7,000.00	101.39	709,730.00	4	10,139,000.00	4.00%	405,560.00	0.009863	4,000.00	3,000.00	300.00
5	100,000.00	7.00%	7,000.00	101.39	709,730.00	5	10,139,000.00	4.00%	405,560.00	0.009863	4,000.00	3,000.00	300.00
6	100,000.00	7.00%	7,000.00	101.39	709,730.00	6	10,139,000.00	4.00%	405,560.00	0.009863	4,000.00	3,000.00	300.00
7	100,000.00	7.00%	7,000.00	101.39	709,730.00	7	10,139,000.00	4.00%	405,560.00	0.009863	4,000.00	3,000.00	300.00
8	100,000.00	7.00%	7,000.00	101.39	709,730.00	8	10,139,000.00	4.00%	405,560.00	0.009863	4,000.00	3,000.00	300.00
9	100,000.00	7.00%	7,000.00	101.39	709,730.00	9	10,139,000.00	4.00%	405,560.00	0.009863	4,000.00	3,000.00	300.00
10	100,000.00	7.00%	7,000.00	101.39	709,730.00	10	10,139,000.00	4.00%	405,560.00	0.009863	4,000.00	3,000.00	300.00
11	100,000.00	7.00%	7,000.00	101.39	709,730.00	11	10,139,000.00	4.00%	405,560.00	0.009863	4,000.00	3,000.00	300.00
12	100,000.00	7.00%	7,000.00	101.39	709,730.00	12	10,139,000.00	4.00%	405,560.00	0.009863	4,000.00	3,000.00	300.00
	TOTALS		84,000.00		8,516,760.00				4,866,720.00		48,000.00	36,000.00	3,600.00

Figure 3.6 Interest Rates Increase in US

If interest rates increase in the US by 1%, the cost of borrowing for the Japanese firm increases to $84,000, whereas costs of borrowing for the American firm would remain the same. This may lead to a decline in borrowing by foreign companies.

Scenario 4. Interest Rates in Japan increase by 1%

Conversely, if interest rates in Japan increase by 1%, the US firm will end up paying more for its Japanese borrowings.

| | AMERICAN FIRM - AMERICAN BORROWING | | | | | JAPANESE FIRM BORROWING | | | | | SWAP SPREAD | BANK'S COMMISSION |
| | BORROWING IN $ | | | | | BORROWING IN YEN | | | | | | 10% |
	LOAN AMOUNT	RATE	EMI $	YEN RATE	in Y		LOAN AMOUNT	RATE	EMI Y	$ RATE	in $		
1	100,000.00	6.00%	6,000.00	101.39	608,340.00	1	10,139,000.00	5.00%	506,950.00	0.009863	5,000.00	1,000.00	100.00
2	100,000.00	6.00%	6,000.00	101.39	608,340.00	2	10,139,000.00	5.00%	506,950.00	0.009863	5,000.00	1,000.00	100.00
3	100,000.00	6.00%	6,000.00	101.39	608,340.00	3	10,139,000.00	5.00%	506,950.00	0.009863	5,000.00	1,000.00	100.00
4	100,000.00	6.00%	6,000.00	101.39	608,340.00	4	10,139,000.00	5.00%	506,950.00	0.009863	5,000.00	1,000.00	100.00
5	100,000.00	6.00%	6,000.00	101.39	608,340.00	5	10,139,000.00	5.00%	506,950.00	0.009863	5,000.00	1,000.00	100.00
6	100,000.00	6.00%	6,000.00	101.39	608,340.00	6	10,139,000.00	5.00%	506,950.00	0.009863	5,000.00	1,000.00	100.00
7	100,000.00	6.00%	6,000.00	101.39	608,340.00	7	10,139,000.00	5.00%	506,950.00	0.009863	5,000.00	1,000.00	100.00
8	100,000.00	6.00%	6,000.00	101.39	608,340.00	8	10,139,000.00	5.00%	506,950.00	0.009863	5,000.00	1,000.00	100.00
9	100,000.00	6.00%	6,000.00	101.39	608,340.00	9	10,139,000.00	5.00%	506,950.00	0.009863	5,000.00	1,000.00	100.00
10	100,000.00	6.00%	6,000.00	101.39	608,340.00	10	10,139,000.00	5.00%	506,950.00	0.009863	5,000.00	1,000.00	100.00
11	100,000.00	6.00%	6,000.00	101.39	608,340.00	11	10,139,000.00	5.00%	506,950.00	0.009863	5,000.00	1,000.00	100.00
12	100,000.00	6.00%	6,000.00	101.39	608,340.00	12	10,139,000.00	5.00%	506,950.00	0.009863	5,000.00	1,000.00	100.00
	TOTALS		72,000.00		7,300,080.00				6,083,400.00		60,000.00	12,000.00	1,200.00

Figure 3.7 Interest Rates Increase in Japan

This is illustrated above where interest rates in Japan increase to 5%. There is no impact on the actual cost of borrowing in the US for the Japanese borrower, but borrowing costs certainly increase for the American borrower in Japan.

Swaps and the Shariah

The concept of swapping financial assets seems to have no issue with the *shariah,* what may present itself as a *shariah* issue is the idea of trading swap contracts in a secondary market. Were original parties to a swap contract to sell their obligation or transfer their obligation to a 3rd party for a consideration, this would create a secondary market for swaps. A secondary market provides liquidity and an opportunity for original parties to exit their obligations in an environment of changing circumstances or expectations. As we have seen in the chapter so far, swaps behave like contingent liabilities, as it is not necessarily known who would end up with a net pay out to the counterparty.

However, in an environment based on *wa'ds,* one can avoid the aversion to uncertainty and develop financial products that learn to deal with uncertainty, to price uncertainty and benefit from uncertainty instead of avoiding it. Swaps can be executed under the concept of *muabadla,* and as such profit rate swaps have reached a stage of maturity where *mubadalatul arbaah* or profit rate swaps have been standardised, and documentation for the contract has been accepted by the International Swaps and Derivatives Association, Inc.

In fact swaps have gained popularity in many IFIs and are currently on the product offering shelves of many Islamic Banks.

Conclusion

In this chapter we simply wished to illustrate the concept of swaps and the incentives behind them. Swaps are arrangements between 2 parties that hold 2 different assets or liabilities. These assets or liabilities may be in the shape of a sequence of profit payments to be received (assets) or made (liabilities), and they may be in one currency or another. Each party merely swaps one asset (or liability) with that of another having certain expectations in mid of changes in profit rates or in currency exchange rates. One party may have an opposing view from that of the other party altogether and therefore simply to swap with each other. One party becomes the beneficiary (or liable to perform) for the others payments and vice versa. The application of this transaction has many fold, whether in money markets, in currency markets, in bond markets or in markets for *shariah* compliant instruments. Islamic Banks may help arrange swaps for clients, or may agree to be a counterparty to a swap arrangement and thus incurring a contingent liability or asset. In the conventional industry contracts of swaps are bought and sold in a secondary market, where the original parties to the contract may no longer be involved. A contract that swaps fixed rates cash flows of $100M may be swapped for one with floating rates embedded, and these contracts may be traded on spreads that reflect the expectations of whether it is advantages to hold a fixed rate contract or a floating rate contract.

Companies in the Muslim world are entering into more and more complex transactions every day. Companies like Emaar and Emirates Airlines purchase millions of dollars of fuel for their aircraft, and they require the flexibility offered to them by swaps arrangements where they may swap a contract of fixed prices for oil with a contract for floating prices of oil to hedge against different risks. They also borrow heavily from banks and such companies have to approach conventional banks for derivatives products and remain with Islamic Banks for traditional sale based products, they will not be able to benefit from their relationships with their bankers who price products on what is known as a TRB or a Total Relationship Basis, which takes into account, all the business a client gives to a bank.

CHAPTER 4

ISLAMIC PROFIT RATE SWAPS

Of one of the innovation that Islamic Financial Institutions came up with is the Islamic Profit Rate Swaps. This is a two way agreement between the parties to make regular or fixed payment to each other in an arranged set of intervals, usually with a form of exchange between two cash flows: one based on fixed profit rate and one floating profit rate, in order to hedge against any adverse profit rate movements. Done within the same currency, the Islamic Profit Rate swaps in other words are used to manage the duration gap that occurs in the Islamic Financial Institutions.

Before going into the mechanism of Islamic Profit Rate Swaps, let us refresh ourselves with the concept of duration gap and rate sensitivity of asset and liabilities.

Generally, a normal bank would have the following activities: take in deposits and give out financing, in the case of Islamic banks, and or loans in the case of a conventional bank. These activities are recorded in their balance sheet asset and liabilities accordingly: the asset side of the balance sheet, which shows the financing or loans given out to the clients, and the liability side of the balance sheet, which shows the deposits.

These two sides of the balance sheet would differ in terms of the price sensitivity of the assets and the price sensitivity of liabilities towards a change in market interest rates. That is, the changes in the interest rates would affect the bank's position due to the asset liability mismatches. The duration gap would show this risk by measuring how well matched is the timings of the cash inflows from assets and the cash outflows from the liabilities. The following shows the duration gap calculation:

Duration gap = Asset duration - Liabilities duration x (liabilities/ assets)

For instance, a bank's average asset duration is 3 years and the average liability duration is 5 years. The total asset held amounted to $ 500 million and the total liabilities held is $450 million; the duration gap would be as follows:

Duration gap = Asset duration – Liabilities duration x (liabilities/assets)
$$= 3 \text{ years} - 5 \text{ years} (\$450 \text{ Million}/ \$500 \text{ Million})$$
$$= 3 \text{ years} - 4.5 \text{ years}$$
$$= -1.5 \text{ years}$$

Hence the duration gap for the scenario above would be a negative duration gap of -1.5 years.

The ideal situation is when the duration gap is zero. This implies that the bank is immune against the interest rates changes in the market, whereby the duration of the liabilities equal to the duration of the assets. But this situation is nearly impossible to achieve as there are many factors that contribute to a definite mismatch between asset and liability. This includes factors such as the various patterns of payments of assets and liabilities, the different maturities of each instruments, and sometimes even the prepayments that has already been made also the defaulted payments can also distort the duration gap and asset liability mismatch. Hence banks usually hedge their position to ensure that the duration gap position is aimed to zero.

A bank can have either positive duration gap or a negative duration gap. Positive duration gap occurs when the bank duration of the asset exceeds the duration of the liability. On the contrary, a negative duration gap is the situation whereby the duration of assets is less than the duration of the liability. Depending on what kind of duration that the bank has, the impact of the rise and fall of the interest rate can be different.

A negative duration gap, as shown in the previous calculation, is where the duration of the asset is less than the duration of the liabilities. In the event of rise of interest rates, the decrease of value of the liability would be more as compared to the decrease in value of the asset, hence increasing the overall value of the bank's equity. Conversely, when the interest rates go down, the opposite happens: bank's liabilities will gain more value as compared to the assets, hence would result in an overall decrease in the bank's equity. In other words, the liabilities are more rate-sensitive as compared to the assets.

The other situation is where the duration of the asset is greater than the duration of the liability. A positive duration gap means greater risk, that is, the payables to liabilities are, in simple terms, due earlier before the receivables from the asset. In this situation, when the interest rates rise, the assets will lose more value than the liabilities. This results in a drop in the overall value of the bank's equity, and vice versa.

The impacts of changes in interest rates towards the overall value of a bank can be illustrated below:

SCENARIO 1 DECREASE IN INTEREST RATES

Supposedly ABC bank has average asset duration of 4 years and average liabilities duration of 3 years. Its assets have a total value of $600 and its liabilities amounted to $400 million, the duration gap would be as follows:

Duration gap = Asset duration – Liabilities duration x (liabilities/assets)
= 4 years – 3 years ($400 Million/ $600 Million)
= 4 years – 2 years
= 2 year

When there is a decrease of interest rate from 5% to 4%, the total change in net worth would be:

Change in net worth = (-4 years x (-1%/1+5%) x $600 million)-(-3 years x (-1%/1+5%) x $400 million
= $ 22,857,142.83 – $ 11,428,571.42
= $ 11,428,571.41

As we can see from the formula above, a decrease in the interest rates would result to an increase in overall value of the net worth when the asset-liability duration gap is positive.

SCENARIO 2 INCREASE IN INTEREST RATES

Same scenario above with ABC bank, when there is an increase of interest rate from 5% to 6%, the total change in net worth would be:

$$\text{Change in net worth} = (-4 \text{ years} \times (1\%/1+5\%) \times \$600 \text{ million})-(-3 \text{ years} \times (1\%/1+5\%) \times \$400 \text{ million}$$
$$= -\$ 22{,}857{,}142.83 - (-\$ 11{,}428{,}571.42)$$
$$= -\$ 11{,}428{,}571.41$$

As we can see from the computation above, an increase in the interest rates would result to a decrease in the overall value of the net worth when the asset-liability duration gap is positive.

Since the financing or loans that banks give out are usually at a longer period as compared to the deposits that they take in, the average asset duration is usually more than the average liabilities duration. That is, mostly banks are with a positive duration situation. Hence the above scenario would apply.

In this case, conventional banks would normally hedge themselves through using derivatives such as forwards or futures; use adjustable loan interest rates; and or using interest rate swaps.

Islamic Profit Rate Swap functions similarly like how interest rate swaps function for conventional banks. This instrument is used by Islamic Financial Institutions to hedge their profit and or net worth against any adverse movement in the interest rate within the market. It is true that by right, Islamic Financial Institutions are interest free, and supposedly not affected by any changes in the market. However, it is to be noted that currently most of the Islamic Financial Institutions are being run side by side with the conventional banks within a dual banking system.

There is still a flow between funds from the Islamic and the conventional banking system and as a resultant, any changes in the interest rates from the conventional side would mean that the cost of fund in the Islamic banking side is affected as well.

In a simpler example, supposed that XYZ bank has $400 million more of rate-sensitive asset as compared to the rate-sensitive liabilities. Notice that this is a simpler form of asset-liability mismatch which is also a form of interest risk and a fraction of the duration mismatch between the two. To help manage this duration gap, the Islamic Profit Rate Swap comes into the picture. This rate-sensitive gap of (a positive)$400 means that the rate-sensitive assets are more than the rate-sensitive liabilities. A negative gap would mean otherwise.

XYZ bank then engages in IPRS to hedge its position to protect itself in the event of adverse changes in interest rates.

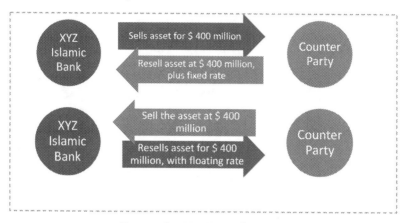

Figure 4.1 IPRS Mechanism

As seen above, there are a few stages involved in the IPRS mechanism. First stage is when XYZ Islamic bank sells the asset to counter party, consequently the counterparty would sell it back to XYZ Islamic bank at the notional rate plus fixed rate. This way, XYZ Islamic bank is obligated to pay the notional amount plus the fixed rate (agreed profit rate) at a determined period in the future. The fixed rate determined at the start of the contract would remain the same until the end of the agreement.

Next stage is when the XYZ Islamic bank buys an asset for $400 from the counter party and then resells it at notional amount plus the floating rate. This way, XYZ Islamic bank would receive the floating rate payment, usually referenced to and index, for instance, benchmarked against LIBOR or any other applicable benchmark rate at an agreed period. This floating rate payment would be determined at every settlement date.

There are several Shariah compliant concepts that are used as the underlying contract for this instrument. The example above can be broken down into the usage of a few Shariah contracts, namely Bai-Inah, Muqassah, and Wa'ad.

At the inception stage, both parties each undertake a unilateral promise to enter into the Bai-Inah transactions on a certain agreed date. Consequently, they will undertake the above bai-inah contract.

After each of the above stages are executed, the payments between both parties are net off. When they net off the payments, the concept applied is Muqassah. Therefore XYZ Islamic bank would pay the net cash flow, which is the fixed profit rate, at the end of stage one. The counter party would also only have to pay the floating rate to XYZ Islamic bank at the end of stage two.

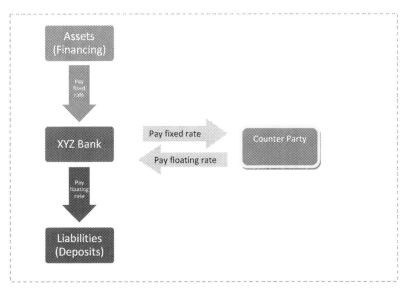

Figure 4.2 IPRS for hedging

The above figure shows the resultant of the IPRS mechanism. This way XYZ Islamic bank's position is hedged against any adverse changes in the interest rates within the market.

An alternative contract for IPRS would be *Murabahah Tawarruq*, which is more acceptable in the Middle East and other Islamic countries, which uses actual commodities as the underlying asset for the transaction. This structure can be either involve 3 parties or 4 parties (including the commodity brokers), but ultimately has the same end result as the *Bai-Inah* IPRS.

Related to our discussion about swaps, there is another form of hedging against the risk brought about by globalization. This is also one of the most needed form of hedging, considering the fact that we live in an environment that is interconnected across jurisdictional boundaries, which will be discussed in the next chapter.

CHAPTER 5

ISLAMIC FOREIGN EXCHANGE SWAPS

As the growth of Islamic banking and finance reaches out globally Islamic entities would not be hidden from the ever volatile foreign currency exposure. Islamic finance market players, academician, and Islamic scholars have all been working on the best shariah compliant solution for the management of currency risk as it may be one of the problems that may affect an entity's earnings greatly.

Foreign currency exposure would entail to many things. An entity can be exposed to foreign exchange exposure when it deals with payments in foreign currency. When an entity strike up an agreement with determined price in foreign currency and its delivery date, it would be faced by the risk of the change in the exchange rates between the foreign currency and the home currency. The amount of money that would be received at the agreement date in the home currency, for instance, might not be the same as what the entity will actually receive later on the settlement date because the exchange rate between the two would now be different. That is, any movement in the rates can affect the payment made or received by the entity. Some other entities have it more complex, when they have many branches globally. For reporting purposes, when they consolidate the reports into one, the prevailing exchange rate would affect the total values of the entity.

By far, there are two methods for managing currency risk: the On-Balance-Sheet approach and the 'Off-Balance-Sheet' approach. Since years ago, the majority of Islamic jurists are proponents of the 'On-Balance-Sheet' approach to currency risk management. 'On Balance Sheet' approach refers to the method that focuses on operational techniques such as timing of payments and receipts, where the entity would time the payments made in one foreign currency and the receipts would be around the same period; invoicing in home currency, that is, when the entity prices all the purchases and sales in the home currency regardless of the client's domicile; and netting the exposures towards the foreign currency, where the 'buy' is matched to the 'sell' of the same foreign currency so that it would be net-off. In general this method affects the business conducts of the entity.

Unlike Off-Balance-Sheet method, this method avoids the use of derivatives like options, swaps, future and forwards. By doing the On-Balance-Sheet method, the entity may be able to pass the currency risk to the counter parties. This would be a very effective method to avoid any adverse impact due to the changes in the exchange rates, but at the same time would be quite far-fetched as this may impact on other things such as the competitiveness of the entity as the dealings with its clients or customers are bounded by such rigidity. Unless they have the power in a monopoly market, this way they may be able to dictate on the terms and conditions.

Due to these limitations, there were pleads and appeals directed to the Islamic scholars to reconsider the prohibition of use on derivatives and other Off-Balance-Sheet methods. This was the turning point where some Islamic scholars and jurists agree that some derivatives such as forwards, futures and options are allowed following a certain criteria. For example, these transactions are allowed when they are based on shariah compliant contracts such as Salam Sarf and Wa'ad and only allowed specifically for hedging purposes only.

Basically an Islamic Foreign Exchange swaps is also one of the alternative products that Islamic Financial Institutions came up with to hedge against the changes in foreign exchange rates. The common underlying contract used to facilitate this transaction is the Tawarruq structure.

Two tawarruq transaction would be executed in this case. For instance, an investor has MYR 3 million and wishes to invest in USD. At the point of time, the current exchange rate would be MYR 3 for every US dollar. If the investor exchanges his ringgit to dollar he would get USD 1 million on day 1.

Supposed he did invest the money in the bank, after 3 months the exchange rate changes into MYR 3.5 for every US dollar. Which means that at the end of the 3 months period, he would receive his capital back at MYR 3.5 million, and make a capital gain of MYR 500,000, apart from the profit or interest that he would gain from the investment. However, what if the situation turns out that the exchange rate changes into MYR 2.5 for every one US dollar. Which in this case, at the end of the 3 months period, he would only receive his capital back at MYR 2.5 million, and make a capital loss of MYR 500,000, regardless from the profit or interest that he would gain from the investment. Even though he might benefit from the first scenario where MYR appreciated against USD, he would also be exposed to the possibility that the USD would appreciate against MYR.

To lock his position on the exchange rate and preserve his capital, he would like to protect himself against this exposure thus this is where the foreign exchange swap comes in. This product would protect him from the fluctuation or the rates through the following:

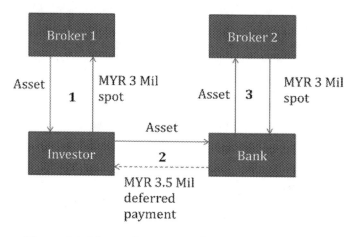

Figure 5.1 Islamic Foreign Exchange Swap: Tawarruq 1

Step 1. Investor has MYR 3 million cash, and buys commodity on spot payment from broker 1. Hereby, the bank would act as the agent of the investor and buys the commodity on his behalf.

Step 2. The bank would buy this commodity from the investor for MYR 3.5 million, which payment would be done on a deferred basis after 1 year.

Step 3. The bank, once in possession of the commodity, would sell it to Broker 2, and get MYR 3 million on the spot.

This is end of the first tawarruq contract. The bank now has in its hand, MYR 3 million, and an obligation to repay the investor an amount of MYR

3.5 million in a year time. While this can give the investor a net of profit of MYR 500,000, this does not fulfill his purpose of investing in USD. In order to execute this, the bank needs USD.

Hence, this brings us to step 4. The bank exchanges MYR 3 million into USD 1 million (based on bay al-sarf) on spot. This money is then used to buy commodity from Broker 3 for USD 1 million on spot payment.

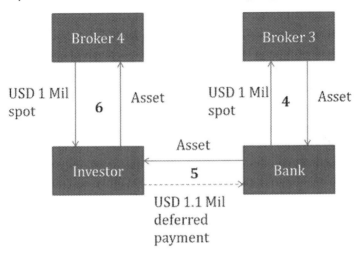

Figure 5.2 Islamic Foreign Exchange Swap: Tawarruq 2

Step 5. The bank the sells this commodity to investor for USD 1.1 million on deferred payment after 1 year.

Step 6. Investor then sells this to Broker 4 for USD 1 million in cash. This is done through the bank as the agent.

Therefore the net transaction is that the bank has the obligation to pay the investor an amount of MYR 3.5 million in a year. The investor now hold cash USD 1 million and also at the same time has the obligation to pay the bank USD 1.1 million in a year time.

The result of this whole transaction, is that the investor gets the USD 1 million cash which he can invest for one year. At the end of 1 year term, he would receive MYR 3.5 million, and has to make a payment of USD 1.1 million for the purchase of commodity in step 5. This way, both parties has locked the conversion of USD to MYR at a fixed rate in the future at MYR 3.5 million for USD 1.1 million.

Another method to deal with foreign exchange swaps is using Wa'ad. In Islam, a Wa'ad is not legally binding, even though to a certain extent it is morally binding and muslims are encouraged to fulfil all the promises that they have made. Under the common law, Wa'ad may or may not be considered obligatory and can be challengeable in the court of law[3]. Nevertheless, the OIC Fiqh Academy is of the view that a breach of Wa'ad would be deemed to be equivalent to a breach of contract especially if the unilateral promise is made in a commercial transaction and can cause one to incur liabilities or losses.[4] More about this contract will be discussed in the next chapter.

Using the same example above, through Wa'ad, the investor who is looking for the hedge, would provide an undertaking or promise to purchase the foreign currency at an agreed rate after an agreed period. That is, the whole transaction would involve a bay al sarf (normal spot exchange of currencies between two parties) at the beginning, and then the carrying out of another exchange of these currencies in the future based on the rate agreed today.

Based on the same example above, the investor has MYR 3 million and wants to invest in USD. At the beginning of the transaction, the investor and the bank would usually both sign a master agreement, and then conduct bay al sarf. Investor would give the bank MYR 3 million in exchange of USD 1 million credited to his account by the bank using the spot rate prevailing at that moment. Next step is when the investor would undertake the promise to purchase MYR 2.9 million for USD 1 million after 3 months. Hence, this way, the investor locks himself against the potential loss that he can suffer should the exchange rate worsen for USD.

These two system are the most common mechanism being implemented currently. However, notice that all these methods are not quite exactly straight forward. In the next chapters, we propose a few alternative ways to do an

---

3   Muhammad, M., Yaacob, H., & Hasan, S. (2011), "The Bindingness And Enforceability Of A Unilateral Promise (wa'ad): An Analysis From Islamic Law And Legal Perspectives," ISRA Research Paper No 30/2011, Kuala Lumpur.

4   Organization of the Islamic Conference (OIC) Islamic Fiqh Academy, (1988), "The Binding Nature of Promise and Murabaha Transaction," Resolution No 40-41, http://www.fiqhacademy.org.sa/qrarat/5-2.htm, site accessed September 2014.

Islamic Foreign Exchange swap. Whether it is viable or not viable, we leave the matter open for your thoughts.

Effective Forward Currency Sale using *bai muajal*

The following structure behaves like a forward currency sale transaction using a combination or sequence of 2 sale transactions with spot delivery but deferred payments. However, unlike as in the case of *inah,* where the 2 sales are for the same subject matter, but differ in price, in this structure they differ in the currency of the sale transactions.

We illustrate the product using a simple scenario involving 2 parties A and B. Party A has Malaysian Ringitts and wishes to exchange them for US $ in 90 days. Party B has US $ and wishes to purchase Malaysian Ringitts in 90 days. Both parties wish to lock in a rate for the sale of Malaysian Ringitts for US $, (from A's perspective) and for US $ to Malaysian Ringitts in 90 days.

If the transaction is executed in the shape of a sale of one currency for another currency. The transaction must be in spot to abide by the rules of *bai al sarf.* We propose a structure where the end result is that of a "sale" of one currency for another by using back to back deferred sale transactions under *bai muajjal.*

Contract Initiation

Party A sells an asset, (CPO) to B for $1,000,000 with delivery on spot but payment in 90 days. Subsequently, Party B sells CPO to A for RM 3,500,000 with delivery on spot but payment in 90 days.

Contract Conclusion in 90 days.

A receives a payment of $1,000,000 in 90 days from B. B receives a payment of RM 3,500,000 in 90 days. Both parties are able to lock in a currency exchange rate today, but for a transaction to be executed in the future.

The net result of the two transactions is that A is able to dispose off Malaysian Ringitts in exchange for US $ and B is able to do the exact opposite, i.e. exchange US $ for Malaysian Ringitts. The "sale/purchase price" for each sale is determined at the time of contract initiation. B will accept a price agreed upon in US Dollars for the first purchase and A will accept a price in Malaysian Ringitts for the second sale.

This structure differs from *bai al inah*, in that both sales are for deferred payments and spot deliveries. Conditions of a valid sale are fulfilled by spot delivery in both circumstances.

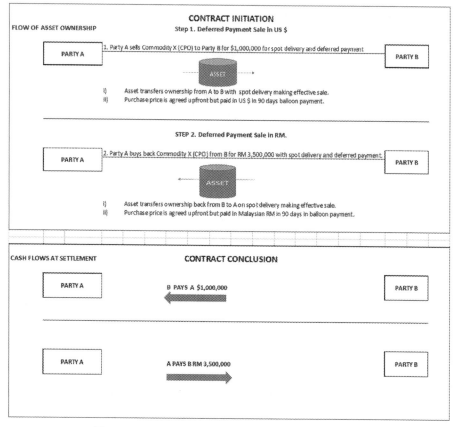

Figure 5.3 FX Forward Sale using *bai muajjal*.

Forward Foreign Currency Sale using *Tawarruq*.

A forward foreign currency sale can be executed using the concept of *tawarruq*.

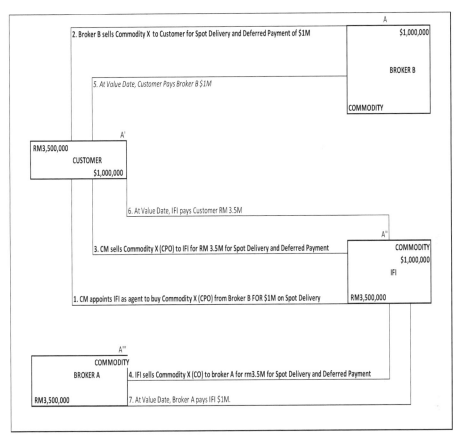

Figure 5.5 Forward Currency Sale using *tawarruq*

At contract initiation the following steps are undertaken.

Step 1. A Customer appoints an Islamic Bank as an agent to purchase Commodity from a broker for spot delivery but deferred payment. The purchase price is agreed at $1 Million.

Step 2. The Broker transfers ownership of the underlying from itself to the Customer and the Customer owes the Broker a payment of $1 Million, due in 90 days.

Step 3. The Customer, sells the Commodity with spot delivery and deferred payment for RM 3.5 Million to the Islamic Bank. The Islamic Bank obtains ownership of the underlying Commodity and owes the Customer a payment of RM 3.5 Million due in 90 days.

Step 4. The Islamic Bank sells the Commodity to Broker A (or any other broker) for spot delivery and deferred payment of RM 3.50 Million. Ownership of the Commodity is transferred from the Islamic bank to the Broker. Each party to this sequence of transactions owes a counterparty a deferred purchase price either in RM or in $.

At contract conclusion in 90 days the following steps are followed.

Step 5. The Customer pays the Broker for the Commodity purchased on credit, $1Million.

Step 6. The Islamic Bank pays the Customer, RM 3.5 Million as purchase price for the Commodity the Islamic bank bought on credit from the Customer.

Step 7. Broker A pays the Islamic Bank $ 1 Million.

The net results of these transactions are as follows. The Customer who had $1 Million at contract initiation experiences at cash outflow at t = 90 of $1Million and a cash inflow of RM 3.5 Million. In essence the Customer has been able to lock in a rate of $1 = RM 3.5M at time t = 0 for converting $1 Million to RM 3.5 Million in 90 days. The Bank which supplies the RM 3.5 Million experiences an outflow of RM 3.50M and a subsequent inflow of $ 1 Million in 90 days as well.

These methods are being adopted by some Islamic banks in GCC and Malaysia to hedge foreign currency exposure for themselves and their clients.

CHAPTER 6

WA'D BASED CONTRACTS

The discourse on Islamic Finance thus far has been based on sale based or lease based contracts especially on the asset side of Islamic banks and their credit based portfolios. Contracts that emerge on the liability side are *wadiah, qard, wakalah and mudharabah.* Being contracts of *bai,* or trade, these contracts must fulfill all requirements of bilateral contracts of sale and purchase.

Contracts which are bilateral in nature must not have any elements of uncertainty, speculation or elements of chance embedded in them. A sale transaction must be clear in terms of the subject matter, the price and the delivery. Unilateral contracts however offer far more flexibility, especially arrangements based on promises. Almost all contracts have embedded promises in them, the least of them being a seller promises that the subject matter meets the given description. Such promises however, become implicit features of a contract and thereby become enforceable by law. In general though promises are not deemed enforceable.

Shariah rulings on *wa'd.*

The most comprehensive document on *wa'd* is offered by Bank Negara Malaysia in its Exposure Draft, "*Wa'd – Shariah* Requirements and Optional Practices, BNM/RH/CP 028-6, dated December 6th, 2013. The substance of this Exposure Draft is further backed by the Islamic Financial Services Act of 2013. The 2 pieces of legal content are probably the most prolific developments in Islamic Finance since the engineering of *commodity murabahah* products and reflects the vision and commitment of Bank Negara Malaysia and Governor Zeti.

The legal nature of *wa'd* has only been recognized in Malaysia where transactions based upon *wa'd* are deemed enforceable, and parties to *wa'd* arrangements are required to fulfil their promises by law. Thus if one party promises to sell a certain asset to a counterparty in the future at a specific price, the fulfilment of the promise does not come under the contract of forward sales but rather that of *wa'ds* and at least in Malaysia is thus enforceable. If Party A promises to sell $100M to a second party B at an exchange rate of $1 = RM 3.10 for RM310M in 30 days, if A fails to come up with $100 in 30 days, or B fails to come up with RM310M in 30 days, either parties are seen to have defaulted and are treated as such by regulators and market participants. For financial institutions being treated as defaulters by market participants, be they depositors, investors, fund managers, and other banks, is far more a serious cause of concern than the penalties levied by regulators. Penalties can be absorbed from profits, but a negative rating from market participants can eliminate chances of doing future business especially as banking is fundamentally based upon trust, the trust one party has in another to perform its commitments, either to pay back borrowed moneys, or have enough liquidity to manage a balance sheet, or have certain assets available for sale in trade transactions.

We shall highlight some key clauses from the Exposure Draft mentioned above. Under the normenclature of Bank Negara, Malaysia, the following clauses are cited as "Standards" and must be followed by all Islamic Financial Institutions operating in Malaysia. Standards are defined as "requirement or specification that must be complied with. Failure to comply may result in one or more enforcement actions". [5]

Clause S 7.1 "*Wa'd* literally, a promise or undertaking, refers to an expression of commitment given by one party to another to perform certain action(s) in the future."[6]

"Clause S 8.1 *Wa'd* is neither a contract nor an agreement. It is a unilateral promise which is not binding in nature.

Clause S 8.2 Notwithstanding paragraph 8.1, *wa'd* it is binding and enforceable on the promisor if it fulfils certain requirements.

---

[5]   Bank Negara Malaysia, Exposure Draft on *Wa'd*. Clause 5.2 www.bnm.gov.my / documents/SAC/11_%20Wa'd.pdf

[6]   Bank Negara Malaysia, Exposure Draft on *Wa'd*. Clause 7.1 www.bnm.gov.my / documents/SAC/11_%20Wa'd.pdf

Clause S 9.7 Any term or condition mutually agreed upon which does not contravene Shariah shall be binding on the parties involved.

Clause S 11.2 A fee shall not be imposed on a *wa'd*.

Clause S 12.2 The promisor shall fulfil his *wa'd*, upon occurrence of the specified event.

Clause S 12.3 The promisor is considered to have breached the *wa'd* if he does not fulfil his *wa'd* upon the occurrence of the specified event at its specified time.

Clause S 12.4 Where the promisor has breached his promise, the promisee may claim for compensation for any actual loss suffered and the promisor shall to fulfil the claim by the promisee".[7]

The remaining clauses come under the Guidelines which are defined as such. Guidelines "denotes guidance which may consist of such information advice or recommendation intended to promote common understanding and sound industry practices which are encouraged to be adopted."[8]

Clause G 13.1 In a *wa'd* to purchase, a promisor may provide the promisee a security deposit (*Hamish jiddiyah*) to secure the undertaking to purchase the asset. The security deposit may be used to compensate the promisee against actual losses incurred in the event the promisor breaches his binding *wa'd*.

Clause G 13.4 The promisor may enter into a binding *wa'd* to sell an asset which is yet to be owned by him provided that the promisor possesses the asset or possesses authority to sell the asset at the time of execution of the sale contract. [9]

---

7   Bank Negara Malaysia, Exposure Draft on *Wa'd*. www.bnm.gov.my /documents/ SAC/11_%20Wa'd.pdf

8   Bank Negara Malaysia, Exposure Draft on *Wa'd*. www.bnm.gov.my /documents/ SAC/11_%20Wa'd.pdf

9   Bank Negara Malaysia, Exposure Draft on *Wa'd*. www.bnm.gov.my /documents/ SAC/11_%20Wa'd.pdf

Simple *wa'd* arrangement.

STEP 1.

STEP 2.

The same transaction can also be seen from B's point of view.

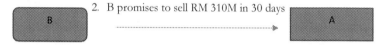

Figure 6.1 *Wa'd* based forward sale.

In the illustration above, Parties A and B enter into a promissory arrangement, where A promises to sell B $100M in exchange for RM310M in 30 days. Neither parties require any consideration or collateral from their counterparty to ensure performance of the promises. Each party knows that in financial markets, failure to perform on a promise is as good as closing down. However, A can request B for some sort of collateral to ensure performance and vice versa. This "collateral" can take the shape of cash kept in a margin account which is not controlled by A or B, but by a 3rd party, a trustee or an exchange. The monies kept in this account will be used to compensate that party which is able to fulfil their end of the promise, but the promisor is unable to do the same.

If either party fails to perform on their promise in 30 days, the counterparty can claim damages. Another consequence of the failure to perform on A's part for instance, would be that no other market participant would trust A any longer, and A would not be able to transact in the currency markets.

The concept of *wa'd* opens up the doors to engineer a wide range of financial products. Islamic banks can develop products based on *wa'd*, where they can promise a certain rate of return to depositors but not guarantee it, promise to buy or sell financial assets with other institutions in the future at either spot price, market prices or average prices over specific intervals. ***Wa'ds can be the underlying concept between the trade of rabbawi items like currency that must be traded on spot as is the case with foreign currency swaps, or foreign currency forward transactions.***

Wa'd can also be the premise for futures contracts where a buyer agrees to buy an asset in the future from a seller, and agrees to pay a margin for the asset under consideration. As the transaction is not one of *bai,* a margin purchase is considered to be permissible. The buyer to the transaction can also promise to resell the same asset to a third party before taking delivery of the underlying. *Wa'ds* therefore allow for the development of a futures and forwards industry within Islamic Finance. Whether such *wa'ds* are customized between 2 counters and traded on an Over the Counter Basis or they are standardized and traded on an exchange becomes irrelevant, however, again as in the case of swaps, the argument would be how *wa'ds* can be traded in a secondary market. Offering a *wa'd* and accepting a *wa'd* between 2 original parties is one thing, the question arises is can one party to the promise, "sell" his obligation at par, discount or at a premium to a third party and if so for what consideration.

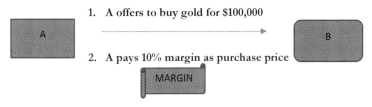

Figure 6.2 *Wa'd* with margin.

The margin serves as an implicit collateral to the arrangement for a gold sale.

Charging a fee for *wa'd.*
Shariah scholars have been averse to allowing a promisor to charge a fee for a promise. The current practice however, is to build a price for the *wa'd,* into the price of the underlying asset. For instance of A promises to sell 1 ounce of gold to B for $1,500 on the spot, for $1,501 in 30 days, and $1,502 in 60 days. A has added a fee for the obligation of selling gold in the future to compensate for holding costs, opportunity cost of investing proceeds of spot sales, and for not selling to another party. This fee becomes part of the final price of the underlying. If B accepts the offer, there is no impermissibility in the arrangement.

Wa'd, Hawalah and *Hibah*

Once a mechanism is developed for pricing *wa'ds,* we can now develop a mechanism for trading them. A wishes to exit the obligation to sell gold to B at $1,501 in 30 days. A approaches Party C, to take over the obligation of A due on B, under the contract of *hawalah.* C agrees to do so as C feels that a profit can be made from the trade, as C has inventory of gold purchased at low prices. If C accepts the obligation the promise is transferred from A to C, whether B is aware of the arrangement or not. A question arises is if C can charge a fee for accepting the obligation from A? In standard discussion on *hawalah, a fee cannot be made part of the arrangement.* Typically *hawalah* is discussed within the context of debt, where one party transfers his debt to a third party. However, we are not discussing debt here but promises and wonder if the *shariah community* at large would recognize this difference. Alternatively, A can however offer C a monetary gift under the contract of *hibah,* but this too cannot be made conditional to the *hawalah* arrangement.

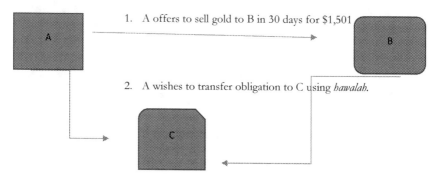

1. A offers to sell gold to B in 30 days for $1,501

2. A wishes to transfer obligation to C using *hawalah.*

3. B promises to sell to C before taking delivery from A for $1,502

Figure 6.3 *Wa'd* with *hawalah*

Wa'd and hedging

There does not seem to be any other mechanism of trading a *wa'd* other than transferring either the rights or the obligations from one party to another using *hawalah* or by entering into offsetting positions with other parties. A may offset a promise to sell in 30 days, by entering into a promise to buy with a 3rd party, and B may offset its buy position by entering into a sale promise with a 3rd party. As A and B will be offsetting promises with a set of other promises both parties would be in a position to hedge themselves against any fluctuations in prices of the underlying assets. A may offset the exposure on the price of gold in 30 days, buy entering into options contracts or promises to buy gold from another party for a price lower than $1,501.

B can hedge its position of buying gold for $1,501 by finding another buyer willing to purchase gold for $1,502. Given the flexibility allowed in *wa'd* structures, each party can enter into subsequent arrangements without the first arrangement concluding.

Wa'd and short selling

This latter leg can be in the shape of transferring rights to the original promise, or by merely making a separate promise to C to sell the gold to C in 30 days, without having taken delivery from A for a price of $1,502. In this manner B A is able to sell the gold to C without taking delivery of the asset in the first place and circumvents the *shariah* ruling of selling an asset not in one's ownership by not entering into a contract of *bai,* but a contract of *wa'd.*

Conclusion

The concept of *wa'ds* offer a window of opportunity to develop financial products and Islamic Derivatives. We shall subsequently look at the various derivatives structures like futures and options to explore the possibilities offered in a *wa'd* based environment. A *wa'd* based environment requires legal recognition of the status of promises, which so far has only been developed in Malaysia. This legal status accompanied with market perceptions can help develop financial products that are free from the restrictions levied by contract law.

CHAPTER 7

CREDIT DEFAULT SWAP / CREDIT LINKED NOTES

Let us examine a system where Credit Risk, Market Risk, and Liquidity Risk is involved. The system below represents a system of risk. A bank mobilises $600,000 worth of funds from various sources, and lends out these monies to various borrowers of varying credit worthiness and books receivables worth $ 600,000 to be repaid over 10 years.

For simplicity sake we refer to a good quality borrower as A1 and a medium quality borrower as B1,B2 and a poor quality borrower as B3. The safer counterparty is extended a larger loan albeit at a lower interest rate of 7%, whereas the slightly riskier counterparties are extended smaller loans but with higher interest rates. On one loan of $300,000 to A, the bank earns $21,000, whereas on 3 loans of $100,000 to Parties B1,B2 and B3, the bank earns $31,000 in interest income. The probability of default however is higher for B category loans but they provide the bank higher yield. Total lending is $600,000.

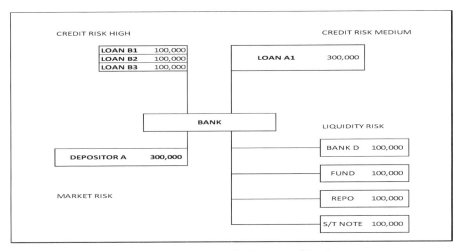

Figure 7.1 A Simple System of Risk

Each party provides collateral for the loans they have secured, and we observe the values of these collaterals in Figure 7.2. The value of these collaterals certainly reduce the net exposure the bank has on the borrowers. The value of this net exposure depends greatly on the value of collateral posted by the borrowers, and therefore the strength of the real estate market in the system (assuming the loans are residential mortgages). The value of collaterals offer the first exposure of our system to an external risk, which is the risk posed by changes in real estate prices. The real estate market is in turn linked to various other factors, such as availability of credit, interest rates, population growth, demand, disposable income, political stability, each having its own impact on real estate prices.

The system is exposed to credit risks, or the risk that the borrowers will default. This risk has repercussions on the entire system. The entire system functions as long as borrowers are able to repay their loans. The bank is able to pay back the money sourced from depositors and other counterparties, compensate them with interest expense and earn it's owns spreads. The credibility of the borrowers and their overall ability to repay the loans is a fundamental factor of this entire system, far more important than the value of collaterals. Credit risk is therefore coloured in red and orange with the former reflecting high credit risk and the latter lower credit risk.

	AMOUNT	EXPOSURE	%AGE OF TOTAL	COLLATERAL	UNRECOVERABLE AMOUNT	TENOR YEARS	INTEREST RATE	INCOME	PROBABILITY OF DEFAULT
LOAN A1	300,000	300,000	50.00%	250,000	50,000	10	7.00%	21,000	4.00%
LOAN B1	100,000	100,000	16.67%	75,000	25,000	10	10.00%	10,000	9.00%
LOAN B2	100,000	100,000	16.67%	75,000	25,000	10	10.00%	10,000	9.00%
LOAN B3	100,000	100,000	16.67%	75,000	25,000	10	11.00%	11,000	10.00%
TOTAL LENDING A1B1B2B3	600,000	600,000		475,000	125,000			52,000	
WIGHTED AVERAGE		600,000		475,000	125,000		8.667%		6.67%

Figure 7.2 Details of Credit Financing Within The System

Each borrower provides collateral to the bank which can be liquidated in the event of default. Each loan is classified on the basis of risk. Loan A1 offers low risk and therefore the borrower is charged a low interest rate. However, the bank has taken a rather large exposure on the borrower of $300,000. Loans B1,B2 and B3 are extended to high risk borrowers, the bank charges a credit risk premium of 3% from B1 and B2 and 4%from B3 and extends smaller loans of just $100,000 to each borrower. Three loans extended to class B borrowers are of $100,000 each but earn a higher yield for the bank.

	AMOUNT	TENOR IN YEARS	TENOR IN DAYS	AMOUNT AS %AGE OF TOTAL	DEPOSIT TENOR AS %AGE OF TOTAL ASSET TENOR	INTEREST EXPENSE	INTEREST EXPENSE	NET INCOME
FUNDING								
DEPOSIT A	300,000	0.167	60	50.00%	1.67%	4.00%	12,000	
BANK D	50,000	0.250	90	8.33%	2.50%	4.65%		
FUND	50,000	0.250	90	8.33%	2.50%	4.50%	2,250	
REPO	100,000	0.083	30	16.67%	0.83%	3.85%	3,850	
S/T NOTE	100,000	0.167	60	16.67%	1.67%	3.95%	3,950	47,050
TOTAL	600,000							
WEIGHTED AVE						3.68%		

Figure 7.3 Details of Sources of Funding

The Islamic bank funds its assets using deposits of $300,000, interbank borrowing from Bank D for $50,000, partially via a structured product offered to a fund for $50,000, repo transactions for $100,000 and short term notes of $100,000. Each source of funding is for a different tenure and carries a different cost.

The system here, or the bank is exposed to several risks, one such risk is credit risk, or the risk of default from borrowers. Another risk is market risk, that depositors and other banks may demand a higher return on the funds they provide the bank. This will reduce the net interest margins for the bank. Depositors do not have an in depth understanding of the assets on the bank's balance sheet. Their demand for returns on demands are linked to prevailing market interest rates and the tenor for which they fix their deposits. Institutional fund providers may not also have the same visibility over a bank's assets in the same manner that other banks would. Their demand for returns is also linked to market rates and the tenor of placements. Lending banks however, have limited access and knowledge of the assets a bank holds on its balance sheet. Banks particularly lend to each other on the basis of each other's credibility. A bank's credibility is based on the quality of its asset portfolio so is in effect derived from the creditworthiness of its borrowers. If a bank has high risk loans on its books, lenders like other banks who have knowledge of such information charge higher interest rates for placing money with the borrowing bank.

An indication of the quality of a bank's assets is the rate at which they borrow money from other banks. This rate is publicly available and is known as the Interbank Over Night Rate. Banks in UK lend to each other at the London Interbank Over Night Rate or LIBOR. Banks lend to each other for as short a tenor as 1 night, to 10 years depending on the maturity of the interbank market. Banks borrow funds for varying tenors to match their asset and liability gaps known as funding gaps. The concept of funding gap has been explained in our previous work.

Each bank discloses its own rates for borrowing from the interbank market for varying tenors. Higher rates reflect a lack of comfort in the mind of lenders regarding the asset quality on the borrowing banks books. An incentive to underquote Inter Bank Borrowing Rates is to window dress the asset quality on a banks books. As interbank rates are quoted and made available to the public, rising rates would send a warning signal to depositors and lenders as to the creditworthiness of a bank.

The interest rate at which a bank lends to a customer is a reflection of the creditworthiness of the customer, interbank rates are an indication of the creditworthiness of the bank itself.

Risk Mitigation

The bank has 2 methods of mitigating credit risk. One is to maintain reserves from its income which are known as general provisioning reserves. These reserves are based on mathematical calculations of Expected Losses, where EL = PD * EAGD * LRGD.

This is calculated as below:-

	LOAN	EAGD	COLLATERAL	LRGD	PROBABILITY OF DEFAULT	EXPECTED LOSSES
LOAN A1	300,000	300,000	250,000	16.67%	4.00%	2,000
LOAN B1	100,000	100,000	75,000	25.00%	9.00%	2,250
LOAN B2	100,000	100,000	75,000	25.00%	9.00%	2,250
LOAN B3	100,000	100,000	75,000	25.00%	10.00%	2,500
TOTAL LENDING A1B1B2B3	600,000	600,000	475,000	20.83%		
WIGHTED AVERAGE	600,000	600,000	475,000		0.00%	8,750

Figure 7.4 Expected Losses

The bank would keep a reserve of $8,750 to cover for what is known as the unrecoverable amount of $125,000. The amount lent to a borrower that cannot be recovered from the sale of any collateral. This is amount is simply the difference between any outstanding exposure less the collateral provided by the end user.

Another method of covering risk is holding collateral. For every loan disbursed the bank maintains a certain amount as collateral. For the bank in question, $600,000 worth of loans are secured by $475,000 of collateral. This collateral can be liquidated if all the borrowers default, however the probability of all borrowers defaulting is simply the product of all the individual default probabilities in the system as shown in the following table:-

	AMOUNT	PROBABILITY OF DEFAULT
LOAN A1	300,000	4.00%
LOAN B1	100,000	9.00%
LOAN B2	100,000	9.00%
LOAN B3	100,000	9.00%
TOTAL LENDING A1B1B2B3	600,000	
WIGHTED AVERAGE		6.50%

Figure 7.5 Probability of Default

However, if this rare event does occur the bank can liquidate the collaterals provided the collaterals maintain their values. If the loans above are house loans and the collaterals offered are all homes, if there is a depreciation in housing prices, the values of the collaterals may decline, thus increasing the net exposure of the bank. The value of the collaterals is an important component of the overall system of credit and changes in the market values of these houses held as collateral can adversely affect the risk profile of the system as a whole. However, if housing prices increase, the banks can in fact increase their exposure to borrowers by lending them more money against the value of their houses.

Selling the Risk

Another option available to the bank is to sell the receivables at a discount to another bank or counterparty. The loans booked by the bank constitute a set of receivables due to be paid to the bank over a period of 10 years. For the sake of simplicity we have kept all the loans for 10 year tenors. The bank can bundle the receivables into a single instrument reflecting the aggregate of all receivables or can sell each receivable individually. In fact each instalment in each receivable can be sold individually to another bank. In this manner the bank recovers the principal amounts extended to borrowers and recovers a certain percentage of the interest income. The bank that buys the portfolio or the repackaged portfolio is now exposed to the credit risk of the entire portfolio. The purchasing bank however does not incur the operating costs associated with loan origination and in fact the original borrower may not be aware that the loan has been sold to a third party.

	EXPOSURE	TENOR YEARS	CASH FLOW SEQUENCE										
LOAN A1	300,000.00	10	1	30,000 1	30,000 2	30,000 3	30,000 4	30,000 5	30,000 6	30,000 7	30,000 8	30,000 9	30,000 10
LOAN B1	100,000.00	10	2	10,000 1	10,000 2	10,000 3	10,000 4	10,000 5	10,000 6	10,000 7	10,000 8	10,000 9	10,000 10
LOAN B2	100,000.00	10	3	10,000 1	10,000 2	10,000 3	10,000 4	10,000 5	10,000 6	10,000 7	10,000 8	10,000 9	10,000 10
LOAN B3	100,000.00	10	4	10,000 1	10,000 2	10,000 3	10,000 4	10,000 5	10,000 6	10,000 7	10,000 8	10,000 9	10,000 10
TOTAL LEN	600,000.00			60,000 1	60,000 2	60,000 3	60,000 4	60,000 5	60,000 6	60,000 7	60,000 8	60,000 9	60,000 10
WIGHTED	600,000.00												

	CASH FLOW SEQUENCE										
	1	28,000 1	28,000 2	28,000 3	28,000 4	28,000 5	28,000 6	28,000 7	28,000 8	28,000 9	28,000 10
	2	8,000 1	8,000 2	8,000 3	8,000 4	8,000 5	8,000 6	8,000 7	8,000 8	8,000 9	8,000 10
	3	8,000 1	8,000 2	8,000 3	8,000 4	8,000 5	8,000 6	8,000 7	8,000 8	8,000 9	8,000 10
	4	8,000 1	8,000 2	8,000 3	8,000 4	8,000 5	8,000 6	8,000 7	8,000 8	8,000 9	8,000 10
		52,000 1	52,000 2	52,000 3	52,000 4	52,000 5	52,000 6	52,000 7	52,000 8	52,000 9	52,000 10

Figure 7.6 Selling the Risk

As per the illustration the bank would recover $520,000 and the purchasing bank would obtain a portfolio worth $600,000 for only $520,000 making a profit of 15.38% provided the borrowers do not default. Although the selling bank may earn less interest from the loan portfolio, it has walked away from all the credit risk involved. This originate and dispose model has become quite common in banks and is used frequently. Banks often sell their portfolios and simultaneously buy other banks portfolios as well.

Credit Ratings

When receivables are packaged and sold to third parties the instruments thus created resemble what can be called asset backed securities. The mortgage cash flows highlighted above represent a financial asset themselves The values of these receivables are linked to the creditworthiness of the borrowers and so these receivables can be assigned a credit rating as an implicit composite rating of the ratings assigned to each individual borrower.

The buying back ought to conduct its own credit assessment of each individual borrower before buying the portfolio, however, when the number of borrowers run into thousands this is not a cost effective proposition. Instead samples are taken at random to assess the quality of the loan portfolio as a whole, or the opinion of credit rating agencies is sought on the quality of the portfolio and the quality of the collaterals that are linked to the receivables.

A fundamental flaw however in this mechanism is that it is the selling bank that secures the credit assessment of its portfolio from rating agencies and not the buying bank. The selling bank pays the rating agency for the opinion offered by the latter. The agency discloses the methodology and assumptions used in coming to certain conclusions of asset quality, however, these assumptions are rarely scrutinized in detail by investors. Nevertheless, the rating agency could also assess the credit worthiness of the portfolio at the request of the buying bank.

Transferring the Risk

Loans come with credit risk. The ability of borrowers to repay loans is assessed at the point of loan origination. However, borrowers may default for a variety of reasons. There could be wilful and deliberate default on the part of the borrower who has the capacity to repay but not the willingness. There could be the occurrence of a negative "life event" such as loss of a job caused by an economic downturn, or relocation of factories or due to medical illnesses or a host of other factors which could not have been anticipated at the time of loan origination and affect the borrower's capacity to pay. Certain factors can be in the control of borrowers other factors can be out of the control of borrowers.

Banks can hedge against a fall in the value of stocks, bonds and foreign currency they hold on their balance sheets using hedging tools such as options and futures contracts. Even adverse changes in interest rates can be thwarted by purchasing interest rates swaps to cover for increases or decreases in market rates. But how can banks cover themselves from credit risk, the risk that is a major component of their basic business, that of lending. Collateral is considered to be a risk mitigant, but values of collateral can fluctuate. Banks have to go through detailed legal proceedings before liquidating houses in the case of mortgage loans. Furthermore, at the time of liquidation of collateral banks may not be able to recover the market value of the asset but what is known as a Forced Sale Value, which can be considerably lower. Banks maintain reserves from their income to offset losses incurred by borrower's defaults. Collateral values may offer a stop loss mechanism to banks but as sighted above often are difficult to liquidate and often do lose considerable value when actually sold in the marketplace.

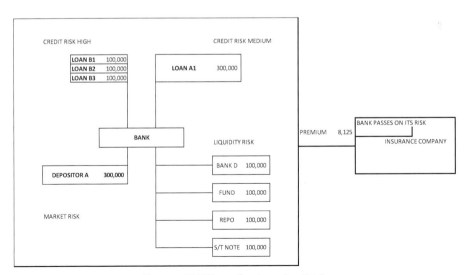

Figure 7.7 Transferring the Risk

Banks however have managed to develop a mechanism to transfer credit risk to third parties by simply buying credit insurance policies on their portfolios. Certain insurance companies and other institutions have in the conventional space, offered to protect banks from credit default against the payment of a premium. The product resemble a normal insurance policy that a reader may be familiar with, the only difference here is that the peril under consideration is credit default on a particular basket of financial assets or loans. These credit insurance policies can be structured in the following manner. Bank A with $600,000 of outstanding loans has classified its portfolio according to the risk profile of the borrowers. So if Loan Series A1 for $600,000 has a rating of AAA, and Loans B1,B2 and B3 have ratings of BBB, the likelihood of default in the B Series is greater than the likelihood of default of the A Series. Therefore, the insurance policy that protects the Bank from defaults will have higher premiums for the riskier B Series loans than the A Series Loan.

Counterparties willing to take the credit risk have thereby absolved the banks from holding onto credit risk while still allowing them to hold the asset on its balance sheet and maintaining the client relationship. Such counterparties are also assigned the rights to liquidate all collateral held by the banks.

Premiums on these credit insurance policies are calculated in a manner similar to the manner any normal policy is priced, where Risk Contribution is simply the product of Probability of Peril * Sum Assured or Payout. In the case above if we were to price insurance premiums for Loan A defaulting, we would come up with the same number as we did for Expected Losses.

Were a bank to maintain reserves to provision for losses, it would be one thing. An alternative would be to pay the same amount calculated as a reserve as a premium to a 3rd party to cover for credit defaults. Option 2 is more expensive in a way, as if no defaults occur, the bank cannot recover the amounts paid in premiums, but if the same bank had maintained reserves to cover for losses, and no losses occurred, the bank could credit the reserves to its Profit and Loss account and paid it as a reserve.

An important point to note is that a reserve for Expected Losses is a mathematical figure. Were the bank to maintain reserves for Loan A to default, over a period of 2 years it would have reserves of $4,000. If in 2 years Loan A for $300,000 does default, and assuming the bank is able to liquidate the collateral for $250,000, the reserves of $4,000 would not be sufficient to cover the loss of $50,000 to the bank. However, if the bank had purchased an credit insurance policy, the insurance company would simply pay the Bank $300,000 and it would bear a loss of $50,000 instead of the bank. The insurance company would liquidate the collateral, but the net amount of $50,000 would a loss on its books. Thus purchasing Credit Default Swaps in this manner offers banks an additional credit cover and serves as an additional risk mitigant along with collateral and reserves.

Credit protection is not new to the banking industry but so far has been reserved for depositors. The governments of many countries agree to guarantee all deposits placed within the banking system to provide stability to the financial sector. Depositors are seen as creditors to banks and in the event that banks re unable to pay their depositors, government run deposit insurance schemes step in and make good the losses. However, such credit protection had been made available to depositors under government run deposit insurance schemes. The insurance premium for this coverage is paid by the banks and not the borrowers.

It was a matter of time before this concept could be applied to banks who sought protection from the possibility of default of their borrowers from the private sector. The premium paid on the insurance policy taken by a bank would reflect again the quality of the underlying asset portfolio, or the creditworthiness of the portfolio.

CDS and the Financial Crises

Credit Default Swaps or Credit Insurance Policies gained in popularity for one major reason. Institutional investors in the US were running short of AAA rated assets to invest in. Funds managers, pension funds, insurance companies and various asset management companies have seen in recent years competition from Sovereign Wealth Funds with astronomical balance sheets. The mere purchasing of these SWFs has inflated asset prices and also reduced the supply of good assets available for sale. Therefore, private funds managers looked to invest in the credit portfolios of commercial banks. But banks had to not only repackage their credit portfolios by a process known as securitization, but also had to provide credit enhancements so that their loans could be "bought over" by fund managers.

Banks in the US are no longer in the distribution business of loans. Many large, well known commercial banks bought mortgage loans in the 2000s from reputable finance companies, who actually did the laborious work of identifying borrowers, booking loans, disbursing loans and then monitoring them. These finance companies that approached international ratings agencies to rate their portfolios. Rating agencies also did not look at all loans one by one, but checked tranches of loans. Tranches is a complicated word for a basket of financial assets. If we assume one basket has 1 loan of AAA, 2 loans of BBB and 1 loan of B-, the basket has an average rating of BBB+ (for instance) and therefore becomes investment grade quality. Such mechanisms of packaging good quality loans with poor quality loans is no different than throwing in a few rotten potatoes with some good ones and selling a 5kg basket at the grocery store for a discount. In this manner the grocery store gets rid of its rotten inventory along with its good stock. In fact the good inventory is used to disguise the poor inventory and this is what was done in the case of home mortgages in the US.

Finance companies managed to use this process to secure investment grade ratings for bundles of good and bad inventory of loans and sold these portfolios to commercial banks. Commercial banks purchased credit insurance policies from AIA insurance to further package the loans and sell them to fund managers. AIA also calculated its risk exposure based on the credit ratings provided by ratings agencies and failed not only to conduct its own due diligence and also failed to buy reinsurance for this exposure.

Neither of the players expected 30% of the borrowers to default on their house loans, or for housing prices to drop by 30% in just 1 quarter making the values of the collateral utterly useless against the loans extended.

Due Diligence

The counterparty or insurance company should have an in depth knowledge of the quality of the portfolio and should price the risk on the bank based upon the creditworthiness of the bank's underlying borrowers. In essence creditworthiness itself becomes an asset. A higher premium reflects higher risk, and lower premiums reflect lower risks. The banking industry developed Credit Default Swaps that behave much like an insurance policy on loans, however, the premiums paid on the credit protection themselves and the insurance contracts became tradable contracts.

Not only were certain parties willing to issue the insurance policy, certain parties developed tradable products linked in value to the insurance premiums paid by the banks seeking coverage. Unlike normal insurance premiums that do not change during a policy period, these credit default swap contracts changed in value with a change in the financial situation of the bank and the quality of the receivables. If a bank begins to experience a growing number of defaults in its portfolio, the cost of purchasing credit default protection will increase. The contract of credit default protection itself began to be traded as a financial product and the value of this contract was seen as a creditor's assessment of a banks finances. Just as shareholders reflect the quality of a company's assets in share prices, creditors now interpreted the value of insurance premiums paid on credit protection as a value of the creditworthiness of the banks finances.

In 2008 as these contracts came to be traded, banks were going through daily trading and settlements, investors could daily gauge the changes in a banks position on an ongoing basis without having to wait for quarterly announcements from the banks. Financial markets began to play closer attention to the price at which banks insurance policies were being traded than they were paying to the price of the companies' stock. The value of a bank's stock is although meant to indicate the strength of a banks books, given the heavy volume of speculative secondary trading, and low cost of borrowing, the "markets" valuations could no longer be relied upon. The credit default swap not only became a product that could be traded it also become a means of valuing the portfolio of a bank, its creditworthiness and its expected earnings.

Islamic Credit Default Swap

The Credit Default Swap behaves as a contract of *takaful*. An Islamic bank trying to seek coverage for credit default becomes a participant in a plan offered by a specialized *takaful* company or any other counter party like an Islamic Hedge Fund that is willing to take the risk for a certain price. However, to curtail the speculative features of CDS trading it would be prudent to limit the trading of Islamic Credit Default Swap contracts. Islamic banks seeking to purchase credit protection from a counterparty willing to offer it may enter into a contractual relationship under the concept of *takaful*. The *takaful* company offering the protection should conduct due diligence on the loan portfolio they wish to underwrite and should seek out *re-takaful* to limit their exposures. *Takaful* companies can begin to provide cover for certain economic sectors only to penetrate the market of credit risk with care.

It would be interesting to see if a secondary market can be developed for insurance policies that cover for credit risk. Who would be the players in such a market and how would insurance policies be bought and sold. For instance of Bank A has purchased $100M worth of credit protection from Party B for $1M, can either A or B sell this contract to C? If A feels their credit portfolio has stabilised and no longer needs the credit cover can A sell its rights under the policy to C for $950,000. Now C would be the beneficiary of an insurance policy. Would C have cover for its own portfolio of loans, would C have to be a bank or could the cover be applied to any other financial assets with similar rating and maturity as the assets of Bank A?

The concept of trading *takaful* policies is to date unheard of within the Islamic Finance Space, but it is possible to explore this area. A secondary market for any asset provides support to a primary market and an incentive for institutions to experiment with new products and structures as a liquid secondary market allows for easy exist.

Credit Linked Notes

Another mechanism of transferring risk or sharing risk with a third party is to issue Credit Linked Notes. A CLN is a hybrid instrument that looks like a fixed income instrument but can behave like equity as there is an element of risk sharing embedded in the structure.

A CLN is basically a bond whose returns are linked to the returns of an underlying portfolio of receivables or financial assets. The bond offers a premium coupon to investors over vanilla bonds as in the event the issuing entity suffers some deterioration in the value of its receivables these can be passed onto the note holders in the shape of either reduced coupon payments or reduced principal repayment at the maturity of the note. In effect the purchaser of the note is not only an investor in a bond but also a credit protection seller, whereas the note issuer is not only a bond issuer but also a protection buyer. The instrument can fund liquidity needs and also provide credit protection at the same time.

An issuer of a CLN however, may or may not have any receivables on its balance sheet and maybe issued by an unrelated entity speculating on the credit quality of an unrelated lender. From a *shariah* point of view this may well be an impermissible application of the structure.

We can illustrate the CLN in the following manner:-

A bank has a portfolio of car loans worth $100M offering a return of 5% per annum. The bank decides to fund this asset using a CLN instead of a plain vanilla bond issue.

LIABILITY		ASSET
OPTION A VANILLA BOND $100,000,000		CAR LOANS $100,000,000
ISSUED AT PAR VALUE	$100	
TENOR	2 YEARS	
COUPON	120BPS	
REDEEMED AT MATURITY	$100	
RATING	AAA	
OPTION B CLN $100,000,000		
ISSUED AT PAR VALUE	$100	
TENOR	2 YEARS	
COUPON	200BPS	
REDEEMED AT MATURITY	$100 OR LESS	
RATING	AAA	

Figure 7.8 Credit Linked Note Illustration

The bank offers investors a coupon rate of 200BPS with the added clause that if the bank experiences more than 5% of defaults on its loan portfolio, the bank will redeem the note not at $100 but at $95. Investors are offered a premium of 80BPS for sharing the risk on the credit portfolio with the bank

The bank can offer a floating coupon mechanism whereby if it experiences an upgrade in its credit rating the bank will offer a lower coupon payment, say of 180BPS and conversely if the bank experiences s downgrade in its credit rating the bank will pay an increased coupon payment of 220BPS.

The coupon payment can also be linked to the credit spreads earned by the bank. Any increase in cost of funds is shared with the CLN holder in terms of reduced coupon payments.

The CLN offers considerable opportunities for product development and alternative sources of funds for Islamic Banks and the industry as a whole as it is a hybrid instrument offering features of debt and equity.

Conclusion

The Islamic Financial Industry could well develop hybrid instruments that have features of both equity and debt. A bond issued to finance a credit portfolio is a fixed income debt instrument if all coupon payments on the bond and its principal amount repayment are unaffected by returns on the credit portfolio. The same instrument becomes a hybrid instrument if the pay outs are adversely affected if there is a credit event that affects the portfolio. The instrument of *sukuk,* has attempted to capture the best features of both equity and debt but thus far has been absorbed into the market as a debt instrument and has often been referred to as a Islamic bond, which is as true to its essence as saying Islamic interest payments.

Investors are averse to enjoying ownership rights over assets, as their claims are then downgraded to a residual status. In the event of poor returns, all other obligations in terms of expenses, salaries and so on are settled before proceeds from a liquidated asset are transferred to the ownership of an investor. However, where investors are financiers or lenders, their rights supersede even those of the employees of a company that is being liquidated. Under such a legal environment, investors prefer to be lenders rather that equity stake holders. This market sentiment, and the insistence of *sukuk* issuers to please investors with such mind sets has polluted the concept of *sukuk.*

Furthermore, providing credit cover, or *takaful* cover on credit events is a bold step, for which Islamic Financial Institutions are not ready. Islamic *takaful operators* are still treading the safer waters of general and family *takaful,* and are still not able to provide cover for large projects or entities including even the Ka'aba, which is in fact covered by Tokyo Marine Insurance Company. It will be some years before the *takaful* industry will venture into providing cover for credit events, however, there is no harm in laying the ground work for the conceptual framework.

CHAPTER 8

STRUCTURED PRODUCTS

EXPENSE ON LIABILITY		LIABILITY - FUNDING SOURCE		ASSET- UTILIZATION OF FUNDS		INCOME FROM ASSET		NET INCOME		ASSET CLASS
EXPENSE	RATE	ACCOUNT TYPE	AMOUNT MOBILISED	ASSET	AMOUNT ALLOCATED	RATE	INCOME	SPREAD	NET INCOME	
-	0.00%	CURRENT ACCOUNT	200,000,000	CREDIT CARDS LOANS	100,000,000	14.00%	14,000,000	14.00%	14,000,000	DEBT INSTRUMENTS
3,000,000	1.00%	SAVINGS ACCOUNT	300,000,000	AUTO LOANS	250,000,000	10.00%	25,000,000	9.00%	22,000,000	
15,000,000	3.00%	FIXED DEPOSIT	500,000,000	HOME MORTGAGES	490,000,000	8.00%	39,200,000	5.00%	24,200,000	
4,000,000	2.00%	REPURCHASE AGREEMENTS	200,000,000	BUSINESS LOANS	200,000,000	7.00%	14,000,000	5.00%	10,000,000	
400,000	2.00%	EQUITY LINKED DEPOSIT	20,000,000	S$P SHARIAH 500	20,000,000	3.00%	600,000	1.00%	200,000	CAPITAL MARKETS INSTRUMENTS
200,000	0.50%	SUKUK LINKED DEPOSIT	40,000,000	SOVEREIGN SUKUK	40,000,000	1.00%	400,000	0.50%	200,000	
200,000	2.00%	GOLD FUND	10,000,000	GOLD	10,000,000	3.00%	300,000	1.00%	100,000	COMMODITIES
250,000	2.50%	OIL FUND	10,000,000	OIL	10,000,000	4.00%	400,000	1.50%	150,000	
800,000	4.00%	ALUMINUM FUND	20,000,000	ALUMINUM	20,000,000	6.00%	1,200,000	2.00%	400,000	
1,050,000	3.50%	FOREIGN EXCHANGE FUND	30,000,000	$,GBP, YEN, EURO	30,000,000	5.00%	1,500,000	1.50%	450,000	FOREIGN CURRENCY
10,500,000	7.00%	REIT FUND I	150,000,000	COMMERCIAL RE	150,000,000	9.00%	13,500,000	2.00%	3,000,000	REAL ESTATE
2,000,000	5.00%	REIT FUND II	40,000,000	RESIDENTIAL RE	40,000,000	7.00%	2,800,000	2.00%	800,000	
250,000	5.00%	EM FUNDS	5,000,000	GCC, ASEAN	5,000,000	7.00%	350,000	2.00%	100,000	EM
		CASA & EQUITY		CASH AND SHORT TERM NOTES	312,500,000	2.00%	6,250,000	1.00%	3,125,000	CSTN
37,650,000		TOTAL LIABILITIES	1,525,000,000	TOTAL ASSETS	1,677,500,000		113,250,000		75,600,000	

	EQUITY	152,500,000			
	TOTAL LIABILITIES + EQUITY	1,677,500,000	TOTAL ASSETS	1,677,500,000	

Figure 8.1 Balance Sheet

For our discussion on structured products we shall for the time being ignore regulatory issues, and banking models. We shall assume that banks are free to mobilise deposits and funds in any way they choose and allocate these funds in any way they choose.

We shall also assume for the time being that all deposits and funds are principal guaranteed and indicative rates of returns are also guaranteed. The balance sheet indicates a simplistic example where we can assume that funds mobilised from current accounts are only used to finance credit cards. This may not be the actual case, current account funds may also be used to finance purchase of stocks and bonds. Further funds mobilised from equity linked deposits may be used to fund credit based assets.

What is important to understand here that the in top part of the balance sheet the bank's assets are loan contracts that generate interest income for the bank. Some of these loans are collaterized and others are not. We also see that profit rates (or interest rates) embedded in these assets are pre-determined, so the bank knows what earnings to expect from this portfolio. This portfolio also offers the highest returns to the bank. The remainder of the balance sheet requires of the bank to buy financial assets, commodities and real estate. Only fixed income bonds offer a pre-determined interest rate and the rental on various real estate assets. Returns from stocks come from unpredictable dividends and from capital gains, i.e. the difference between the buying price and the selling price.

We can call the former portfolio a debt based or loan based portfolio and the latter a trade based portfolio. Each portfolio presents the banks with its own risks, and the bank has tools for each kind of risk it is exposed to. It mitigates credit risk, with collateral, and impairment reserves. Market risk is mitigated using variable rate asset structures and liquidity risk is managed by keeping a certain number of liquid assets on the balance sheets. For equities, banks maintain certain inventories of put options as protection and use interest rate swaps to mitigate interest rate risk, in case interest rates increase and the current bonds held offer lower yield than the ones on the market. Each mitigant also comes at its own price.

Losses accrued from investments in equities can be covered by income earned from credit cards for instance, to ensure customers get their required rate of return. The balance sheet looks like a poorly managed insurance company, where different funds exist to cover different risks, but the funds are co-mingled between each asset and risk class. Each liability class also poses its own risk, customers may wish to withdraw funds either on demand or over a period of say 30 days, 60 days or 90 days. Most customers place funds in fixed deposits for not longer than 90 days. The bank in this scenario would therefore have to mobilize new funds at the same costs to maintain a certain spread. This may not always be easy to do. It is rather difficult to match any liability fund with a specific asset, as most assets are long term in nature and do not match the "behaviour" of the liabilities that fund them.

Fund providers however can be classified according to their risk appetite. Risk averse customers may want their deposits to only fund credit based assets, and may demand principal and profit guarantees. Banks may offer lower returns in exchange for these guarantees as the bank would have to make provisions for any losses incurred such that they are not passed onto depositors. Risk averse customers may not want their deposits to fund purchases of equities, or real estate or emerging markets sovereign bonds or *sukuks*.

The bank could theoretically therefore "ring fence" the funds of risk averse customer's deposits from those of risk prone depositors. Certain customers may prefer to take on certain risks in exchange for higher returns. The bank could map such customers and design different products with varying combinations of principal guarantee or returns guarantees. For instance the bank could offer products shown in Figure 8.2

PRODUCT	PRINCIPAL GUARANTEE	PROFIT GUARANTEE	POSSIBLE PROFIT RANGES
ABC	100%	NIL	1% TO 3%
DEF	98%	NIL	1% TO 5%
GHI	95%	NIL	1% TO 9%
JKL	90%	NIL	1% TO 14%

Figure 8.2 Structured Products

Funds can be mobilised according to the risk profiles and then asset allocation within the balance sheet can be determined based upon these risk profiles. Surplus returns from any one asset class CAN fund deficits in any other asset class and if all assets experience lower than expected returns than the fund providers either must absorb losses or be compensated by the shareholders. Obviously someone has to take the hit.

Structured Products

The example above is a kind of structured product and we can look at how these products look without any clothes on.

Structured Product ABC

PRODUCT	PRINCIPAL GUARANTEE	PROFIT GUARANTEE	POSSIBLE PROFIT RANGES
ABC	100%	NIL	1% TO 3%

Figure 8.3 Structured Product ABC

ABC may fund assets in the following way:-

ASSET CLASS	PERCENTAGE EXPOSURE
DEBT	70%
CREDIT CARDS 10%	
AUTO LOANS 20%	
HOUSE LOANS 30%	
BUSINESS LOANS 40%	
CONSTRUCTION 10%	
TELECOM 30%	
WHEAT FARMS 20%	
MINING 10%	
AUTO MANUF 5%	
ELECTRONICS MANUF 5%	
RETAIL & WHOLESALE 20%	
FIXED INCOME *SUKUK*	20%
FOREIGN CURRENCY	10%

Figure 8.4 ABC Exposure

We can see that even the debt portfolio is segregated by economic sectors, to diversify the bank's loan book and minimise exposure to any one given sector. However, one can also conduct certain "stress test" to establish the correlation between the various debt sectors. For instance if the telecom sector is a big employer in the country, and experiences a negative downturn, this may in fact impact the repayment capacity of various borrowers in the consumer sector. Laid off employees of the telecommunication sector may not be able to pay bills on credit cards, on auto loans or home mortgages, and therefore the poor performance of one borrower may impact the performance of other borrowers as well. It is likely that vendors of telecommunication companies may also suffer due to the negative performance and may also default on loan payments as well. In this manner one asset class has negative impacts on other asset classes.

We shall just name each loan type and assign it a rating for explaining further.

ASSET CLASS		SERIES NAME		STAND ALONE RATING	CORRELATION TO OTHER ASSETS
DEBT					
CREDIT CARDS	10%	CREDIT CARDS	10%	B-	.8
AUTO LOANS	20%	AUTO LOANS	20%	B+	.9
HOUSE LOANS	30%	HOUSE LOANS	30%	B	.95
BUSINESS LOANS	40%	BUSINESS LOANS	40%	A	.60
CONSTRUCTION	10%	CONSTRUCTION	10%	A-	.75
TELECOM	30%	TELECOM	30%	A+	.40
WHEAT FARMS	20%	WHEAT FARMS	20%	B-	.30
MINING	10%	MINING	10%	C	.30
AUTO MANUF	5%	AUTO MANUF	5%	B+	.65
ELECTRONICS	5%	ELECTRONICS	5%	B	.65
RETAIL & WHOLE	20%	RETAIL & WHOLE	20%	A-	.85

Figure 8.5 ABC Exposure with Ratings

All sectors of the economy are interrelated. Correlation measures the "connectiveness" of one sector to another, or one risk to another. What is the probability that a decline in demand in the telecommunication sector will cause a default in the bank's books, and what is the probability that this will trigger off defaults in other parts of the bank's books. Will credit card holders default, will auto loan holders default. Certainly if a major portion of employment is focused on the telecommunication sector, losses in the sector, may spread to other sectors like an oil spill we would have a default spill. Low demand for cars would impact revenues of auto manufacturers which might trigger off further defaults. Low demand for housing triggered off by poor economic prospects may trigger a decline in house loans and therefore on the construction industry. Banks in such a system would all be impacted differently based upon the nature of their portfolio.

Each asset class has a standalone risk, but no income earner functions on a standalone basis, ultimately, one borrower's fate is linked to others within the system. This risk be it unsystematic or systematic within the system, grows as banks portfolios grow. Ironically, as banks do diversify their portfolios, their risks of default continue to increase because the cobbler depends on the plumber, the plumber depends on the car mechanic who in turn depends on the car dealership, who in turn depends on the fate of the telecom workers in the community. Diversity in the portfolio does not hedge risks, because each economic agent lent to depends on income from another economic agent. The only way diversifying a loan portfolio reduces risk, is if the fate of each borrower is entirely unrelated to the fate of other borrowers, which is rarely the case.

It would also be rather difficult to quantify the relationship each borrower has with other borrowers, but we have assigned a correlation factor to the loans in the portfolio. Note that credit cards has the highest CF, as being a consumer loan, the consumer relies on income provided from the other sectors of the economy to pay his (or her) bills. The telecommunication loans have the lowest CR factor as its revenues do not depend so much on other sectors, but yet, it would be consumers who work for other sectors such as construction, mining, agriculture, retail etc. that would be purchasing cell phones and their packages. No one is earning income from paradise. How banks conduct stress tests is unknown to me, and seems to be a fruitless exercise if they are not able to determine the interconnectivity within an economy of various borrowers or asset classes. (it is frightening to see leading banks in all economies have very similar exposures to various sectors of the economy, so much for diversification).

Anyhow, to return to our discussion on structure products (we shall revert back to the concept of risk again).

Structured Product DEF

PRODUCT	PRINCIPAL GUARANTEE	PROFIT GUARANTEE	POSSIBLE PROFIT RANGES
DEF	98%	NIL	1% TO 5%

Figure 8.6 Structured Product DEF

Product DEF may have an asset allocation looking something as follows:-

ASSET CLASS	PERCENTAGE EXPOSURE
DEBT	40%
FOREIGN CURRENCY	20%
CORPORATE *SUKUK*	20%
SOVEREIGN *SUKUK*	15%
EQUITIES	5%

Figure 8.7 DEF Exposure

Product DEF offers returns linked to debt, trading in currencies, coupon payments on *sukuks,* and capital gains accrued from trading *sukuks.* As there is a principal loss component involved, the bank takes a 5% exposure on equities as well.

Structured Product GHI

PRODUCT	PRINCIPAL GUARANTEE	PROFIT GUARANTEE	POSSIBLE PROFIT RANGES
GHI	95%	NIL	1% TO 9%

Figure 8.8 Structured Product GHI

Product GHI allows the bank to take on certain additional risks as well.

ASSET CLASS		PERCENTAGE EXPOSURE
DEBT		20%
FOREIGN CURRENCY		10%
CORPORATE *SUKUK*		10%
SOVEREIGN *SUKUK*		10%
EQUITIES		15%
COMMODITIES		10%
ASSET CLASS	**PERCENTAGE EXPOSURE**	
GOLD	40%	
COPPER	20%	
ALUMINUM	20%	
OIL	15%	
ZINC	5%	
REAL ESTATE		5%

Figure 8.9 GHI Exposure

The asset allocation moves away from debt to other asset classes such as fixed income capital market's instruments to equities, commodities and real estate. Income sources move away from interest income to trading income. However, the bank does not take long term exposures on equities or commodities and in fact takes on high frequencies of buy sale trades to earn spreads, in what may be speculative in nature. Additional returns earned are shared with customers as are risks.

Structured Product JKL

ASSET CLASS		PERCENTAGE EXPOSURE
DEBT		10%
FOREIGN CURRENCY		10%
CORPORATE *SUKUK*		10%
SOVEREIGN *SUKUK*		5%
EQUITIES		25%
COMMODITIES		20%
ASSET CLASS	**PERCENTAGE EXPOSURE**	
GOLD	40%	
COPPER	20%	
ALUMINUM	20%	
OIL	15%	
ZINC	5%	
REAL ESTATE		5%
EMERGING MARKETS EQUITIES		15%

Figure 8.10 Structured Product JKL

We can see here therefore, how the asset allocation mix is revised and we move into riskier assets such as emerging markets equities.

The universe of assets may seem limited to a reader, but multinational banks are able to make investments in various asset classes all over the world. However, with the world segregated into 3 broad markets, Developed, Emerging and Frontier Markets, banks may not find a wide spectrum of low risk assets available for sale. After all there may be a large chunk of real estate available for sale in Singapore for instance, but its owners may not be willing to sell. Companies in China may have large market capitalization and excellent prospects but regulations may limit the investments foreign banks can make in domestic companies. It is no secret that banks compete with each other to purchase quality assets and this at times drives up prices such that when banks do liquidate their holdings they are unable to sell the asset for a decent spread as the asset was acquired at an inflated price.

Hedging

All banks try to hedge the risks they are exposed to. Credit risk is the most difficult risk to hedge, as there are few players out there wiling to cover credit risk. Credit risk can be covered by credit default swaps, where banks pay a sort of insurance premium to a counterparty, where a pay off is triggered by a credit event.

Market risk is absorbed by having variable rate liabilities and variable rate assets, along with such instruments as interest rate swaps. Investments in foreign currencies are hedged using fx swaps. Exposures to prices of equities are hedged using call and put options. Exposure to fluctuations in commodities are hedged using options and futures contracts. All these instruments are either traded by bespoke contracts, Over The Counter, or by standardised contracts on various exchanges. Each hedging tool comes at a price and an associated risk. Hedging does not eliminate any risk, it allows one party to share risk with another counterparty, but if the counterparty is unable to cover their end of their risk the bank is left with all the exposure. These instruments do not offer a 100% fix, nor do they come for free. Often enough, banks themselves sell such instruments to other institutions and clients and are exposed to contingent liabilities in the case certain events occur that trigger a pay off as in cases of performance guarantees etc.

Shariah Perspective

From a *shariah* standpoint an Islamic bank would in any case only invest in *shariah* compliant financial assets, alternative assets and commodities, so sharing profits from such investments with capital providers would be of no concern.

Conclusion

Structured Products link returns paid out to fund providers not just from a banks debt or credit portfolio but from a whole menu of other assets as well. Various products have a different mix of debt based and equity based exposure, and pay outs are streamlined to offer customers monthly returns. Obviously not all assets generate returns on a monthly basis, and therefore banks secure a stream of payments by maintaining reserves such as Profit Equalisation

Reserves and such. Various structures offer a varying risk and return mix, with some products offering the possibility of higher returns with a limited chance of loss of principal.

Traditionally banks have been in the business of lending money to individuals households, corporations of varying sizes and turnover, local governments, state governments, federal governments and international governments, international households and international companies. This has been the bread and butter of banks until of late. Yet there is an inherent problem in the lending model. Banks identify the best borrowers first, the doctors, lawyers and professionals of a community, or the well established companies of a certain industrial sector. After having lent to this low risk sector, banks are forced to find borrowers with slightly volatile and unpredictable earnings, or borrowers that present higher risks. With each subsequent loan given, the credit quality of the borrower (theoretically) depreciates. Within a span of time, and aided with technology, outsourcing models and such, banks quickly ran out of good borrowers and then had to find ways to package loans to poor borrowers. The incentive to originate and dispose came precisely from this predicament as the industry matured. The incentive to also make earnings from capital gains by speculative activity in currencies and other assets also became more acute.

Sharing interest income with depositors was the traditional way bank's customers got rewarded. However, as interest rates declined over the years, depositors also opted for products that compromised a certain percentage of their capital with the added caveat of offering higher returns. Banks used such depositors funds to invest in currency trading, commodities speculation, emerging markets equities, and such. Now, some depositors were sharing in another source of income through banks but also put their capital at risk.

Banks may offer depositors a share of the earnings from credit portfolios, as after all it is their money the bank is lending out, but through structured products, banks are able to use depositors money to invest in a whole range of financial assets, and share capital gains instead of just interest income with customers.

CHAPTER 9

EQUITY LINKED STRUCTURED DEPOSIT

Structure Products are merely mechanisms of offering customer's opportunities of earning a higher yield by investing part of funds deposited with the bank in other instruments and products offered by either the bank itself or by a third party. In an environment of reducing interest rates, structured products offer a variety of options to customers to divert part of their funds into the equities market, or the fixed income market, or even the commodities market. Certain products are structured such that the principal deposited is not guaranteed whereas other offer principal guarantees. A certain percentage of return is guaranteed and an additional yield can be earned provided certain market movements are favourable in financial and commodities markets where exposure is taken.

We shall examine several structured deposits and see how they can be adapted by Islamic banks. We revert to a hypothetical balance sheet to assess the motivation behind this product.

EXPENSE	RATE	ACCOUNT TYPE	AMOUNT MOBILISED	ASSET	AMOUNT ALLOCATED	RATE	INCOME	SPREAD	NET INCOME	ASSET CLASS
EXPENSE ON LIABILITY		LIABILITY - FUNDING SOURCE		ASSET - UTILIZATION OF FUNDS		INCOME FROM ASSET		NET INCOME		
-	0.00%	CURRENT ACCOUNT	200,000,000	CREDIT CARDS LOANS	100,000,000	14.00%	14,000,000	14.00%	14,000,000	DEBT INSTRUMENTS
3,000,000	1.00%	SAVINGS ACCOUNT	300,000,000	AUTO LOANS	250,000,000	10.00%	25,000,000	9.00%	22,000,000	
15,000,000	3.00%	FIXED DEPOSIT	500,000,000	HOME MORTGAGES	490,000,000	8.00%	39,200,000	5.00%	24,200,000	
4,000,000	2.00%	REPURCHASE AGREEMENTS	200,000,000	BUSINESS LOANS	200,000,000	7.00%	14,000,000	5.00%	10,000,000	
400,000	2.00%	EQUITY LINKED DEPOSIT	20,000,000	S$P SHARIAH 500	20,000,000	3.00%	600,000	1.00%	200,000	CAPITAL MARKETS INSTRUMENTS
200,000	0.50%	SUKUK LINKED DEPOSIT	40,000,000	SOVEREIGN SUKUK	40,000,000	1.00%	400,000	0.50%	200,000	
200,000	2.00%	GOLD FUND	10,000,000	GOLD	10,000,000	3.00%	300,000	1.00%	100,000	COMMODITIES
250,000	2.50%	OIL FUND	10,000,000	OIL	10,000,000	4.00%	400,000	1.50%	150,000	
800,000	4.00%	ALUMINUM FUND	20,000,000	ALUMINUM	20,000,000	6.00%	1,200,000	2.00%	400,000	
1,050,000	3.50%	FOREIGN EXCHANGE FUND	30,000,000	$,GBP, YEN, EURO	30,000,000	5.00%	1,500,000	1.50%	450,000	FOREIGN CURRENCY
10,500,000	7.00%	REIT FUND I	150,000,000	COMMERCIAL RE	150,000,000	9.00%	13,500,000	2.00%	3,000,000	REAL ESTATE
2,000,000	5.00%	REIT FUND II	40,000,000	RESIDENTIAL RE	40,000,000	7.00%	2,800,000	2.00%	800,000	
250,000	5.00%	EM FUNDS	5,000,000	GCC, ASEAN	5,000,000	7.00%	350,000	2.00%	100,000	EM
		CASA & EQUITY		CASH AND SHORT TERM NOTES	312,500,000	2.00%	6,250,000	1.00%	3,125,000	CSTN
37,650,000		TOTAL LIABILITIES	1,525,000,000	TOTAL ASSETS	1,677,500,000		113,250,000		75,600,000	

	EQUITY	152,500,000		
	TOTAL LIABILITIES + EQUITY	1,677,500,000	TOTAL ASSETS	1,677,500,000

Figure 9.1 Balance Sheet

In an environment where interest rates are high, banks can earn a significant spread between a profit rate charged on financing contracts and a profit rate paid to depositors. With interest rates at 6%, banks can offer depositors 3% and still walk away with a 3% spread. However, if interest rates on loans and financing contracts are as low as 1%, neither banks nor depositors stand to make any returns on investments.

In such an environment, banks and depositors seek high yields on investments, forcing an environment of financial innovation. The balance sheet above reflects total deposits and funds to a tune of $1.530 billion and assets of $1.530 billion. Deposits and funds are sourced from 13 different account types and customer categories, each offering a unique return. These include CASA deposits, Fixed Deposits, Equity Linked Deposits, *Sukuk* Linked Deposits, Commodities Funds and Foreign Exchange Funds. Assets are classified into 13 categories ranging from loans to investments in Emerging Market Funds. Setting aside issues of regulation, ring fencing of retail deposits we conclude that the balance sheet offers returns from a variety of cash flow streams generated by 13 different asset classes to reward 13 different liability classes. We also assume that income generated from one asset class can be used to compensate income generated from an underperforming asset class to fulfil obligations to depositors. We also assume that although fund providers are segregated by their risk appetite, funds are distributed amongst all the asset classes without restrictions.

The returns paid to any one depositor are also not linked to the performance of any specific asset class as returns from assets are pooled into a common income General Ledger account and then distributed amongst funds providers and the subsequently shareholders.

From the perspective of *shariah*, funds can be mobilised under either *wakalah, wadiah, qard, mudharabah, or reverse murabahah*. These contracts have all been addressed earlier in how they function. The reader can refer to Contracts and Deals in Islamic Finance by Hussain Kureshi for clarifications.

Equity Linked Convertible Deposit

An equity linked deposit is a structured product that has enjoyed considerable popularity in conventional banking. Its structure lends itself very easily to be adapted as a *shariah compliant* product. An ELCD is a product by virtue of which deposit is mobilised using any of the contracts mentioned above. The funds are capital guaranteed and are used to fund normal financing assets based on *murabahah, and ijarah.* Deposits are mobilized for varying tenors, typically 90 days and assets have an average tenure of 5 years. To offer the depositor additional yield, a portion of the deposit is used to purchase call options on a basket of *shariah compliant* stocks each with a specific exercise price. If any of the call options purchased fall In the Money, before the deposit is matured, the bank will share the earnings from exercising the option with the depositor on a *mudharabah* basis, or deliver the purchased shares to the depositor.

The contract of deposit may be a combination of *wadiah* and *mudharabah, qard* and *mudharabah* or even *wakalah* and *mudharabah*. What is important to realize here is that the bank in this case will a invest a portion of these funds in financial assets that are not developed by the bank itself, but in financial products sold on listed exchanges and offered by third parties.

Let us examine this product in detail:-

Deposit Amount	= $100,000	:	Tenor	= 90 day	:	Return = 2%
Call Options Price	= $1	:	Contract Size	= 10 shares		
Underlying Share	= IBM	:	Share Price	= $ 999		
Option Exercise Price	= $1,000	:	Options Purchase	= 10		

The bank receives $100,000 in deposit on January 1st 2000. $10 from the deposit is used to purchase 10 options in IBM shares. The remainder of the funds are allocated to fund assets on the balance sheet. The bank has to pay the customer $100,500 to the customer in 90 days as committed.

If the price of IBM stock goes beyond $1,000 to say $1,001 by March 31st, the bank can exercise the options on behalf of the customer utilising the $100,500 that has now matured in the customer's account. The 10 options will entitle the customer to purchase 10 shares per option at an Exercise Price of $1,000. The cash outlay required would be $100,000 for purchasing 100 shares of IBM at a price of $1,000. The bank can either deliver these shares to the customer or can sell them at market prices of $1,001 and credit the customer's account with the residual profit of $1 per share or $100 less any brokerage commissions paid. Not accounting for brokerage fees, the bank can retain $.50 as a share of the profits, and the customer would earn an additional $50 as return on a deposit of $100,000. The customer also has a final option to hold the stocks for longer period and benefit from an increase in share price of IBM for an even higher return.

The effective return for the depositor is $100,550 in 90 days or 2.2% on an annualized basis. The options provided an additional .2% yield for the depositor. However, if the stock price of IBM does not move favourably and the options are not In The Money when they deposit reaches maturity, the depositor can opt to extend the term of the deposit in anticipation of favourable price movements, or the options would retire worthless, yet the depositor will receive $100,500 at maturity. The cost of purchasing the options would be borne by the bank.

Such an arrangement would offer the depositor an opportunity to benefit from the upside and not be exposed to any downside events in the stock markets for additional yield. The Bank would have to ensure that the cost of the options purchased is covered either by the bank's share of profits on the trade, or from income generated from funding assets from the $100,000 deposit. The Bank could also arrange with the broker who purchases the options and shares on behalf of the customer to earn a certain commission from the buy and sale transactions.

Shariah Perspective

A *shariah* perspective on the product would be limited as there is no consensus as yet amongst the *shariah* community on the concept of options. We shall discuss this later in detail. Suffice it to say at this point that the share purchased would have to undergo *shariah* screening and must remain compliant for the time the bank holds the asset or the option on the asset.

Conclusion

Different variations of this product may be structured. Funds mobilised may be invested in call and put options or in index futures, linking returns to the performance of the stock markets without committing the full amount of the funds. Derivatives instruments allow depositors to earn additional yield if by investing in instruments that offer exposure to movements various markets for a variety of asset classes. What is important to understand here is that funds mobilised are not restricted to funding credit portfolios, but instead can also be used to fund a stock portfolio or a portfolio of options or a combination of both. A certain percentage of the customer's deposits may be kept in cash to manage liquidity, a certain percentage may be allocated to funds the bank's credit portfolio, and the remainder may be used to purchase stocks, or invest in equities indices or in options and other capital markets instruments.

A customer would enjoy predictable returns on a certain portion of his (or her)deposit, and may have a risk appetite to avail the opportunity to earn variable returns based on how well the bank bets on the markets. Investments in stocks coupled with purchase of an adequate number of call and put options can hedge a customer's position (with a cost) and not only limit losses, but offer a customer a predictable rate of return.

Such products can be customized to suit a client's needs, and may not always guarantee returns but ought to guarantee principal amounts, especially if they are held under contracts of *wadiah or qard*. Equity linked deposits can be structured under the contract of *mudharabah* where even the principal amount is not guaranteed.

CHAPTER 10

ISLAMIC *SUKUK* LINKED DEPOSITS

This concept may not require a dedicated chapter, however, Islamic banks can develop products that link returns to returns on some specific *sukuks*, a basket of *sukuks*, or a *sukuk index*. The conventional bond market is exceedingly well organized in this area with the US government Treasury Bills dominating the sovereign issue market. In fact the returns on US Treasury Bills are considered as global benchmark risk free rates. Bonds indices are developed keeping in mind either the issuer, or the region of the issuer or the risk ratings of issuers. Indices can be developed for issues of bonds for AAA rated sovereign issuers of the Organization of Economically Developed Countries. Alternatively, indices can track returns on AAA corporate bond issues. Typically bonds are fixed income instruments, they carry a fixed coupon rate, these coupon payments do not change, but yields on investing in bonds change as a function of the price for which bonds are traded. The price of a specific bond in the secondary market is a function of prevailing interest rates. A 10 bond issued in 2000 may be offering a coupon rate of 7%. In 2005, if interest rates increase to 8%, holders of a 7% bond would want to sell the bond and use the money to purchase the new issue of bonds offering 8%. Thus, the price of the 7% bond will decline. The opposite would happen if interest rates rise.

A **Global Sukuk Index** can be developed which tracks yields on various sovereign issues and corporate issues. Islamic Banks could offer products that offer returns linked to the performance of this index, or any other index which may have a basket of regional issues or local issues with particular ratings.

CHAPTER 11

ISLAMIC REPURCHASE AGREEMENTS

Repurchase Agreements are a type of transaction that allows banks to sell securities to another bank with the agreement (or binding promise) that the buying bank will resell the same securities back to the seller at a future date at another price.

There are 2 parties to the transaction, one the Seller of Securities and the other the Buyer. At time t = 0 the Seller would sell certain securities in its ownership to the Buyer for a Price P0. After a specific duration the Buyer would then sell back the securities to the original Seller for a Price P1. The Buyer in this case would earn a profit of P1 – P0.

The motivation behind this structure is for the Seller to raise funds equivalent to the Price P0 for a short term for a premium of P1 – P0. The Seller would in effect be raising a loan for the amount P0, using securities as a collateral, and for an effective interest rate of P1 – P0 / P0.

Let us illustrate using an example. Bank ABC is short of liquid cash but owns $100M of A rated shares in IBM. Bank XYZ has a surplus of cash and is looking for short term and secure placements.

Repo Transaction

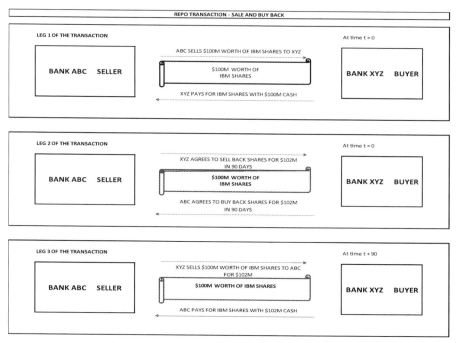

Figure 11.1 Repo Transaction Process Flow

The diagram above represents the process flow of a repo transaction. Effectively, ABC Bank raises funds for an effective rate of 2% per annum known as the repo rate. This rate is the cost of borrowing $100M for 90 days while placing shares worth $100M as collateral.

SALE PRICE	REPO PRICE	TENOR	DAYS BASIS	COLLATERAL TYPE	COLLATERAL AMOUNT
100,000,000	102,000,000	90	360	SHARES IN IBM	$100,000,000
RATE P.A.	TENOR	REPO RATE		PRICE PER SHARE	NUMBER OF SHARES
2.00%	0.25	0.50%		$1,000	100,000

Figure 11.2 Repo Illustrated

The same transaction is seen as a reverse repo from the perspective of Bank XYZ, that enters into a buy and sale back agreement as opposed to a sale and buy back agreement.

Reverse Repo Transaction

From the Buyers point of view the transaction is seen as a reverse repo.

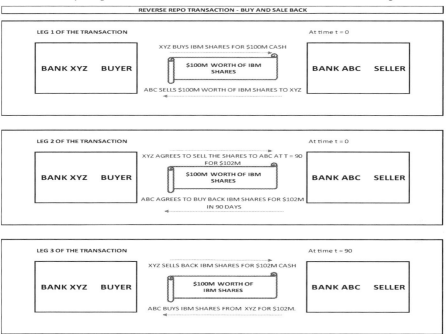

Figure 11.3 Reverse Repo

Credit Risk

Bank XYZ as the buyer of IBM shares worth $100M is effectively taking exposure on Bank ABC. ABC is required as per the agreement to repurchase the same shares for cash in 90 days for $100M and a $2M premium. ABC can default on this final leg of the transaction leaving XYZ looking to either keep the shares on its books or sell them to another buyer. In this manner XYZ is exposed to credit risk on ABC.

Market Risk

Bank XYZ holds 100,000 shares of IBM with a market price of $1,000 per share as collateral. However, the market value of the shares may increase or decrease. In the event that they decrease in value, Bank XYZ will be faced with a shortfall in the event that ABC defaults. The share price for IBM may decline for a number of reasons, such as an increase in interest rates in bonds, that leads to a sell off in equities, an increase in the prices of commodities and gold, or any other asset class. It can also be a result of some poor sales performance reported at IBM. Nevertheless, XYZ needs to protect itself from such events.

XYZ would recommend a "hair cut" on the value of the shares. If the market value of IBM shares is $100M at contract initiation, XYZ may consider buying them for only $90M and agreeing to sell them back to ABC for $92M in 90 days

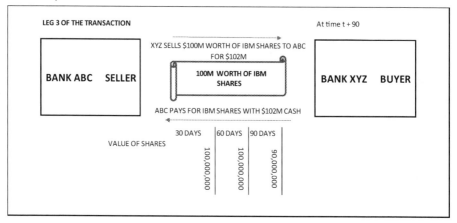

Figure 11.4 Final Leg of the Transaction

The transaction with a "haircut" would look something like this. XYZ's position would be covered for a 10% decline in the value of shares of IBM.

SALE PRICE	REPO PRICE	TENOR	DAYS BASIS	COLLATERAL TYPE	COLLATERAL AMOUNT	HAIR CUT
90,000,000	92,000,000	90	360	SHARES IN IBM	$100,000,000	$10,000,000
RATE P.A.	TENOR	REPO RATE		PRICE PER SHARE	NUMBER OF SHARES	
2.22%	0.25	0.56%		$1,000	100,000	

Figure 11.5 Repo with a Haircut

In this manner XYZ is covered for 10% decline in the value of the shares sold by ABC. In essence XYZ buys $100M worth of shares from ABC for only $90M and sells the same shares back to ABC for $92M in 90 days. The shares kept with XYZ serve as collateral for the transaction. XYZ can sell these shares to a 3rd party, but must have in hand similar assets in terms of credit rating and quality to sell back to ABC.

Mark to Market.

The concept of mark to market is rather simple. Assets held on bank's balance sheet can be reported at cost, market value or fair value. Collateral held by a bank is also reported in a similar manner. To illustrate, in 2014, a specific house has a cost price or market price to a buyer of $150,000. The bank extends a loan of $125,000 to help finance the loan. The $25,000 deduction is referred to as a haircut in industry terms. The loan is well secured as collateral provided is 120% the value of the loan. However, if by 2017, the outstanding amount of the loan is $110,000, but the value of the property is only $100,000, only 90.9% collaterised. The bank would have to report the value of the collateral at $100,000 in 2017, i.e. at market value. It would mark the value of the collateral to the market value.

Similarly, banks hold stocks in their balance sheet as assets. We assume a bank bought shares in IBM for $1000 in 2014. In 2017, the shaare price hikes to $1004, at what price should the bank report the asset on its balance sheet, at cost or $1,000 or at market value or $1004. If it reports the value at $1004, the asset has been marked to market.

In contracts where finanical assets are provided as collateral, borrowers may often find themselves in situations of increasing the amount of assets placed in collateral to counter a fall in prices. In our example above, the bank sells 100,000 shares to XYZ at a value of $1000 per share. The value of shares sold to XZY is thus $100M and XYZ pays ABC $100M. If the prices of the shares falls to $950, XYZ would be holding only $95M worth of shares as collateral against a loan disbursed of $100M. Were XYX to mark to markte the value of shares held, it would require ABC to place another 5,263.16 shares with XYZ to maintain a collateral value of $100M.

		NO. OF SHARES BOUGHT	MARKET PRICE / SHARE	INC/DEC PER SHARE PRICE	COLLATERAL NEEDED	CURRENT COLLATERAL VALUE	SHORTFALL /EXCESS IN $	SHORTFALL/ EXCESS IN SHARES
							MARK TO MARKET	
DAY	1	100,000.00	1,000.00		100,000,000.00	100,000,000.00	-	
DAY	2	100,000.00	999.00	(1.00)	100,000,000.00	99,900,000.00	(100,000.00)	(100.10)
DAY	3	100,000.00	998.00	(1.00)	100,000,000.00	99,800,000.00	(200,000.00)	(200.40)
DAY	4	100,000.00	999.00	1.00	100,000,000.00	99,900,000.00	(100,000.00)	(100.10)
DAY	5	100,000.00	1,000.00	1.00	100,000,000.00	100,000,000.00	-	-
DAY	6	100,000.00	1,001.00	1.00	100,000,000.00	100,100,000.00	100,000.00	99.90
DAY	7	100,000.00	1,000.50	(0.50)	100,000,000.00	100,050,000.00	50,000.00	49.98
DAY	8	100,000.00	1,000.25	(0.25)	100,000,000.00	100,025,000.00	25,000.00	24.99
DAY	9	100,000.00	1,000.00	(0.25)	100,000,000.00	100,000,000.00	-	-
DAY	10	100,000.00	1,000.25	0.25	100,000,000.00	100,025,000.00	25,000.00	24.99
DAY	11	100,000.00	1,000.50	0.25	100,000,000.00	100,050,000.00	50,000.00	49.98
DAY	12	100,000.00	1,000.75	0.25	100,000,000.00	100,075,000.00	75,000.00	74.94
DAY	13	100,000.00	1,000.50	(0.25)	100,000,000.00	100,050,000.00	50,000.00	49.98
DAY	14	100,000.00	1,000.25	(0.25)	100,000,000.00	100,025,000.00	25,000.00	24.99
DAY	15	100,000.00	1,000.00	(0.25)	100,000,000.00	100,000,000.00	-	-
DAY	16	100,000.00	999.50	(0.50)	100,000,000.00	99,950,000.00	(50,000.00)	(50.03)
DAY	17	100,000.00	999.75	0.25	100,000,000.00	99,975,000.00	(25,000.00)	(25.01)
DAY	18	100,000.00	999.50	(0.25)	100,000,000.00	99,950,000.00	(50,000.00)	(50.03)
DAY	19	100,000.00	999.65	0.15	100,000,000.00	99,965,000.00	(35,000.00)	(35.01)
DAY	20	100,000.00	999.85	0.20	100,000,000.00	99,985,000.00	(15,000.00)	(15.00)
DAY	21	100,000.00	999.90	0.05	100,000,000.00	99,990,000.00	(10,000.00)	(10.00)
DAY	22	100,000.00	999.75	(0.15)	100,000,000.00	99,975,000.00	(25,000.00)	(25.01)
DAY	23	100,000.00	999.50	(0.25)	100,000,000.00	99,950,000.00	(50,000.00)	(50.03)
DAY	24	100,000.00	999.45	(0.05)	100,000,000.00	99,945,000.00	(55,000.00)	(55.03)
DAY	25	100,000.00	999.40	(0.05)	100,000,000.00	99,940,000.00	(60,000.00)	(60.04)
DAY	26	100,000.00	999.35	(0.05)	100,000,000.00	99,935,000.00	(65,000.00)	(65.04)
DAY	27	100,000.00	999.50	0.15	100,000,000.00	99,950,000.00	(50,000.00)	(50.03)
DAY	28	100,000.00	999.55	0.05	100,000,000.00	99,955,000.00	(45,000.00)	(45.02)
DAY	29	100,000.00	999.00	(0.55)	100,000,000.00	99,900,000.00	(100,000.00)	(100.10)
DAY	30	100,000.00	998.75	(0.25)	100,000,000.00	99,875,000.00	(125,000.00)	(125.16)
DAY	31	100,000.00	998.50	(0.25)	100,000,000.00	99,850,000.00	(150,000.00)	(150.23)
DAY	32	100,000.00	998.25	(0.25)	100,000,000.00	99,825,000.00	(175,000.00)	(175.31)
DAY	33	100,000.00	998.00	(0.25)	100,000,000.00	99,800,000.00	(200,000.00)	(200.40)
DAY	34	100,000.00	997.75	(0.25)	100,000,000.00	99,775,000.00	(225,000.00)	(225.51)
DAY	35	100,000.00	998.00	0.25	100,000,000.00	99,800,000.00	(200,000.00)	(200.40)
DAY	36	100,000.00	998.25	0.25	100,000,000.00	99,825,000.00	(175,000.00)	(175.31)
DAY	37	100,000.00	998.50	0.25	100,000,000.00	99,850,000.00	(150,000.00)	(150.23)
DAY	38	100,000.00	998.75	0.25	100,000,000.00	99,875,000.00	(125,000.00)	(125.16)
DAY	39	100,000.00	998.80	0.05	100,000,000.00	99,880,000.00	(120,000.00)	(120.14)
DAY	40	100,000.00	998.85	0.05	100,000,000.00	99,885,000.00	(115,000.00)	(115.13)
DAY	41	100,000.00	998.90	0.05	100,000,000.00	99,890,000.00	(110,000.00)	(110.12)
DAY	42	100,000.00	999.00	0.10	100,000,000.00	99,900,000.00	(100,000.00)	(100.10)
DAY	43	100,000.00	999.25	0.25	100,000,000.00	99,925,000.00	(75,000.00)	(75.06)
DAY	44	100,000.00	999.50	0.25	100,000,000.00	99,950,000.00	(50,000.00)	(50.03)
DAY	45	100,000.00	999.75	0.25	100,000,000.00	99,975,000.00	(25,000.00)	(25.01)
DAY	46	100,000.00	1,000.00	0.25	100,000,000.00	100,000,000.00	-	-
DAY	47	100,000.00	1,000.25	0.25	100,000,000.00	100,025,000.00	25,000.00	24.99
DAY	48	100,000.00	1,000.50	0.25	100,000,000.00	100,050,000.00	50,000.00	49.98
DAY	49	100,000.00	1,000.75	0.25	100,000,000.00	100,075,000.00	75,000.00	74.94
DAY	50	100,000.00	1,001.00	0.25	100,000,000.00	100,100,000.00	100,000.00	99.90
DAY	51	100,000.00	1,001.25	0.25	100,000,000.00	100,125,000.00	125,000.00	124.84
DAY	52	100,000.00	1,001.50	0.25	100,000,000.00	100,150,000.00	150,000.00	149.78
DAY	53	100,000.00	1,001.75	0.25	100,000,000.00	100,175,000.00	175,000.00	174.69
DAY	54	100,000.00	1,002.00	0.25	100,000,000.00	100,200,000.00	200,000.00	199.60
DAY	55	100,000.00	1,001.75	(0.25)	100,000,000.00	100,175,000.00	175,000.00	174.69
DAY	56	100,000.00	1,001.50	(0.25)	100,000,000.00	100,150,000.00	150,000.00	149.78
DAY	57	100,000.00	1,001.25	(0.25)	100,000,000.00	100,125,000.00	125,000.00	124.84
DAY	58	100,000.00	1,001.00	(0.25)	100,000,000.00	100,100,000.00	100,000.00	99.90
DAY	59	100,000.00	1,001.00	-	100,000,000.00	100,100,000.00	100,000.00	99.90
DAY	60	100,000.00	1,001.00	-	100,000,000.00	100,100,000.00	100,000.00	99.90
DAY	61	100,000.00	1,001.00	-	100,000,000.00	100,100,000.00	100,000.00	99.90
DAY	62	100,000.00	1,001.25	0.25	100,000,000.00	100,125,000.00	125,000.00	124.84
DAY	63	100,000.00	1,001.50	0.25	100,000,000.00	100,150,000.00	150,000.00	149.78
DAY	64	100,000.00	1,001.75	0.25	100,000,000.00	100,175,000.00	175,000.00	174.69
DAY	65	100,000.00	1,001.50	(0.25)	100,000,000.00	100,150,000.00	150,000.00	149.78
DAY	66	100,000.00	1,001.25	(0.25)	100,000,000.00	100,125,000.00	125,000.00	124.84
DAY	67	100,000.00	1,001.00	(0.25)	100,000,000.00	100,100,000.00	100,000.00	99.90
DAY	68	100,000.00	1,000.75	(0.25)	100,000,000.00	100,075,000.00	75,000.00	74.94
DAY	69	100,000.00	1,000.50	(0.25)	100,000,000.00	100,050,000.00	50,000.00	49.98
DAY	70	100,000.00	1,000.25	(0.25)	100,000,000.00	100,025,000.00	25,000.00	24.99
DAY	71	100,000.00	1,000.00	(0.25)	100,000,000.00	100,000,000.00	-	-
DAY	72	100,000.00	1,000.25	0.25	100,000,000.00	100,025,000.00	25,000.00	24.99
DAY	73	100,000.00	1,000.50	0.25	100,000,000.00	100,050,000.00	50,000.00	49.98
DAY	74	100,000.00	1,000.75	0.25	100,000,000.00	100,075,000.00	75,000.00	74.94
DAY	75	100,000.00	1,001.00	0.25	100,000,000.00	100,100,000.00	100,000.00	99.90
DAY	76	100,000.00	1,001.25	0.25	100,000,000.00	100,125,000.00	125,000.00	124.84
DAY	77	100,000.00	1,001.50	0.25	100,000,000.00	100,150,000.00	150,000.00	149.78
DAY	78	100,000.00	1,001.00	(0.50)	100,000,000.00	100,100,000.00	100,000.00	99.90
DAY	79	100,000.00	1,000.50	(0.50)	100,000,000.00	100,050,000.00	50,000.00	49.98
DAY	80	100,000.00	1,000.25	(0.25)	100,000,000.00	100,025,000.00	25,000.00	24.99
DAY	81	100,000.00	1,000.00	(0.25)	100,000,000.00	100,000,000.00	-	-
DAY	82	100,000.00	1,000.25	0.25	100,000,000.00	100,025,000.00	25,000.00	24.99
DAY	83	100,000.00	1,000.50	0.25	100,000,000.00	100,050,000.00	50,000.00	49.98
DAY	84	100,000.00	1,000.75	0.25	100,000,000.00	100,075,000.00	75,000.00	74.94
DAY	85	100,000.00	1,000.50	(0.25)	100,000,000.00	100,050,000.00	50,000.00	49.98
DAY	86	100,000.00	1,000.25	(0.25)	100,000,000.00	100,025,000.00	25,000.00	24.99
DAY	87	100,000.00	1,000.00	(0.25)	100,000,000.00	100,000,000.00	-	-
DAY	88	100,000.00	999.50	(0.50)	100,000,000.00	99,950,000.00	(50,000.00)	(50.03)
DAY	89	100,000.00	999.75	0.25	100,000,000.00	99,975,000.00	(25,000.00)	(25.01)
DAY	90	100,000.00	1,000.00	0.25	100,000,000.00	100,000,000.00	-	-

Figure 11.6 90 Days Prices for shares

The table above reflects changes in the price of IBM shares over a period of 90 days. At times the price of shares falls below the $1,000 level and at times the prices of IBM shares goes beyond the $1,000 level. If XYZ has bought these shares without a haircut, ABC would have to beef up the collateral by additional shares, each time the value of IBM's shares falls below the $1,000 level.

Figure 11.7 Chart for IBM prices.

As per the chart above this happens frequently during the initial days of the contract when prices fall well below the $1,000 levels.

		NO. OF SHARES BOUGHT	MARKET PRICE / SHARE	INC/DEC PER SHARE PRICE	COLLATERAL NEEDED	CURRENT COLLATERAL VALUE	SHORTFALL /EXCESS IN $	SHORTFALL/ EXCESS IN SHARES
							MARK TO MARKET	
DAY	1	100,000.00	1,000.00		100,000,000.00	100,000,000.00	-	
DAY	2	100,000.00	999.00	(1.00)	100,000,000.00	99,900,000.00	(100,000.00)	(100.10)
DAY	3	100,000.00	998.00	(1.00)	100,000,000.00	99,800,000.00	(200,000.00)	(200.40)

Figure 11.8 1st 3 Days if Trading

As per the table above, on Day 2, prices for IBM shares fall to $999, therefore the level of collateral held with Bank XYZ is valued at $99,900,000. ABC will therefore have to beef up the collateral with additional 110.10 shares which will have to be "sold" to Bank XYZ.

Nature of asset sold

In repo transactions the assets that can be sold and bought back can include physical assets, financial assets, receivables, stocks, bonds, *sukuks,* pretty much any asset class that is agreeable to both parties, has a liquid market and an efficient and transparent pricing mechanism. In the context of financial assets, the assets in the 2 legs of the transaction need not be the same. If for instance US Treasury Bills of AAA Rating are sold in the first leg of the transaction. The counterparty need only furnish similar securities with similar maturity dates to the original seller.

Islamic Repurchase Agreements

Islamic Repurchase Agreements can be structured using the concept of *wa'd.* A repurchase agreement, combines 2 sales contracts with a promise. One sale contract of *bai* is linked to another sale contract (the buy back) with a promise. Each sale transaction in the process will be documented using a separate Sale and Purchase Agreement. The first sale will be based upon the First Agreement and the Buy back on the Third Agreement.

First Agreement: The Selling Bank (SB) enters into a Sale and Buy Back Agreement (SBBA) with the Buying Bank (BB), to sell a certain number of specific securities at a specific price under the contract of *bai musawamah or murabahah.*

Second Agreement: The Buying Bank promises under a *wa'd* arrangement to sell back the same securities to the Selling Bank at a specified price at a specified date in the future. The 2 prices in both the agreements may not be related.

Third Agreement: The Buying Bank sells the same or similar securities back to the Selling Bank at a specified price under the contract of *bai musawamah or murabahah.*

Reporting of Transaction

First Transaction
    SB sells assets to BB for cash.
        CR ASSETS HELD FOR TRADE
        DR CASH

By reducing Assets Held for Trade on ABC's books the bank lowers its capital charges.

Transfer of ownership of assets from seller to buyer is a must.

Second Transaction

SB promises to Buy Back the same shares in future for a pre-agreed price. Alternatively, the BB promises to sell the shares back to the SB as well. Within the legal jurisdiction of Malaysia, this promise to buy back shares in the future on behalf of the SB is treated as a contingent liability as the SB has to perform a certain act in the future.

Third Transaction

SB Buys Back the assets from the BB and ownership of the assets is transferred back into the Balance Sheet of the SB.

    DR ASSETS HELD FOR TRADE
        CR CASH.

The SB will record the difference between the 2 prices as a capital loss, as the SB buys back assets for a price higher than what it sold the assets for.

One can clearly see how a binding *wa'd* links 2 contracts of *bai*. The assets sold in the 2 *bai* contracts are the same yet the price in both transactions is different.

Issues of Price in Repo Transactions

If for instance the subject matter of the first sale are 1,000 shares in IBM and they are sold at a market price of $100, both parties can agree to a buy back price of $102. The $2 difference will be the cost of funds for the first seller. If at the time of the buy back the market price of shares is at $103, the counterparty would have incurred an implicit loss. Repo transactions may be structured such that the buy back price is decided upfront, or a mechanism can be put in place by virtue of which a buy back price can be determined. For instance the buy back price be the average price of the asset from the date of the first sale to the date of the buy back as in the case of an Asian option, or the original seller may also sell call options to the buyer for an exercise price well in excess of the pre-agreed buy back price.

The controversy of price versus a pricing mechanism surfaces here again, but as we are dealing with *wa'd* where uncertainty is tolerated Islamic banks could engineer products that allow for a fluid pricing mechanism for buy back agreements.

Assets funded by repo.

Bank ABC will utilise the funds raised by mobilising deposits or through the repurchase agreements to fund assets. $100M worth of deposits mobilized at 3%, funds assets worth $100M which earn 5%. The net spread of 2% is the income of the bank. However, funds mobilized using a repo transaction carry a lower cost of fund, as the bank places highly rated securities as collateral with the counterparty. If the repo rate is 2.20% on an annual basis, ABC will earn a higher spread of assets funded by funds mobilised from the repo desk. This spread is 2.8% on this transaction.

Alternatively, the bank must maintain a capital of 8% for all assets funded by deposit. The capital requirement for assets funded by proceeds from repurchase agreements are more relaxed and allows banks more room to manouver with lower capital charges.

LIABILITIES		ASSETS	
DEPOSITS	100,000,000.00	MORTGAGES	100,000,000.00
		RISK WEIGHTAGE	70%
REPO	100,000,000.00	CAPITAL	
CAR	8.00%		
K	5,600,000.00		

EXPENSE		INCOME		NET INCOME
DEPOSIT RATE	3.00%	LOAN RATE	5.00%	
EXPENSE	750,000.00	1,250,000.00		500,000.00
REPO RATE	2.20%			
REPO EXPENSE	550,000.00			700,000.00

Figure 11.9 Assets Funded by Repo

Conclusion

Repo transactions can be short term, as low as overnight to 30 days. Certain repo transactions can be of a long term nature and are referred to as term repo. Funds mobilised with repo transactions typically carry much lower costs of funds as opposed to interbank borrowing and deposits. Repos are the first financial product that we have discussed under the concept of *wa'd,* outside of profit rate and currency swaps. We shall be looking at more instruments closely to see how the concept of *wa'd* applies to various financial instruments.

CHAPTER 12

INDICES

The best way to explain indexes is by using a very simple example. We imagine a fund manager that has investments in 9 different companies. The portfolio consists of 4,500 shares of IBM, TESLA, BMW, Mercedes, Exxon, Apple, Google, Time and AT&T. The number of shares purchased in each company are highlighted below, with 800 shares in IBM constituting 17.78% of the portfolio, 500 shares in TESLA constituting 11.11%, 900 shares in BMW constituting 20%, 100 shares in Mercedes constituting 2.22% and so on. The composition of the portfolio does not change over time, however, the share price of each stock does change. At time t = 0, the value of the portfolio as a whole is $455,500. At time t =1, with movements in the value of the share prices in the portfolio, the value of the portfolio increases by $3,100 to $458,600, offering a return of 0.06%. At time t = 2, the portfolio has a value of $458,800, offering the fund manager a cash inflow of $3,300 offering a .12% return over a benchmark at time t = 0. If we look at cash flows in a time series manner the portfolio offers an additional inflow from the period t+30 to t+60 of $458,800 - $458,600 = $200. The same portfolio has a value of $461,700, offering a positive cash inflow of $6,200 to the fund manager for a return of 0.34% from the time the portfolio was developed. In a time series flow the cash inflow from time t + 60 to time t + 90, the fund manager enjoys a cash inflow of an additional $2,900 ($461,700 - $458,800).

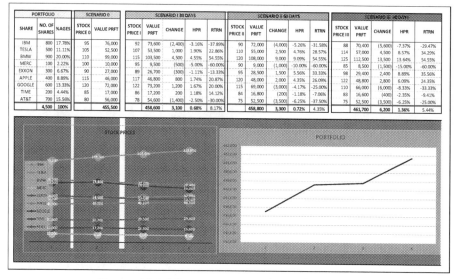

PORTFOLIO			SCENARIO 0		SCENARIO I 30 DAYS					SCENARIO II 60 DAYS					SCENARIO III 90 DAYS				
SHARE	NO. OF SHARES	%AGES	STOCK PRICE 0	VALUE PRFT	STOCK PRICE I	VALUE PRFT	CHANGE	HPR	RTRN	STOCK PRICE II	VALUE PRFT	CHANGE	HPR	RTRN	STOCK PRICE III	VALUE PRFT	CHANGE	HPR	RTRN
IBM	800	17.78%	95	76,000	92	73,600	(2,400)	-3.16%	-37.89%	90	72,000	(4,000)	-5.26%	-31.58%	88	70,400	(5,600)	-7.37%	-29.47%
TESLA	500	11.11%	105	52,500	107	53,500	1,000	1.90%	22.86%	110	55,000	2,500	4.76%	28.57%	114	57,000	4,500	8.57%	34.29%
BMW	900	20.00%	110	99,000	115	103,500	4,500	4.55%	54.55%	120	108,000	9,000	9.09%	54.55%	125	112,500	13,500	13.64%	54.55%
MERC	100	2.22%	100	10,000	95	9,500	(500)	-5.00%	-60.00%	90	9,000	(1,000)	-10.00%	-60.00%	85	8,500	(1,500)	-15.00%	-60.00%
EXXON	300	6.67%	90	27,000	89	26,700	(300)	-1.11%	-13.33%	95	28,500	1,500	5.56%	33.33%	98	29,400	2,400	8.89%	35.56%
APPLE	400	8.89%	115	46,000	117	46,800	800	1.74%	20.87%	120	48,000	2,000	4.35%	26.09%	122	48,800	2,800	6.09%	24.35%
GOOGLE	600	13.33%	120	72,000	122	73,200	1,200	1.67%	20.00%	115	69,000	(3,000)	-4.17%	-25.00%	110	66,000	(6,000)	-8.33%	-33.33%
TIME	200	4.44%	85	17,000	86	17,200	200	1.18%	14.12%	84	16,800	(200)	-1.18%	-7.06%	83	16,600	(400)	-2.35%	-9.41%
AT&T	700	15.56%	80	56,000	78	54,600	(1,400)	-2.50%	-30.00%	75	52,500	(3,500)	-6.25%	-37.50%	75	52,500	(3,500)	-6.25%	-25.00%
	4,500	100%		455,500		458,600	3,100	0.68%	8.17%		458,800	3,300	0.72%	4.35%		461,700	6,200	1.36%	5.44%

Figure 12.1 Movements in Values of Portfolio

The cash flows generated from this portfolio are represented in the following table

TIME	PORTFOLIO VALUE	10% of PORTFOLIO	CHG FROM DAY 0	HPR	ANNUAL	CHG FROM PREV T
DAY 0	455,500.00	45,550	-			-
30 DAYS	458,600.00	45,860	3,100.00	0.68%	8.17%	3,100.00
60 DAYS	458,800.00	45,880	3,300.00	0.72%	4.35%	200.00
90 DAYS	461,700.00	46,170	6,200.00	0.34%	5.44%	2,900.00

Figure 12.2 Returns from 0 to 90 Days

A Synthetic product can be developed that mirrors the cash flows of this portfolio. Investing in stocks requires heavy cash outlays, foregone returns from alternative investment choices, and brokerage and commission fees. An index can be developed that tracks the behaviour of a portfolio. The index is developed by matching the weightages assigned to different shares in a portfolio. Thereby the index would offer the same returns that the benchmarked portfolio offers. What if a counterparty sells a product to an investor for a notional amount far less than the actual $455,500 required to invest in the portfolio above, yet promises to offer the same returns that the portfolio offers as a whole? So let's say a counterparty offers the fund manager to invest in an index by placing only 10% of the running value of the portfolio in a margin account which can be utilised by counterparty for making investments. This means the fund manager would keep adjusting the balance maintained with the counterparty with the fluctuating value of the portfolio and subsequently the index.

TIME	PORTFOLIO VALUE	10% of PORTFOLIO	CHG FROM DAY 0	HPR	ANNUAL	CHG FROM PREV T
DAY 0	455,500.00	45,550	-			-
30 DAYS	458,600.00	45,860	3,100.00	0.68%	81.67%	3,100.00
60 DAYS	458,800.00	45,880	3,300.00	0.72%	43.47%	200.00
90 DAYS	461,700.00	46,170	6,200.00	0.34%	54.45%	2,900.00

Figure 12.3 Running Portfolio Values

The 10% requirement as indicated in Figure 12.3 tracks the changes in the value of the portfolio. This amount is placed by the fund manager at all times with the counterparty.

The counterparty estimates that the maximum cash outlay required over a 90 day period would be $6,200. This means the counterparty must find suitable assets that will generate returns of $6,200 in 90 days with just an investment of $45,550. The required return on these assets would be 13.61% over a period of 90 days or 54.45% on an annualized basis.

FUND	45,550.00
REQ RET	6,200.00
PAYOUT	51,750.00
TENOR	90
HPR	13.61%
RETURN	54.45%

Figure 12.4 Counterparty's Return

The counterparty invests these funds of $45,550 in the stock market using an active trading policy, or in alternative assets like options, or commodities to compensate the fund manager with the required $6,200 cash outlay in 90 days. In 90 days the fund manager will terminate the contract, the counterparty would have to return the 10% funds kept in margin with the counterparty and would also pay the fund manager a return of $6,200 to track the performance of the benchmark portfolio. The example so far does not take into consideration adjustments in margin for increasing values of the portfolio.

From the funds manager's point of view a cash inflow of $6,200 with an investment of $455,000 over 90 days offers a return of just 5.44% on an annualized basis. But the same return offered on a cash outlay of just $45,550 reflects a return of 54.44% an improvement of 10 times or 1000%. However, in this product, the $45,550 is returned back to the fund manager as the funds kept in margin are not used to purchase the shares.

The counterparty can retain a fee for this service of say 5% of the average amount of funds kept in the margin account. For simplicity sake if we simply calculate this against $45,550, this amount becomes $2,775. If this fee is taken upfront, in addition to the 10% margin, this allows the counterparty flexibility to invest its own fees to achieve the required $6,200 pay out to the fund manager at the end of 90 days. This means the counterparty will manage $45,550 + $2,700 to generate $6,200 in 90 days.

FUND	48,250.00
REQ RET	6,200.00
PAYOUT	54,450.00
TENOR	90
HPR	12.85%
RETURN	51.40%

Figure 12.5 Closer Look at Counterparty's Returns

The fund manager's ACTUAL investment would in fact be $2,700 paid to the counterparty making its return on equity of a phenomenal 918.52% on an annualized basis.

FUND	2,700.00
REQ RET	6,200.00
PAYOUT	
TENOR	90
RETURN	918.52%

Figure 12.6 Fund Manager's Returns

Applications of Indices: Barometers of economic activity, benchmarks or financial products.

Indices offer investors a synthetic exposure to returns on underlying assets that are components of the index. Indices are developed by financial services providers all over the globe, with Dow Jones and Morgan Stanley being market leaders in this area. Indices have been developed for various sectors of industry focusing on manufacturing sectors, telecommunications, software development, automobile, oil and gas and a host of other sectors. Indices can be developed across industrial sectors for large companies, mid size companies or small companies. Company size is measured by market capitalization, (share price * number of outstanding shares). Indices can cover certain regions and can include companies in a variety of economic sectors of varying size, but from specific regions. Thus we have NASDAQ, which looks at companies in the IT sector listed in the United States. We have Nikei 225 –which lists the top 225 firms by market capitalisation listed in Tokyo, we have various indices covering emerging and frontier markets and we have indices that only include equities that meet some *shariah* screening requirements.

Shares in companies within each sector are grouped together to develop an index and returns for each index are calculated. These returns can be either treated as a benchmark or as a product in itself. Indexes are developed in a manner such that a specific level of share price at a specific time for each component asset results in an index level. Thus the Standard and Poors S&P 500, being at a level of 5,000 is reached when prices of shares within the index reach a certain level. If the S&P 500 rises from 5,000 to 5,300, this means that most shares within the index have appreciated in price, and that too considerably. If the S&P 500 falls to 4,800 this means that most shares within the index have fallen in value.

If the S&P 500 offered a return of 15% for a specific year, this means that had any investor invested in shares that mirrors the composition of the index at the beginning of the year, the investor would earn 15% at the end of the year as the value of the shares within that index appreciated.

Returns on indices can serve as benchmarks for performance of fund managers, or can become financial products themselves. Products have been engineered in the conventional industry where returns are linked to the performance of a specific index. It is not necessary that the funds mobilised by selling such products are used to invest in the index, they may be used to invest in gold, but the returns would match the returns of the benchmarked index.

Shariah Perspective on Indices

The usage of indices as benchmarks for performances seems to hold no cause of concern amongst the *shariah* community. In fact currently, returns on many internationally floated *sukuks* are benchmarked to the London Interbank Overnight Rate, which is an interest rate for interbank borrowing. The benchmark used therefore need not be *shariah* compliant. Islamic banks can offer products, the returns on which can be benchmarked against a host of indices, whether they are inclusive of *shariah* compliant assets or not is a different matter, but Islamic Financial Institutions cannot invest directly into non-*shariah* compliant indices or any financial products that are engineered which require investment into non-*shariah* compliant assets. Using indices as benchmarks is one thing, investing into them directly is quite another.

Conclusion

Indices can be developed with any pool of assets, be they equities, bonds, commodities or even rea estate. They are just mathematical representations of changes in the values of a large basket of underlying assets.

CHAPTER 13

OPTIONS

Options are another asset class that are much misunderstood by *shariah* scholars. The accusation that they are purely speculative in nature evidenced by the fact that the "notional" value of options contracts is several multiples of actual trade transactions that need to be hedged, is a result of not understanding how options contracts are reported.

We shall begin with the very basics and move step by step into explaining the contracts to our readers.

What are options, well in common usage of the term they are exactly just that, options, choices, in Arabic *khiyaar*, rights whether exercised or not is at the discretion of the one having the option. In the world of trade, a Buyer may have the option to choose various suppliers, may have an option to purchase a certain input at a certain price in the spot market or in the future. A Seller may have an option to sell products to Buyers at specific prices at a certain time in the future. By virtue of being an option, the holder of any such instrument has the right to exercise the option or walk away from it.

Let us use a simple scenario to illustrate our point. A Farmer seeks to sell his product, which is wheat to a Buyer. The wheat will take 90 days to harvest and bring to market. The current prices of wheat are at $10,000 per ton. The Farmer knows if he grows 10 tons of wheat he can do so at a cost of $8,000 per ton. A selling price of $10,000 is suitable for the Farmer as it locks in a profit of $2,000 per ton. The Farmer of wheat then decides to offer a Buyer an option to purchase 10 tons of wheat in 90 days for $10,000 per ton. We shall refer to this price as the "Exercise Price".

A market Buyer is also looking to hedge his buying price. The Buyer maybe an end user who owns a mill, or may be an intermediary, but in either circumstance wishes to purchase wheat in 180 days at the lowest price possible. The Buyer may enter into the options contract offered by the Farmer and feels that by entering into this contract he not only binds the Farmer to perform delivery of 10 tons of wheat within 90 days, but is also able to lock in a price.

The Farmer and the Buyer can either enter into a futures contract which is merely a contract to buy/sell the wheat at a price of $10,000 per ton in 90 days. However, the Buyer cannot renegade from this contract and is bound to perform. In order to show commitment to perform in fact both parties must place funds in what in known as a margin account. We shall discuss this contract at another time.

The Buyer however, wants a more open ended commitment. He wishes to retain the choice to buy or not to buy at the time the contract matures and requires performance. The Buyer agrees to enter into an options contract with the Seller, which entitles him as the Buyer, the right to buy the wheat for $10,000 per ton if he chooses to do so. This contract does not guarantee the Seller a Buyer or a Price for his goods, but instead binds the Seller to perform in case the option is exercised. As this is not an ideal scenario for the Seller, he decides to charge the Buyer a fee of $10 for entering into such a contract, in effect he sells the contract to the Buyer. This right to buy is referred to as a call option. The Buyer has bought a call option and the Farmer has sold a call option.

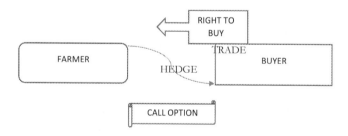

Figure 13.1 Call Options Scenario

Now 3 scenarios may unfold in the wheat market and we shall examine the impact of both scenarios on our transaction.

Scenario 1:

The market price of wheat in 90 days remains at $10,000 per ton, in which case the Buyer and the Seller are indifferent if the option is exercised or not. The Buyer can buy wheat from the Farmer for $10,000 and sell it in the market for $10,000 for no profit. The Seller would not benefit or lose any money by selling to the option holder as the Farmer is getting the same price from the Buyer as he would be getting from the market. However, the Farmer still benefits from the $500 earned from selling the options contract to the Buyer.

Scenario 2:

If in 90 days the market price for wheat is $11,000 per ton the Buyer will exercise his option vis a vis the Farmer, purchase 10 tons of wheat for $10,000 and sell it in the market for $11,000 and make a profit. The Farmer on the other hand is in a loss making situation by being bound to the contract as the Farmer would receive $11,000 from the market instead of just the $10,000 he is getting from the options holder and subsequently the Buyer. To make things worse, if the Farmer does not have the 10 tons of harvest ready to deliver, the Farmer would have to buy the shortfall from the market at $11,000 per ton and sell at $10,000 per ton making an actual loss.

The profit for the Buyer accrues from a market event of rising prices. The profit earned by the Buyer is exactly equal to the loss or implicit loss borne by the Seller who could have sold 10 tons of wheat at $11,000 if he had not offered the Buyer the said option. In a contract of an option, a holder of an option may or may not exercise his right to execute, whereas the issuer of the option does not have that choice. If the Buyer does not exercise the option, the Farmer has no obligation, whereas if the Buyer does exercise an option the Seller must perform. However, in either scenario, whether the option is exercised or not, the Farmer retains the $10 option price, at no stage is this amount made part of the purchase price as is in the case of *khiyaar* or *hamish jiddiyah*. This is a crucial distinction between conventional options in that they carry their own rights and obligations and their own price, and furthermore they are tradable. *Khiyar* and *hamish jiddiyah* do not offer such flexibility, in that the rights offered in either case are not tradable.

An interesting product would be to insure the Buyer or options holder for the performance of the Seller. Where ever counter party risk is involved, insurance can be purchased. The Buyer runs the risk that the Farmer will default on the obligations and thus faces performance risk. The Buyer could obtain certain assets from the Farmer under the contract of *rahn* to hedge against the risk of non performance.

At this stage, there is a financial incentive for the Farmer to actually default on the contract terms, or seek means to exit the contract and sell his crop to the market for $11,000 instead. This risk exposes the Buyer to the risk of will full default on behalf of the farmer. The Buyer is also exposed to performance risk that arises from other factors such as weather, crop yield etc. that would impact the Farmers' ability to deliver the required crop.

The Buyer is also exposed to price risk, in that, he hopes to see market prices continue to increase in order to earn a decent spread between buying and selling prices.

Scenario 3:

Alternatively, if market prices of wheat fall below $10,000 per ton, to say $9,000, the option holder would not exercise the option as it would be cheaper to buy the wheat from the open market. In this circumstance the Seller would benefit if the option was exercised but that would not be likely. Therefore, in this instance the only benefit accrued to the Seller is the option price, or the fee the Seller charged to the Buyer for granting the right to purchase 10 tons of wheat in the future.

SCENARIO 2 MARKET PRICE	$11,000
SCENARIO 1 MARKET PRICE	$10,000
SCENARIO 3 MARKET PRICE	$9,000

Figure 13.2 Possible Prices for Wheat

SCENARIO	1		2		3	
NET BENEFIT	-	-	X			
AMOUNT	-	-	1,000	-1,000	-10	10
	BUYER	SELLER	BUYER	SELLER	BUYER	SELLER

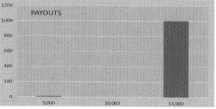

Figure 13.3 and Figure 13.4 Payouts with Scenarios 1,2 & 3.

The options contract in fact here seems rather one sided, with a majority of the benefits being realized by the Buyer if prices increase beyond $10,000 and the only benefit realized by the seller is the $10 earned by Seller or Farmer. The Farmer bears implicit losses or actual losses when prices increase beyond the Exercise Price in terms of foregone profits. When prices increase the Seller could earn greater profits had the Seller not been locked into an options contract. If prices increase to $14,000 per ton of wheat, for instance, the Buyer would realize profits of $4,000 on the resale of wheat, while still incurring a cost of only $10 paid for the options contract. The downside is locked in for the Buyer but is open ended for the Options Issuer.

It is clear that the variables that come into play here are the prices of wheat at the time of contracting, the tenure that is covered by the contract, the Exercise Price agreed upon and most importantly the Expectations of changes in market prices over the specific interval covering the 90 days. The results or net benefits of this contract are diabolically opposed to each other in that the gain of Buyer is exactly the loss of the Seller and vice versa.

As can be seen the options contract does not benefit the Farmer as much as it benefits the Buyer. In fact the contract is exercised only when market circumstances are such that the Farmer would rather sell the wheat to the Market instead of the Buyer. The incentive therefore for the Farmer is then to earn a substantial income from selling the Call Option. In order to price the Call Option the Seller would have to consider the probabilities of various scenarios and the pay outs or implicit losses resulting from those scenarios.

For instance, the probability for market prices reach to $13,000 is 5%. The loss for the Seller in this case is $3,000 (in foregone profit). So the price for protecting oneself from this scenario would be 5% * $3,000 = $150. The probability of prices reaching $12,000 is 6%, with the foregone loss being $2,000. The price for protecting oneself from this scenario would then be $120. The probability of Scenario 2 occurring is 7%, and the foregone profit is $1,000, therefore the Seller covers this event with a price of $70.

The cumulative prices of the above mentioned scenarios with Market Prices hitting $13,000, $12,000 and $11,000 is $150 + $120 + $ 70 = $340. This amount covers the risk and the losses associated with the above market scenarios playing out. Therefore, $340 would be a generic way of the Farmer pricing his Call Option, provided that the Buyer is restricted in exercising his option at Specific Barriers or Prices of $11,000, $12,000 and $13,000.

This formula does not cover the probability calculations of all possible prices occurring between $10,000 and $13,000 such as $10,500 or $11,400.50 for instance. If one were to add the cost of covering ALL these events (from the Sellers point of view), this would become a rather expensive Option to sell.

The Seller or Farmer may alter the contract allowing the Buyer to exercise the Option on specific dates of a month, on a specific maturity date, or anytime up to a maturity date and so on. The more rights are conferred to the Buyer, the more expensive the option would be to cover the opportunity cost of extending those rights. The Seller may also want to limit the exposure on the contract by putting a cap on Market Price at which the Buyer can exercise the option. For instance if market prices go as high as $16,000, the Farmer would incur losses of $4,000 on honouring the option.

Recap

Let us just recap a little here. The Farmer and Buyer wish to make a buy and sale transaction of $100,000 which is the current market price of 10 tons of wheat at $10,000 per ton. The original trade is for $100,000. The Farmer and the Buyer enter into a hedging arrangement to hedge price risk which has a Notional Value of $100,000 as well, although in either possible outcomes the actual cash flows exchanged between the Farmer and the Buyer are just the $10 contract price.

The Farmer can in fact enter into another Call Option with a 3rd Party C, to secure 10 tons of wheat from another source at an Exercise Price of $9,750. This second option would cover the same tenure as first option, and would cover the Farmers risk of non-performance due to a poor crop, or to cover the risk of the Buyer exercising his option as well. In fact, the Farmer can exercise the second option if market prices fall from $10,000 to $9,800 and still make a profit by selling the crop at market prices. The Notional Value of this Hedge will also be $9,750 * 10 = $99,750. The Farmer has passed on some of his risk to a 3rd Party C.

The Buyer can also enter into subsequent contracts that lock in a sale price for the wheat. Such contracts are called Put Options and work in a similar fashion but offer the Holder the right to sell an underlying asset. The Buyer may buy a Put Option from a 4th Party D, that entitles the Buyer to sell 10 tons of wheat at an Exercise Price of $10,200. In this way the Buyer has locked in a minimum profit. We assume the price of this Put Option is $15. The Notional

Value of this contract however, is $102,000. Party D has also absorbed some of the risk associated with the Buyer holding 10 tons of wheat.

To hedge one buy/sell transaction of $100,000, a contract of *bai,* a transaction between just 2 parties, hedging transactions or agreements are entered with notional values of $299,500 with 4 parties. This does not mean that either parties are involved in speculating here, it is not as if a trade transaction of $100,000 has resulted in numerous buy and sale, speculative transactions with an aggregate value of $299,500. In fact Parties C and D have agreed to share some of the risks of bringing 10 tons of wheat to the market and of mitigating the price risk of selling it. If Parties C and D continue to hedge their positions till the wheat finds its way to an end user, 1 trade transaction can generate multiple hedging transactions, in fact multiple layers of hedging contracts.

A large layer of hedging contracts in fact gives an indication of how many intermediaries are involved before goods like wheat reach an actual market of end users.

Option as a stand alone contract

Controversy arises when options contracts are given a life of their own, in the sense that not only do they carry a price independent of the price of the underlying asset, (in our case wheat), but they are traded as an independent asset class on their own. If in our case above the Buyer can sell the Call Option he holds, to a 5th Party E, this raises issues of the intent behind buying the option in the first place. The price of the option will then fluctuate in a secondary market, whereby changes in the price of the underlying asset will affect the price of the option, provided it can be resold.

Shariah scholars feel that the option instrument allows holders to place small bets on the movements of assets with the possible outcome of very large gains. As the price of wheat moves, for instance from $10,000 towards $11,000, a call option entitling the holder to buy wheat at $10,000 would continue to grow in value. In fact an option originally sold for $10, is in this scenario offering a profit of $1,000 to the holder. The option price will still secure the holder a profit if its price alone converged to the spread the option offers i.e. $1,000. Buyers and Sellers of options will continue to purchase the above contract till the cost of purchasing contract is slightly less than $10,000 as it is offering a risk free profit. Many trades would be executed before the price of the option moves from $40 all the way up to $1,000.

Similarly, the option price will diminish in value if the price of wheat falls below $10,000. In this case the Buyer would benefit more by buying from the open market. If the price of wheat falls to $8,000, the value of the option would be near to 0, far below its issue price of $40.

Although, options, like any other assets can be misused, they still need to be tradable for the simple reason that investors prefer to invest in liquid assets. This allows them to exit from a position with ease. Liquidity is a fundamental requirement for assets to be attractive to investors. Liquidity can only be obtained within an active secondary market, and a secondary market is facilitated by market makers and speculators whose frequent buy and sell transactions create a consistent bid ask spread in asset classes and keeps an active market deal flow.

Over The Counter and Exchange Traded

The above scenario can be played out in an Over the Counter framework, where the Farmer/Seller identifies and chooses the Buyer, but neither has any means of holding the other to perform. In a Call Option the Buyer is exposed to performance risk over the Seller. The Buyer could demand collateral from the Farmer to ensure performance but that would make the terms of the contract heavily in favour of the Buyer.

The same contracts could be traded on an Exchange. An Exchange is basically a marketplace for financial products where buyers of financial products, typically seen as investors meet sellers of financial products, typically investment banks, hedge funds and the like. Some banks may be selling these financial products to benefit from their sale and purchase or they may simply earn a fee for developing products on behalf of clients for developing them and transacting with them. For contracts to be traded on an Exchange, they must exist in standardised form so that there is ease in monitoring deal flow, in executing trades, in displaying trades on electronic screens, in interpreting data like trade volumes and in pricing contracts.

If a standard options contract for wheat is for 2 tons, the above mentioned contract would be executed with the sale and purchase of 5 options contracts. The price for each contract may be $2, making the sale of 5 contracts being for $10. A contract for 7 tons could not be executed on the exchange as this would require 3.5 contracts which is not possible. Secondly, the Farmer/Seller and the Buyer are not able to issue or trade these contracts on their own. An Investment Bank would have to be commissioned to write the contracts (for a fee), and an agent or broker would have to be obtained who is authorised to buy and sell options contracts on an Exchange. Brokers are licensed companies who are staffed by licensed professionals who know how to execute options trades and are specialists in the trade or profession. Brokers also maintain a certain amount of capital with an Exchange to cover a portion of positions they take for their clients. A Broker can also however take the other side of a trade offered by a client, in the sense if the Farmer approaches a Broker to sell options, the Broker itself may be the Buyer on the other side.

The advantage of Exchange Traded contracts is offered by the fact that an Exchange guarantees the other side of the trade. In our example, the Exchange would guarantee the performance of the Farmer in the event that the Buyer exercises the options traded. This guarantee offered by the Exchange comes under the principle of novation and protects buyers and sellers from wilful and incidental default of counterparties in any trade.

Separate exchanges exist for options. Options can be offered on any asset class from real estate, to commodities to stocks, bonds and a vast array of financial assets.

Pricing of Options

Pricing of options is not a simple matter to discuss and requires a detailed knowledge of mathematics. The concepts are important to understand however. The call option for instance offers rights to a Buyer, the benefits of which far outweigh its costs. However, the holder of the contract is exposed to performance risk of the issuer or seller and must be compensated for this risk. This would be reflected in the price the Buyer is willing to offer for an option. The Seller of the options contract must consider the losses the Seller exposes himself to when issuing an open ended option. For instance if there is no upper limit on the price at which the Buyer can exercise the option, this exposes the issuer to considerable risk. This risk must be priced into the contract and is a function of the terms of the contract which include tenure, and the circumstances surrounding when the option can be exercised, whether on a specific date, on a range of dates etc.

Another crucial element would be the volatility in the price of underlying asset for the period of the contract. If wheat demonstrates stable price trends, there may not be any incentive for a Buyer to hedge positions. If the price of wheat oscillates around $10,000, and deviates by hardly .00001% in either direction over a period of 90 days, it would not be worth it to buy options as the highest the price would probably go to is $10,000.1 and the lowest it would fall to is $9,999.90. Unless the Buyer can buy options for .50c there would be no sense in buying options.

Volatility is a concern to the Buyer as much as it is to the Seller, in that the Seller must anticipate the fullest extent of the exposure that the contract presents. If wheat prices are very volatile, and susceptible to sudden jumps where prices may go up to $16,000 a ton, the Farmer in our example would make considerable losses in terms of foregone profit by offering wheat for only $10,000 to the Buyer who would most certainly exercise the option.

Volatility by itself is not enough. Price movements in the scenarios illustrated below demonstrate the same volatility, except both demonstrate different movements around the Exercise Price of $10,000. Graph A shows the prices of wheat hovering well above $10,000 with more months spent above the $10,000 price range than spent below the $10,000 price range. Graph B is in fact the same curve, but with fluctuations around the $10,000 and below mark being far more frequent

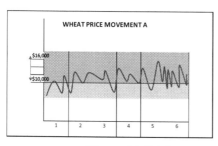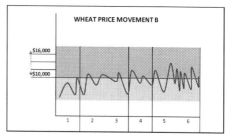

Figure 13.5 Movements A and B in Wheat Prices

From a Buyers point of view, Option A would be more valuable as there is greater likelihood that that prices would reach a range where it would make sense to exercise the option, in that it will be "in the money". Price behaviour for Option B does not offer a good likelihood that prices may cross $10,000 until later in the duration of the contract, say towards the 5th month.

Another important point to track is that the price of the options would track the movements in the prices of the underlying assets. The value of the option increase as prices increase with the option being more and more in the money. The options prices may lag a little behind changes in actual prices in the underlying assets.

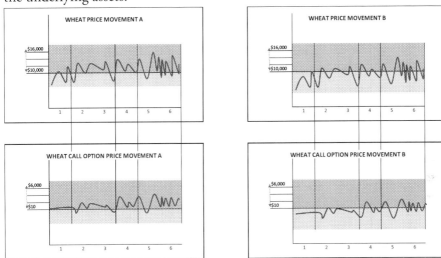

Figure 13.6 Movements in Prices of Wheat and Wheat Call Options

Options prices also demonstrate a certain elasticity to asset prices, where one can gauge the sensitivity of option prices to changes in prices in the underlying. Trading volume would be another variable to consider, where changes in prices of the underlying asset and trading volumes in the underlying assets set of trading in the options markets.

A concise work on options pricing is available and requires a thorough understanding of mathematics which is beyond the scope of this work. The reader is referred to a detailed bibliography at the end of the book that covers titles on the subject.

Put Options

A call option tends to benefit buyers, whereas put options which offer the right to sell are far more beneficial for sellers. We revert back to our Farmer in this case who is seeking to lock in a sale price for 10 tons of wheat after harvest which is within 180 days. The Farmer can sell a call option to a Buyer, but this has limited utility for reasons already discussed. Alternatively, our Farmer here can buy a Put Option from a 3rd Party that entitles the Farmer to sell wheat in 180 days at a predetermined exercise price of $10,000 per ton. At this stage we have 2 parties involved, the Farmer who is growing the wheat and wishes to sell wheat in the future and the 3rd Party who is willing to issue the Put Option to the Farmer.

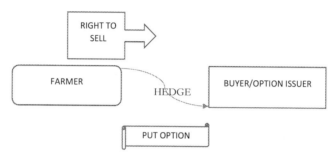

Figure 13.7 Put Options Scenario

For simplicity sake we assume that the issuer of the Put Option is an interested Buyer for the wheat. We shall refer to the issuer of the Put as the Buyer in this illustration. The Put option is structured so as to offer the Farmer the right to sell 10 tons of wheat for $10,000 per ton in 180 days. The value of the put option to the Farmer will depend on how wheat prices fluctuate in the market. If market prices decrease and fall to $9,500 per ton, the Farmer would be glad to have hedged his position by locking in a more favourable price of $10,000. However, if the market prices of wheat increase to $10,500, the Farmer would prefer not to exercise his option and will sell his wheat at market prices. The value or price of a call option and put option are linked to the value of the underlying asset, however, prices for a call option behave in a manner opposite to that of a put option. As a call option offers the holder a right to buy, its value increases when market prices begin to rise, whereas a put option offering a right to sell increases in value at a time when market prices decrease.

The chart below reflects the changes in the value of the put option with changing market prices. As market prices hover below the $10,000 range, the put option enjoys a premium over its issue price of $10. If market prices are at $8,000 per ton, a counterparty may be willing to pay as much as say $1,995 for the option as this would still result in a risk free profit of $5 per ton. The counterparty would buy wheat at $8,000 from the market, purchase the put option for $1,985, and sell the wheat for $10,000 making a risk free profit of $10,000 - $8,000 - $1,995 = $5 per ton.

At market prices above $10,000 the put option has no value as the Farmer would get better prices by offering his wheat in the open market

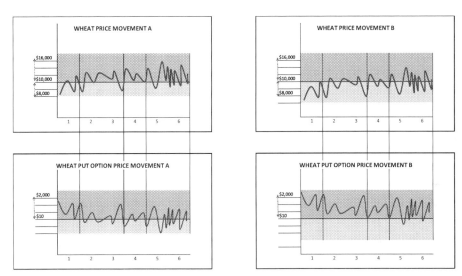

Figure 13.8 Movements in Prices of Wheat and Wheat Put Options Prices

Counterparty Risk.

As with call options, put options holders are exposed to counterparty risk. The seller in this case of a Put option must be ready to purchase 10 tons of wheat from the Farmer if and when the Farmer decides to exercise his option. If market prices fall to $8,000, and the Farmer exercises his option to sell at $10,000, the seller in this case would have to purchase the wheat and either sell it in the market for $8,000 and incur a loss or wait till prices improve to offload the inventory. In the context of a call option when the option holder exercises the option, the issuer must sell the underlying asset to the buyer out of his inventory or by buying the underlying asset from the market. In both call and put options the parties involved are exposed to counterparty risk against the issuer of the instrument.

Physical Settlement vs Cash Settlement.

Let us revert to our call option scenario, where the Exercise Price is fixed at $10,000 and market prices at maturity of the contract are at $12,000 per ton. However, we replace the Farmer with another intermediary or a Commodity Trader A and the Buyer with Trader B. The call option is issued by A. As market prices have hit $12,000, B decides to exercise the option. A must sell 10 tons of wheat to B for $10,000. As A is a trader, A may decide to either sell B from his warehouse a lot of wheat which was purchased at $7,000 the previous year. In this event A still makes a profit of $3,000 on the sale. If A does not hold such an inventory A would be forced to buy from the market at $12,000 and sell to B for $10,000. B would in turn buy from A at $10,000 and sell to the market at $12,000. A would incur a loss of $2,000 and B would make a profit of $2,000 if wheat actually exchanges hands. The warehouse keeper would now receive rent or storage fees from the new owners.

We can assume that both A and B lease space from the same warehouse, and to affect the trade all that the warehouse keeper has to do is reallocate 10 tons of wheat from A's stock in favour of B. No physical movement of stock may be required, just an element of retagging inventory and updated book keeping. B may sell the wheat to Party C, who may also lease space from the warehouse. In this manner the inventory of wheat simply remains exactly where it is, only money changes hands and the ownership of wheat changes hands from A to B to C.

A more expensive alternative would be if A, B and C all held inventories at different locations and costs of transportation will lower the profit margins and increase costs for all parties involved. Cash Settlement offers an interesting alternative, where A just nets off the profit that B will earn from exercising the option and pays him $2,000 in cash. A loses $2,000 on this trade in any case (but no logistical expenses are incurred) and B earns $2,000 on the trade. Neither party incurs any logistical costs or any fees for exchange brokers to buy or sell the wheat on their behalf. This accrues to a considerable savings.

Options contracts are issued on equities and commodities. Options are issued against shares of companies, and with new electronic systems share ownership and transfer now all are executed and settled on electronic platforms with no physical shares changing hands. Options are also issued on commodities and often transactions are executed on crude palm oil, crude Brent oil, crude oil, timber, aluminium, gold, copper, zinc, wheat, rice, rubber and a host of other commodities while these commodities are still in transit on ships or stored in massive warehouses or storage units. There are few storage units in the world through which much of internationally traded commodities is transited, and before a shipment of rubber reaches a port it may well have changed ownership many times over.

However, options contracts help buyers and sellers hedge their risks in bringing goods to market, especially those goods which take considerable time to mine, extract, grow, produce or manufacture and have several unpredictable costs of inputs and volatile prices for outputs. When many of these companies that are involved in the supply chain finance their activities, hedging tools help them to mitigate price risks of inputs and outputs which in fact serve as credit enhancements in dealing with banks. Banks prefer financing those clients that have hedged the costs of their inputs and to a certain degree have locked in prices for their outputs. In fact in certain high risk industries like gold, where close to 250 tons of earth have to moved to extract 250 ounces of gold, banks do not lend unless gold extracting companies have not hedged the prices for their final output.

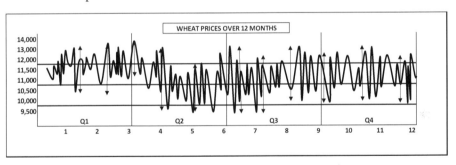

Figure 13.9 Wheat Prices Over 12 Months

Hedging prices makes sense in circumstances of volatile prices. A wheat farmer may be planting seeds in January, the first month of the year and may want to lock in a selling price when the crop comes to harvest in June. In June alone the prices of wheat show fluctuation from prices being as high as $13,000 to as low as $9,000 a band or range of $4,000. If the Farmer is unlucky enough to come to market in July when prices have dropped to $9,500, the Farmer would have to incur storage costs to hold onto inventory till mid-August when prices are expected to rise to $12,000. It might be cheaper for the Farmer to purchase certain put options at various prices to secure maximum profits and avoid losses. If a Farmers production costs are $9,700, prices below that threshold will inflict heavy losses on the Farmer.

As the above example indicates that buy or selling an option is no different that buy or selling insurance. It can done in a *shariah* compliant manner with restrictions on how the contract is traded or it can be done in a manner that inflates prices unnecessarily or distorts the markets for goods.

Link to Underlying

We have demonstrated that an option is an instrument that offers certain rights of sale or purchase of an underlying asset, we did not address the issue of whether an entity, must own the particular asset for which the entity is issuing certain rights. For instance must a Trader own 10 tons of wheat before offering a counterparty an option to buy the wheat in the future? What if the trader has covered the call by another call option the trader holds entitling him to purchase 10 tons of wheat?

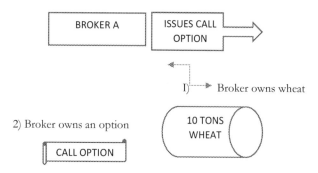

Figure 13.20 Link to Underlying

Another issue arises if even the issuer of the second option held by the trader is also not backed by real inventory and stock? How could one determine who actually owns any of the underlying asset?

TRADER	TRADER	TRADER	TRADER	TRADER	TRADER	TRADER	TRADER	TRADER	TRADER	TRADER	TRADER
TRADER	10 TONS	10 TONS	10 TONS	10 TONS	10 TONS	10 TONS	10 TONS	10 TONS	10 TONS	10 TONS	TRADER
TRADER	10 TONS	10 TONS	10 TONS	10 TONS	10 TONS	10 TONS	10 TONS	10 TONS	10 TONS	10 TONS	TRADER
TRADER	10 TONS	10 TONS	10 TONS	10 TONS	10 TONS	10 TONS	10 TONS	10 TONS	10 TONS	10 TONS	TRADER
TRADER	10 TONS	10 TONS	10 TONS	10 TONS	10 TONS	10 TONS	10 TONS	10 TONS	10 TONS	10 TONS	TRADER
TRADER	10 TONS	10 TONS	10 TONS	10 TONS	10 TONS	10 TONS	10 TONS	10 TONS	10 TONS	10 TONS	TRADER
TRADER	10 TONS	10 TONS	10 TONS	10 TONS	10 TONS	10 TONS	10 TONS	10 TONS	10 TONS	10 TONS	TRADER
TRADER	10 TONS	10 TONS	10 TONS	10 TONS	10 TONS	10 TONS	10 TONS	10 TONS	10 TONS	10 TONS	TRADER
TRADER	10 TONS	10 TONS	10 TONS	10 TONS	10 TONS	10 TONS	10 TONS	10 TONS	10 TONS	10 TONS	TRADER
TRADER	10 TONS	10 TONS	10 TONS	10 TONS	10 TONS	10 TONS	10 TONS	10 TONS	10 TONS	10 TONS	TRADER
TRADER	10 TONS	10 TONS	10 TONS	10 TONS	10 TONS	10 TONS	10 TONS	10 TONS	10 TONS	10 TONS	TRADER
TRADER	10 TONS	10 TONS	10 TONS	10 TONS	10 TONS	10 TONS	10 TONS	10 TONS	10 TONS	10 TONS	TRADER
TRADER	10 TONS	10 TONS	10 TONS	10 TONS	10 TONS	10 TONS	10 TONS	10 TONS	10 TONS	10 TONS	TRADER
TRADER	10 TONS	10 TONS	10 TONS	10 TONS	10 TONS	10 TONS	10 TONS	10 TONS	10 TONS	10 TONS	TRADER
TRADER	10 TONS	10 TONS	10 TONS	10 TONS	10 TONS	10 TONS	10 TONS	10 TONS	10 TONS	10 TONS	TRADER
TRADER	TRADER	TRADER	TRADER	TRADER	TRADER	TRADER	TRADER	TRADER	TRADER	TRADER	TRADER

Figure 13.21 Lots of Wheat in Inventory

We imagine a situation where the total supply of wheat stored in warehouses and ready for sale is 1,500 tons. Another 2,000 tons is under harvest, and another 500 tons is in transit at a particular point in time. A total of 4,000 tons of wheat is either available or will be available within say 90 days within the system. Traders, functioning as either brokers for clients or for their own profits are buying and selling lots of wheat. Each lot is of 10 tons of wheat, and at a market price of $10,000, each lot is worth $100,000. At any given time there are 1500 lots for sale in warehouses with another 500 in transit which can also be traded.

Bear in mind if for each transaction of spot buy and sale, there is no need for any hedging transaction as the asset will exchange hands and money will exchange hands immediately. Let us say if at any time 1,000 transactions are being executed, each for 10 tons or 1 lot (very unrealistic). Of these only 200 are spot transactions where a buyer actually takes delivery not for resale but for processing into finished goods. Thus 800 lots are left for future sales. If for 200 future sales, both counterparties cover their positions with a hedging contract, 200 future sales would generate 400 hedging transactions. The notional value of hedging contracts reflect the scale of the possible trade that might be undertaken if the option is exercised.

Therefore in a market of 4,000 tons of wheat with a market price of $10,000 per ton, with a total market value of $40,000,000 of wheat, and 1500 traders how does one ascertain who actually owns the wheat and who is just issuing options while holding what is known as a "naked position", in that he does not possess what he promises to sell.

Here the *shariah* restriction of not selling something that is not in one's possession places natural restrictions on the trading of options. However, if a seller of options holds call options to cover his claim, the situation may be interpreted differently. It is also possible to foresee that an over reliance on options issuance can lead to circumstances for contracts issued which far offer rights to buy or sell wheat in amounts far in excess of actual available inventories. This is highly likely in the circumstances of cash settlement where parties are not interested in physical delivery. This misuse of the system can actually squeeze out actual legitimate hedgers, producers and end buyers, at the hands of mere brokers, traders and speculators.

This can be regulated however, by daily trade limits, restricting licenses issued to speculators and traders to trade in options. All markets need regulation including spot markets where hoarding can inflate prices, or miss-selling can cause losses to buyers. Markets for options would also need regulation for them to function smoothly and actually function in a manner to spread risk amongst different parties and share risk amongst different parties in a market.

Another setback to the current system is that it is typically investment banks that are involved in being the risk sharers along with hedge funds. Manufacturers, producers, miners or farmers and other parties involved in the supply chain are looking for parties to share their risks. Brokers exist to carry out sale and purchase trades. Investment banks help develop the contracts for a fee, so who actually is willing to sell an option or buy one and be the counterparty to the contracts? For large transactions it tends to be hedge funds, and investment banks, those entities that have flexibility in their regulatory environment and can take such risks. It is not likely that a pension fund manager, or an insurance company, or a mutual fund manager will take the other side of the trade, which results in a system where risk is concentrated in a few hands, yet again.

Airlines for instance have the greatest exposure to prices for jet fuel, which is a function of the price of crude oil. The price of oil is affected by a multitude of circumstances including political circumstances in some of the most volatile parts of the world, the Middle East and Russia. With a great percentage of oil passing through the Straits of Hormuz which borders Iran, a country unfriendly to the interests of the Developed world, this risk is further heightened. Increases in the prices of crude oil can be caused by events such as oil leaks caused during transportation of oil where the legal penalties for destroying the environment far exceed the cost of spilled oil. Prices are also affected by instances of structural engineering flaws that may occur 1000s of metres under the sea bed where a oil rig suffers damages. Prices may also be affected by new discoveries, changes in regulation and technology that allow fracking for instance and by developments in alternative energy sources. The problem is not any more complicated by the fact that all oil payments are settled in US$. Changes in interest rates, that further change different countries exchange rates vis a vis the $ automatically affect the cost of buying oil without there being any changes in the price of oil.

For airlines that compete for customers, offering ticket rates for several months in advance, locking in prices for jet fuel are essential to their business. They cannot function without hedging tools that allow them to lock in not one but several prices for their inputs. They must hedge with varying market expectations with calls for environments of increasing prices and puts for environments of decreasing prices (where they could profit from just selling oil directly and not worrying about ticket sales).

Substance over Form

The whole experience may come across as betting against future prices, which in form it may well be, but what distinguishes a hedge from a bet is the intent of the parties involved and the core business of the party undertaking the hedge. However, what *shariah* scholars would have to accept is that if they wish to divert the actions of large corporations in Muslim countries to more *halaal* financial instruments, they will have to open the door to commodity derivatives. Some of the largest airlines in the world now come from the Muslim world, where will they go to hedge their fuel purchasing?

It is also not feasible or possible to buy large quantities of fuel and hold in storage due to not only storage costs but also as large buy orders increases prices which is exactly what an airline is wishing to avoid.

Chapter 14

TYPES OF OPTIONS

Before we proceed with the various types of options traded in financial markets we briefly look at how options prices behave. Below, we offer prices for Crude Palm Oil for 33 trading days. Prices increase for the first 17 consecutive days, and subsequently decrease from Day 18 to Day 33. With an exercise price of $2,850, a call option has no value till the 18th day when market prices go beyond the $2,850 barrier. The value of the call option is 0 for the option holder for the first 17 days. At this stage the option seller is the beneficiary. However, as market prices go beyond $2,850 the value for the option holder begins to increase as does the negative exposure faced by the option seller.

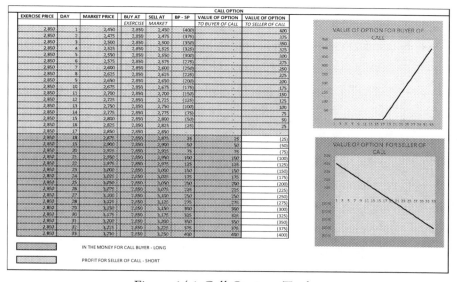

						CALL OPTION	
EXERCISE PRICE	DAY	MARKET PRICE	BUY AT	SELL AT	BP - SP	VALUE OF OPTION	VALUE OF OPTION
			EXERCISE	MARKET		TO BUYER OF CALL	TO SELLER OF CALL
2,850	1	2,450	2,850	2,450	(400)	-	400
2,850	2	2,475	2,850	2,475	(375)	-	375
2,850	3	2,500	2,850	2,500	(350)	-	350
2,850	4	2,525	2,850	2,525	(325)	-	325
2,850	5	2,550	2,850	2,550	(300)	-	300
2,850	6	2,575	2,850	2,575	(275)	-	275
2,850	7	2,600	2,850	2,600	(250)	-	250
2,850	8	2,625	2,850	2,625	(225)	-	225
2,850	9	2,650	2,850	2,650	(200)	-	200
2,850	10	2,675	2,850	2,675	(175)	-	175
2,850	11	2,700	2,850	2,700	(150)	-	150
2,850	12	2,725	2,850	2,725	(125)	-	125
2,850	13	2,750	2,850	2,750	(100)	-	100
2,850	14	2,775	2,850	2,775	(75)	-	75
2,850	15	2,800	2,850	2,800	(50)	-	50
2,850	16	2,825	2,850	2,825	(25)	-	25
2,850	17	2,850	2,850	2,850	-	-	-
2,850	18	2,875	2,850	2,875	25	25	(25)
2,850	19	2,900	2,850	2,900	50	50	(50)
2,850	20	2,925	2,850	2,925	75	75	(75)
2,850	21	2,950	2,850	2,950	100	100	(100)
2,850	22	2,975	2,850	2,975	125	125	(125)
2,850	23	3,000	2,850	3,000	150	150	(150)
2,850	24	3,025	2,850	3,025	175	175	(175)
2,850	25	3,050	2,850	3,050	200	200	(200)
2,850	26	3,075	2,850	3,075	225	225	(225)
2,850	27	3,100	2,850	3,100	250	250	(250)
2,850	28	3,125	2,850	3,125	275	275	(275)
2,850	29	3,150	2,850	3,150	300	300	(300)
2,850	30	3,175	2,850	3,175	325	325	(325)
2,850	31	3,200	2,850	3,200	350	350	(350)
2,850	32	3,225	2,850	3,225	375	375	(375)
2,850	33	3,250	2,850	3,250	400	400	(400)

IN THE MONEY FOR CALL BUYER - LONG

PROFIT FOR SELLER OF CALL - SHORT

Figure 14.1 Call Options Trades

A similar presentation is made for put options.

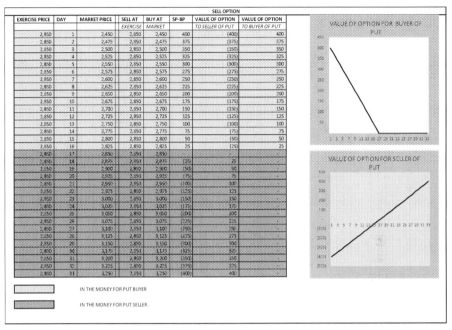

EXERCISE PRICE	DAY	MARKET PRICE	SELL AT	BUY AT	SP-BP	VALUE OF OPTION	VALUE OF OPTION
			EXERCISE	MARKET		TO SELLER OF PUT	TO BUYER OF PUT
2,850	1	2,450	2,850	2,450	400	(400)	400
2,850	2	2,475	2,850	2,475	375	(375)	375
2,850	3	2,500	2,850	2,500	350	(350)	350
2,850	4	2,525	2,850	2,525	325	(325)	325
2,850	5	2,550	2,850	2,550	300	(300)	300
2,850	6	2,575	2,850	2,575	275	(275)	275
2,850	7	2,600	2,850	2,600	250	(250)	250
2,850	8	2,625	2,850	2,625	225	(225)	225
2,850	9	2,650	2,850	2,650	200	(200)	200
2,850	10	2,675	2,850	2,675	175	(175)	175
2,850	11	2,700	2,850	2,700	150	(150)	150
2,850	12	2,725	2,850	2,725	125	(125)	125
2,850	13	2,750	2,850	2,750	100	(100)	100
2,850	14	2,775	2,850	2,775	75	(75)	75
2,850	15	2,800	2,850	2,800	50	(50)	50
2,850	16	2,825	2,850	2,825	25	(25)	25
2,850	17	2,850	2,850	2,850			
2,850	18	2,875	2,850	2,875	(25)	25	
2,850	19	2,900	2,850	2,900	(50)	50	
2,850	20	2,925	2,850	2,925	(75)	75	
2,850	21	2,950	2,850	2,950	(100)	100	
2,850	22	2,975	2,850	2,975	(125)	125	
2,850	23	3,000	2,850	3,000	(150)	150	
2,850	24	3,025	2,850	3,025	(175)	175	
2,850	25	3,050	2,850	3,050	(200)	200	
2,850	26	3,075	2,850	3,075	(225)	225	
2,850	27	3,100	2,850	3,100	(250)	250	
2,850	28	3,125	2,850	3,125	(275)	275	
2,850	29	3,150	2,850	3,150	(300)	300	
2,850	30	3,175	2,850	3,175	(325)	325	
2,850	31	3,200	2,850	3,200	(350)	350	
2,850	32	3,225	2,850	3,225	(375)	375	
2,850	33	3,250	2,850	3,250	(400)	400	

IN THE MONEY FOR PUT BUYER

IN THE MONEY FOR PUT SELLER.

Figure 14.2 Put Option Trades

The price ranges offer opportunities for unique trades. One set of trades for rising prices and another set of trades for declining prices.

EXERCISE PRICE	DAY	MARKET PRICE	BUY AT	SELL AT	BP - SP	VALUE OF OPTION	VALUE OF OPTION	EXERCISE PRICE	DAY	MARKET PRICE	SELL AT	BUY AT	SP-BP	VALUE OF OPTION	VALUE OF OPTION
			EXERCISE	MARKET		TO BUYER OF CALL	TO SELLER OF CALL				EXERCISE	MARKET		TO SELLER OF PUT	TO BUYER OF PUT
2,850	1	2,450	2,850	2,450	(400)	-	400	2,850	1	2,450	2,850	2,450	400	-	400
2,850	2	2,475	2,850	2,475	(375)	-	375	2,850	2	2,475	2,850	2,475	375	-	375
2,850	3	2,500	2,850	2,500	(350)	-	350	2,850	3	2,500	2,850	2,500	350	-	350
2,850	4	2,525	2,850	2,525	(325)	-	325	2,850	4	2,525	2,850	2,525	325	-	325
2,850	5	2,550	2,850	2,550	(300)	-	300	2,850	5	2,550	2,850	2,550	300	-	300
2,850	6	2,575	2,850	2,575	(275)	-	275	2,850	6	2,575	2,850	2,575	275	-	275
2,850	7	2,600	2,850	2,600	(250)	-	250	2,850	7	2,600	2,850	2,600	250	-	250
2,850	8	2,625	2,850	2,625	(225)	-	225	2,850	8	2,625	2,850	2,625	225	-	225
2,850	9	2,650	2,850	2,650	(200)	-	200	2,850	9	2,650	2,850	2,650	200	-	200
2,850	10	2,675	2,850	2,675	(175)	-	175	2,850	10	2,675	2,850	2,675	175	-	175
2,850	11	2,700	2,850	2,700	(150)	-	150	2,850	11	2,700	2,850	2,700	150	-	150
2,850	12	2,725	2,850	2,725	(125)	-	125	2,850	12	2,725	2,850	2,725	125	-	125
2,850	13	2,750	2,850	2,750	(100)	-	100	2,850	13	2,750	2,850	2,750	100	-	100
2,850	14	2,775	2,850	2,775	(75)	-	75	2,850	14	2,775	2,850	2,775	75	-	75
2,850	15	2,800	2,850	2,800	(50)	-	50	2,850	15	2,800	2,850	2,800	50	-	50
2,850	16	2,825	2,850	2,825	(25)	-	25	2,850	16	2,825	2,850	2,825	25	-	25

TRADE
SELL CALL OR BUY PUT FOR THS PRICE RANGE

Figure 14.3 Trade for Increasing Prices

An environment of declining prices presents offers different trades.

EXERCISE PRICE	DAY	MARKET PRICE	BUY AT EXERCISE	SELL AT MARKET	BP - SP	VALUE OF OPTION TO BUYER OF CALL	VALUE OF OPTION TO SELLER OF CALL	EXERCISE PRICE	DAY	MARKET PRICE	SELL AT EXERCISE	BUY AT MARKET	SP-BP	VALUE OF OPTION TO SELLER OF PUT	VALUE OF OPTION TO BUYER OF PUT
2,850	18	2,875	2,850	2,875	25	25	-	2,850	18	2,875	2,850	2,875	(25)	25	-
2,850	19	2,900	2,850	2,900	50	50	-	2,850	19	2,900	2,850	2,900	(50)	50	-
2,850	20	2,925	2,850	2,925	75	75	-	2,850	20	2,925	2,850	2,925	(75)	75	-
2,850	21	2,950	2,850	2,950	100	100	-	2,850	21	2,950	2,850	2,950	(100)	100	-
2,850	22	2,975	2,850	2,975	125	125	-	2,850	22	2,975	2,850	2,975	(125)	125	-
2,850	23	3,000	2,850	3,000	150	150	-	2,850	23	3,000	2,850	3,000	(150)	150	-
2,850	24	3,025	2,850	3,025	175	175	-	2,850	24	3,025	2,850	3,025	(175)	175	-
2,850	25	3,050	2,850	3,050	200	200	-	2,850	25	3,050	2,850	3,050	(200)	200	-
2,850	26	3,075	2,850	3,075	225	225	-	2,850	26	3,075	2,850	3,075	(225)	225	-
2,850	27	3,100	2,850	3,100	250	250	-	2,850	27	3,100	2,850	3,100	(250)	250	-
2,850	28	3,125	2,850	3,125	275	275	-	2,850	28	3,125	2,850	3,125	(275)	275	-
2,850	29	3,150	2,850	3,150	300	300	-	2,850	29	3,150	2,850	3,150	(300)	300	-
2,850	30	3,175	2,850	3,175	325	325	-	2,850	30	3,175	2,850	3,175	(325)	325	-
2,850	31	3,200	2,850	3,200	350	350	-	2,850	31	3,200	2,850	3,200	(350)	350	-
2,850	32	3,225	2,850	3,225	375	375	-	2,850	32	3,225	2,850	3,225	(375)	375	-
2,850	33	3,250	2,850	3,250	400	400	-	2,850	33	3,250	2,850	3,250	(400)	400	-

FIGURE 14.6

```
TRADE
BUY CALL OR SELL PUT FOR THS PRICE RANGE
```

Figure 14.4 Trade for Decreasing Prices

EXERCISE PRICE	DAY	MARKET PRICE	BUY AT EXERCISE	SELL AT MARKET	BP - SP	VALUE OF OPTION TO BUYER OF CALL	VALUE OF OPTION TO SELLER OF CALL	EXERCISE PRICE	DAY	MARKET PRICE	SELL AT EXERCISE	BUY AT MARKET	SP-BP	VALUE OF OPTION TO SELLER OF PUT	VALUE OF OPTION TO BUYER OF PUT
2,850	17	2,850	2,850	2,850	-	-	-	2,850	17	2,850	2,850	2,850	-	-	-

Figure 14.5 No profits for either side.

Types of Options

Up and In Option

An Up and In Option is an exotic option which allows an option holder to exercise an option only if market prices hit a certain barrier price.

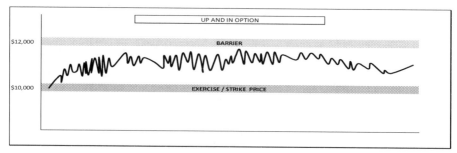

Figure 14.6 Non- Exercisable Up and In Option – Barrier Not Hit

One can see that that although market prices cross the exercise price and the above call option is in the money, the call option holder is only able to exercise the option if market prices cross the barrier of $12,000. As such an option limits the rights of the options holder it is typically less expensive than a normal "vanilla" option.

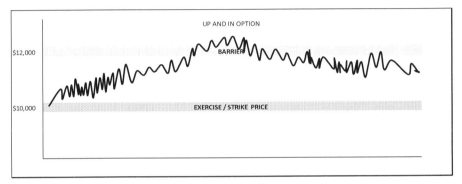

Figure 14.7 Exercisable Up and In Option – Barrier Hit

In the latter case, market prices cross the $12,000 barrier, therefore the option holder is able to exercise the option. The exercise price and the level of the barrier are decided by both parties to the transaction. The upper barrier is referred to as the "knock-in-barrier".

Up and Out Option

The Up and Out options behave entirely in an opposite manner than Up and In options. The option holder can exercise the option only if market prices oscillate between an exercise price and a upper barrier. If prices for the underlying asset cross an upper barrier, the right to exercise the option is automatically revoked and the option becomes worthless. The upper barrier is referred to as the "knock out barrier".

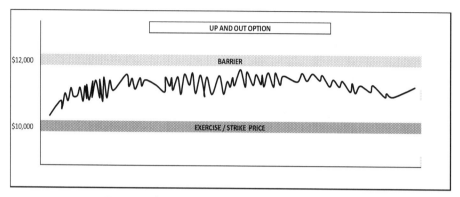

Figure 14.8 Exercisable Up and Out Option

In this scenario as market prices do not hit a certain barrier the option holder can continue to exercise the option.

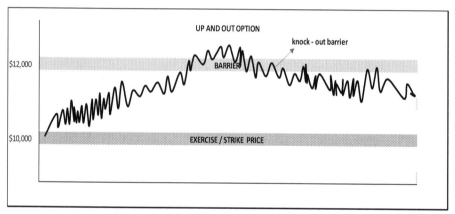

Figure 14.9 Non-Exercisable Up and Out Option

In the second scenario as market prices cross the barrier of $12,000, the contract becomes worthless, as the option holder is not able to exercise the option.

Knock In Option

A "knock in option" is an option which only allows the option holder the right to purchase the underlying asset or sell the underlying asset, if a certain price is reached. A call knock in option behaves like a knock in option. The barrier price must be reached before the contract expires. If the barrier option is not reached the contract would not extend any rights to the holder and for all purposes may never have existed.

Knock Out Option

A "knock out option" behaves like a up and out option where the rights of the holder are revoked if a certain barrier price is reached.

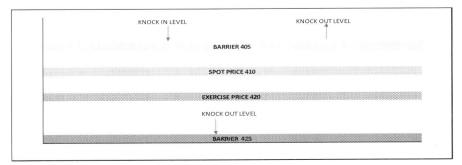

Figure 14.10 Knock In and Knock Out Options

One Touch Option

A one touch option is another form of exotic option which offers a pre-determined pay out to the holder if market prices cross a certain barrier price. Prices need to "touch" the barrier just once for the option holder to be entitled to a profit. If prices do not touch the barrier the option is rendered worthless. The one touch option has become increasingly popular in the commodities market and foreign exchange market.

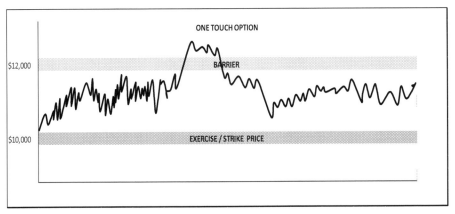

Figure 14.11 One Touch Option

Double Touch Option

The Double Touch Option is similar to the One Touch Option, except that the price of the underlying asset must cross one or more pre-agreed prices barriers. Market prices for the underlying asset must breach both the barriers during the term of the contract.

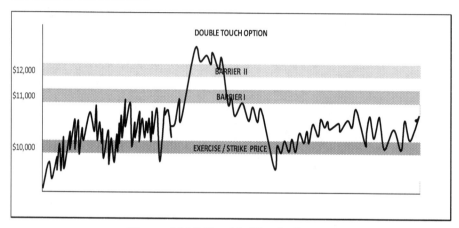

Figure 14.12 Double Touch Option

No Double Touch Option

This version of the option contract offers a pay out to the holder if prices of the underlying asset do not touch any of two barrier prices agreed between the parties.

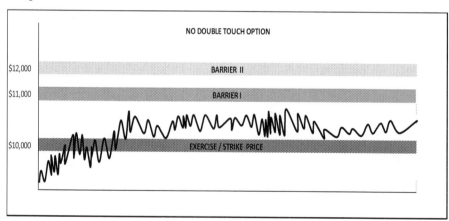

Figure 14.13 No Double Touch Option

Binary Option

Binary Options are very simple contracts where a pay out occurs if prices of an underlying asset hits a certain barrier on a specific date or range of dates before the contract expires. If prices do not reach this barrier price the option holder will not be entitled to any pay out.

Digital Options

A digital option differs from a normal option in that the payout is not linked to the difference between an exercise price and market prices, but is in fact determined upfront and triggered off if an underlying asset's price hits a certain barrier or threshold. Thus, a digital option may be so structured that offers a payout of $3 if the price of an underlying share hits a strike price of $100.

Short Put

Along with being an Olympics event a short put is merely a trade of selling a put option. Selling a put option entitles the counterparty to sell an underlying asset at a specific price referred to as the strike price to the issuer. The put seller would have to perform if the counterparty exercises the option by purchasing the asset. If the put seller expects prices to increase during the term of the contract, it would be prudent to purchase the asset at spot prices in the market and hold inventory till the put buyer exercises the option.

Options Trading Strategies

Investors can and often do purchase call and put options simultaneously in the same asset, for the same exercise price, with the same expiration date, to benefit from price increases or decreases in the underlying. The costs of such trades includes the costs of purchasing the options and the brokerage and commissions fees for purchasing the shares. Several strategies have been developed that involve purchasing various combinations of call and put options, these strategies are known as strip options, straddle options or strap options. We shall demonstrate the strategy behind a strip option.

A strip option strategy simply implies buying 2 put options (in the same asset) for every 1 call option. For ease of explanation we shall refer to an asset which has a market price hovering around $100, call options with a strike price of $100 are available for a cost of $6, and put options for the same strike price of $100. The price of put options is $7 per option.

It is obvious that for call options a break even market price would be $106, as at this price, exercising the option would result in 0 profits or losses. Any price above $106 for the share would yield a dollar for dollar profit for the call option holder.

Similarly, any price below $93 would make sense for a holder of put options, whereby, for instance at $92.50, a put option holder would purchase the underlying at the market price of $92.50, and sell the same for $93 to the issuer of the put and make a profit of $.50.

Were an investor to purchase 1 call and 2 puts, the total costs borne would be $20. At prices above $120, the position of holding 1 call and 2 puts would be profitable, and at prices below $90, the position would be profitable. For prices between $90 and $120, the position would be unprofitable. Yet, in this manner, with this position, the investor can benefit from price swings in either direction, well above $100 and well below $100 as well.

The pay outs are shown in Figure 14.14.

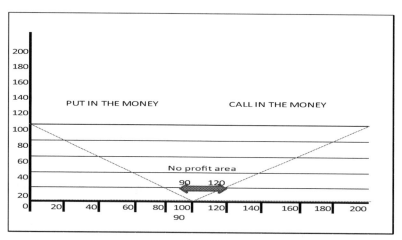

Figure 14.14 Strip Options

The above strategy poises an investor for considerable swings in the in the price of a share, but has a preference for possible decrease in share prices. Such situations are faced when companies are about to launch a new product, where if it is well accepted by the market (like an Iphone 6), company sales, earnings and therefore share prices can escalate, but if the product is not well received like (like the Microsoft Surface Tablet), earnings can disappoint and share prices can fall.

A strategy where 1 call is purchased with the purchase of 1 put is referred to as a straddle. This strategy would have a different break even range, where prices above $113 would make profits and prices below $87 would make profits for the investor. Prices between $87 and $113 would result in losses for the investor.

A strap option would require an investor to hold 2 calls for each put option. In this regard the cost of holding such a position would be $19. At prices above $109.75, an investor would exercise each call option and sell the underlying at market prices making a profit and at prices below $93 the investor would buy the underlying at market prices and sell at the exercise for a profit. At a price range between $93 and $109.75, the position offers no profits to the investor.

Each strategy is based upon expectations of what movements in market prices for an underlying asset. An investor wishing to hedge his positions and make money in either event, price increases or decreases can opt for varying combinations of call and put options.

Shariah Points

There is no clear and simple *shariah* contract hat replicates an option contract. The main features of a conventional option contract are fundamentally that it is a stand alone contract between 2 parties which offers certain rights to certain parties and imposes certain liabilities on others, and more importantly it carries its own consideration and is therefore tradable. An options contract has its own price. Thus, an options contract can neither be developed using the concept of *bai al urbun, wa'd, khiyaar,* or *hamish jiddiyah.* All these contracts and concepts have similarities to options and share certain features with options contracts but they all differ in that they do not carry any consideration of their own and are not tradable.

For instance *urbun* extends rights to a Buyer to make a down payment for an asset, allowing the Buyer to purchase the asset in the future, but does not bind the Buyer to do so. If the Buyer purchases the said asset the *urbun* payment is made part of the final purchase price. If the Buyer decides to forego the right to Buy the asset, the *urbun* payment is left with the Seller. Niether the Buyer or Seller can sell their rights or obligations in the *urbun* contract to a third party.

Hamish jiddiyah is a traditional contract with applications in sales based on *murabahah,* whereby a Buyer promises to purchase a particular asset if a Seller procures the asset from a vendor or manufacturer within a certain time frame. The Seller may demand a deposit from the Buyer in the shape of *hamish jiddiyah* which remains in the ownership of the Seller as a form of collateral or *rahn.* If the Buyer fails to purchase the asset once the Seller has procured it, the Seller may sell the asset to a 3rd party, and if the Seller incurs any losses in doing so, in that the 3rd party purchases the asset for a price lower than that negotiated with the original Buyer, any differences in the price can be deducted from the *hamish jiddiyah.* The concept of *hamish jiddiyah* lends itself more to the idea of margin purchases than it does to the idea of options.

Options cannot be constructed using the concept of *wa'd,* as the only legal contemporary commentary on *wa'd* disallows charging a fee for a *wa'd* and further a *wa'd* cannot be traded.

The concept of *khiyaar* in the traditional texts has been restricted to *khiyaar al shart,* where a Buyer in a sale/purchase contract is accorded some time to inspect the subject matter of the sale, upon delivery, and reserves the right to reject the goods thus delivered if they do not meet certain pre-determined requirements. This right does not lend itself to the idea of conventional options we have discussed so far.

Options are contracts in and of themselves. The issuer of an option, offers certain rights to a counterparty for a consideration, or the options price. The option issuer therefore takes on a contingent liability, if the buyer exercises the option the issuer is required to perform. The option buyer is exposed to performance risk vis a vis the issuer. The issuer of the option charges a price for the rights offered to the counterparty. Here, the authors believe, we enter into a discussion on the sale and purchase of financial rights or *huqquq maaliya.* We have addressed this issue ion detail in subsequent chapters.

Critics of options feel that the instrument leads to speculative trading in assets and have no real economic value. We hope that we have cleared the confusion in that aspect. However, options are financial tools, and like any other tool can be either correctly used or misused. To avoid misuse, a *shariah* compliant market for derivatives could control the players involved in the market regulating daily trading limits and volumes to counter speculators. But this too would require a balanced approach as speculators and market makers are necessary for liquidity and for the market to have scale and enough people to take the other side of the trade.

For instance a certain airline buys $12 billion worth of jet fuel in a year. A 1% saving on the cost of fuel can lead to a saving of $120 million a year. These savings can be passed onto shareholders (which is normal in the conventional world), or they can be passed onto employees, or they can be used in subsidizing Hajj packages for pilgrims, which would actually fulfil some aims of *maqasid al shariah*. A certain number of speculators will have to be tolerated to hedge such a large purchase of oil even if it stretched over a long period of time.

It is how the tool is used that determines whether it is beneficial or harmful to mankind and not the tool itself. To conclude this argument, in the current scenario, with the Muslim world playing a dominating role in the oil industry, and with many airlines carrying the flag of Muslim countries, neither the mechanism, the contracts, the training or the talent exists in the Muslim world to deal with risk and companies are going to conventional banks for solutions. Islamic Banks have a lot of room to grow in this area, whether it comes under the ambit of investment banking, commodities trading or derivatives trading. The hedging will occur, it is better that it happens with the advice of Islamic banks.

CHAPTER 15

FUTURES AND FORWARDS

We will approach the subject of futures with the same simple example of a wheat farmer wishing to sell 10 tons of wheat in 180 days. We construct a market environment to explain the situation. Current market prices are $10,000, and the Farmer seeks to lock in a price of $10,000 in 180 days as well.

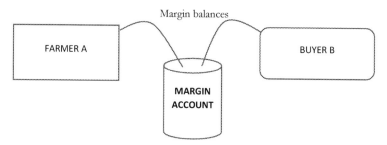

Figure 15.1 Market Scenario

A and B enter into a Futures contract whereby B agrees to buy 10 tons of wheat in 90 days for $10,000 a ton from A. However, prices may fluctuate over 90 days, offering incentives to each party to default on their commitment. If prices increase to $12,000, the Farmer A may wish to default on the contract to sell to B for $10,000 and sell instead to the market for $12,000. To counter this possibility the Farmer agrees to place $2,000 in a margin account (held with a 3rd Party), which eliminates any profit arising from defaulting on the contract. Alternatively, prices may fall by $2,000 to $8,000 a ton offering the Buyer an incentive to default and buy wheat from the market for $8,000 instead of buying from the Farmer for $10,000. To mitigate this risk, the

Farmer A requires the Buyer B to place $2,000 in the margin account to offset any profit that could be earned by defaulting

The payment into the margin account is ongoing, and linked to the movements in prices of wheat in the real markets. This can be compared to the price of a call or put option, but when the contract is concluded the payment into the margin account is made part of the final purchase or sale price. The cost to either party is therefore the opportunity cost of placing funds held in a margin account which may be measured by the prevailing interest rates or profit rates on deposits of a matching tenure.

At the stage of contract conclusion, if both contracts hold the contract to maturity and the Buyer B demands delivery, Farmer A will deliver 10 tons of wheat to Buyer B, and Buyer B will make payment of $100,000 to Farmer A.

The above arrangement is not like *salaam,* in that the Buyer B does not make full payment for the subject matter, instead places a certain amount as a deposit in a margin account. These funds are neither in the control of the Farmer, or the Buyer, but can be utilised at the stage of contract conclusion. If at contract conclusion, the Buyer B, has placed 10% of the purchase price in the margin account, the latter will simply make a balance payment of $90,000 to the Farmer and accept ownership of the wheat. If B is unable to make payment on the due date, A is entitled to retain the full amount placed in the margin account. Alternatively, if Farmer A is unable to make delivery on the due date, B has a right to claim ownership of the funds placed in the margin account by the Farmer.

Buyer B is exposed to performance risk over Farmer A, and the Farmer is exposed to credit risk on B as it may well happen that on the contract maturity date, the Farmer having incurred costs of production has 10 tons of wheat available for delivery but the Buyer does not have the ready cash to make the payment.

In conventional financial systems, however, Buyer B enjoys the right to contract to sell the 10 tons of wheat to other parties before taking actual delivery of the wheat. This is certainly the role played by intermediaries who in effect are not end users of commodities such as wheat, but simply, purchase them in large quantities from producers and sell them to end users or other intermediaries. It would be in the interest of Buyer B to sell to other parties before taking actual delivery, to avoid operating costs of transportation, storage and insurance.

Cash Settlement vs Physical Settlement

The arguments for Physical and Cash Settlement apply to futures contracts as well. If wheat prices increase to $12,000, the Buyer will place $2,000 in the margin account. If A is a genuine farmer, he will continue to harvest his proceeds and move to sell the wheat for an implied loss of $2,000. Party B will on the other hand buy for $10,000 and if B is not an end user of the product, will onward sell the wheat to another Party C for $12,000 making an actual profit of $2,000.

However, if A is not a Farmer and just a trader, he may sell the wheat from his own inventory or may just give B $2,000 cash as the profit on the trade. If B is also not an end user, the cash settlement would do just fine. Alternatively, if prices fall to $7,000 per ton, the Buyer can just "settle" the contract by paying A $3,000 and terminating any commitment to actually perform.

In a futures contract the one long or short can choose to perform or not perform. The party long on the sale, must buy and the party short on the sale must sell, or they may agree to net off cash flows with respect to actual market prices. In simpler words, if both parties to a futures contract are intermediaries or traders looking to benefit from movements in the prices of wheat, gains (for one) and losses (for the other) may be netted off between both the parties without their being any actual delivery of the underlying subject matter.

In fact, in the context of cash settlement trades, a party offering to sell a commodity in the future, may not even have the commodity in its possession or have any intention of procuring the commodity either. The Buyer, offering to buy the commodity too has no intention of taking delivery of the subject matter of the sale. Both parties will simply settle the difference between the agreed upon futures contract price (which can be compared to a exercise price), and the spot market prices on the date of maturity of the contract. If market prices are higher than the contract price, the buyer benefits and if market prices are lower than the contract price the seller will benefit. In this case however, both parties will simply credit each others' account balances in cash for the difference and not undertake the process of actual delivery and sale.

OTC and Exchange Traded

The concepts of OTC and Exchange Traded futures contracts applies to Futures as well. Exchange traded contracts come in standardized forms and performance is guaranteed by the exchange on which the contracts are traded.

Long and Short

In the language of the industry any party that is willing to buy an asset is long on the asset or holds a long position on the asset. Any party long on an asset, is expecting the value of the asset to increase beyond the level at which the asset was purchased. A party short an asset is in a position of selling the asset, possibly without owning the asset. Such a party expects asset prices to fall, so that when it is expected to transfer ownership of the asset to a buyer, this party buys it at a cost lower than for which it is selling the asset for.

In a spot transaction, a seller must own an asset before selling it. In a transaction that is expected to take place in the future, a seller may first purchase an asset, grow it, produce it or manufacture it and then sell it. Another alternative is for a seller to enter into a sale contract for a specific asset, without actually owning the subject matter of the sale, with the hope of purchasing the asset at a lower price from a 3rd party or the market before having to actually deliver the asset to the buyer. In any regard, in a future sale contract, the seller is required to own the asset by the maturity date.

Let us illustrate our point using an example.

Party A is short a futures contract. This means A is on the sale side. The contract is to sell 10 tons of wheat for $10,000 in 90 days. A is also long a futures contract, where A shall buy 10 tons of wheat for $9,800 in 90 days from another party. A has locked in a profit of $200 less the cost of entering the 2 contracts and less the opportunity cost of maintaining margin on both contracts. Let us say that margin requirement for both contracts is 10%. So A will place $1,000 in the first contract that A is short on, and $980 on the second contract that A is long on. A total of $1,980 is kept in non-interest bearing margin accounts or 90 days. If interest rates are 3% per annum for 90 day deposits, the foregone interest is $14.85. If the cost of each contract is $20, Party A has incurred an expense of $54.85 to lock in a profit of $200 in 90 days.

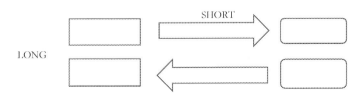

Figure 15.2 Long and Short Positions

As long as margin balances do not increase (note if they increase for one party they will decrease for the other), costs will remain the same. Party A has locked in a net profit of $145.15. A's profit is linked to prevailing interest rates as they offer the opportunity cost of returns earned on the trade. The short position can be compared to holding a put option and the long position can be compared to holding a call option. For simplicity sake, we assume that A can enter 2 trades, (one where the counterparty expects prices to increase), and the other (where the counterparty expects prices to decrease), for the same price and that counterparties are willing to offer both trades, this may not always be so.

It is also prudent to mention that spot trades happen on a different platform, options are issued with OTC or a separate exchange and futures are traded on a separate exchange. What is fundamental to understand tis hat future transactions are a necessary part of spot transactions and are usually entered into to facilitate a spot transaction sometime in the future. A future contract of today is a spot contract in the future. To facilitate a future spot trade, many players with varying motives need to be involved to mitigate price risk and performance risk. Future contracts need to be a discussion forum for Islamic Finance.

Expectation of Price Movements – Contango and Backwardation

The futures markets dynamics are closely linked to expectations of movements in market prices. A trader that expects prices to rise, would like to purchase now and sell in the future. This trade would be restricted by 2 factors. One would be the interest rates foregone if the inventory was sold on spot and the proceeds invested in a bank deposit, the other factor would the cost of storing the inventory. For assets such as shares the element of storage costs have no relevance. Costs associated with storing commodities however are relevant. Storage costs for purchasing gold may be negligible, but costs associated with storing metals like aluminium, copper, or with storing crude palm oil or crude oil can be considerable.

Prices are a function of demand and supply, when demand is high, sellers can get away with disposing their inventories at higher prices. When demand is low, prices too are naturally low. A particular asset may experience multiple cycles of demand and supply in a particular year.

In order to understand futures markets we need to understand two rather simple concepts, that of contango and backwardation. Contango is merely a circumstance where prices for a certain asset in the future are expected to be higher than spot prices today. This is illustrated in Figure 15.3.

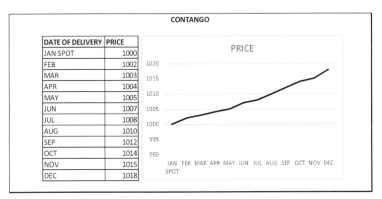

DATE OF DELIVERY	PRICE
JAN SPOT	1000
FEB	1002
MAR	1003
APR	1004
MAY	1005
JUN	1007
JUL	1008
AUG	1010
SEP	1012
OCT	1014
NOV	1015
DEC	1018

Figure 15.3 Contango Prices

Backwardation is merely a condition where futures prices for a particular asset are lower than spot prices.

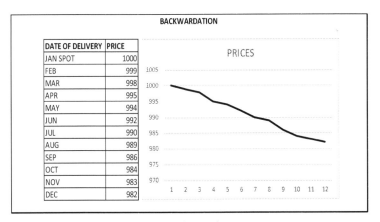

DATE OF DELIVERY	PRICE
JAN SPOT	1000
FEB	999
MAR	998
APR	995
MAY	994
JUN	992
JUL	990
AUG	989
SEP	986
OCT	984
NOV	983
DEC	982

Figure 15.4 Backwardation Prices

We shall examine a hypothetical scenario for jet fuel prices. Airlines experience seasonal demand for air travel coupled with a regular stream of travel during the year. Summer holidays offer an increase in demand as holiday makers decide to make the most of the children's school holidays and parents take 2 weeks of their annual leave at this same time. Another time for peak travel in the West is around Christmas time. Given that Muslims have begun to enjoy increased disposable income, the holidays of Eid offer opportunities for airlines to sell tickets. During these seasons airlines typically fly more aircraft and therefore also consume considerable amounts of jet fuel.

With competitive pricing and holiday packages, airlines would be wise to lock in good prices for their major input, jet fuel. However, jet fuel on average takes 3 months to deliver, so the industry sees peak orders in February and March for delivery in June. A trader sitting in January will expect prices for jet fuel to rise in February and March, a situation where future prices for oil are higher than spot prices because of the ordering for June. This situation where a future price for a commodity, or a price for a commodity to be delivered in the future is higher than spot prices or prices today in the market is referred to as contango.

The seasonal level for jet fuel prices are illustrated in Figure 15.4.

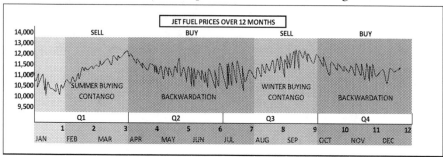

Figure 15.5 Contango and Backwardation

In April prices tend to decline as the airlines have stocked up on their supplies or have already placed their relevant orders with suppliers. The business picks up by May and by August the airlines begin to deplete their jet fuel reserves. Another peak season for air travel (in the West) is around Thanksgiving, Christmas and New Year. These family holidays fall in the months of November and December respectively. Airline place orders as early as mid-August for jet fuel to be delivered by November and the market again experiences an increase in prices.

In between these intervals of rising prices are intervals of reduced demand. These periods fall from late April to mid-July and from October to December.

In these periods prices of jet fuel decline and future prices for oil are lower than spot prices, an environment known as backwardation. In such an environment, it is better to buy inventory in the futures market than in the spot market. However, as all traders would execute this trade the advantages will quickly evaporate from the market.

Traders see these environments of contango and backwardation as opportunities. In an environment of backwardation a trader could sell jet fuel in the spot market (by borrowing it), and buy it in the futures market when prices are lower. This trade could happen if the trader could actually borrow the commodity to cover the short sale. When the trader takes delivery in the futures market where he is long, the trader will replace the jet fuel borrowed in kind with interest in cash. However, this window of opportunity will soon evaporate as traders execute these trades and narrow the gaps between futures and spot markets such that the above trade breaks even. With subsequent sale orders in the spot markets, prices would decline and with increased buy orders in the futures market, prices would increase thus narrowing the spreads between the two, where the sale price is reduced and the buy price is increased. Increased trades of this kind would also increase the cost of borrowing the commodity (possible in the gold market-known as the lease rate) and therefore impact the profits that could be gained.

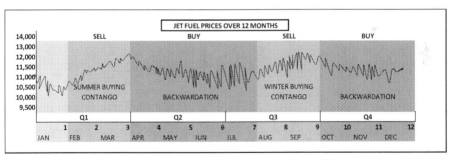

Figure 15.6 Contango and Backwardation Continued

Another variant of the trade would be to merely buy in the backwardation stage and sell in the contango stage. However, with contracts such as call options and futures one need not pay the full purchase price for the buy order. In the event of using futures contracts, commitments are made by just placing certain funds in a margin account. Options are also bought for multiple lots of jet fuel for amounts that reflect a small fraction of actually buying the jet fuel and storing it. One must bear in mind that these costs are borne by the issuer of such options and are priced into the contract and a trader must carefully do the math on his trades. A crucial question to ask is what are you paying to earn an expected profit of $x. If the cost of the trade itself is more than the expected profit from the trade, the trade does not make sense.

Market players in futures markets are constantly watching their screens looking for a shift from contango to backwardation, looking for a trend and traders spend millions of dollars on equipping themselves with the necessary electronic platforms to be able to place orders with brokers in nanoseconds. Successful brokers must also have the tools in place to execute orders in nanoseconds as a window of opportunity may appear and disappear in seconds.

Each market offers its own opportunities given the peculiarities of the commodity or asset class being traded. Gold for instance can be leased from Central Banks for a very low rate, which allows a trader to short on gold in the spot market, only to repay the Central Bank with gold acquired through a long position on a futures contract. Certain commodities are manufactured or processed to certain specific standards. Crude oil for instance comes in specific qualities, such as West Texas Intermediate crude or WTI, North Sea Brent Crude, UAE Dubai Crude. These commodities are priced differently too, with different prices for 30 day delivery, 60 day delivery, or 90 day delivery.

A stickling factor here is of course the currency in which one purchases oil. As per current market practice, oil prices are measured in US$, and settlements for oil imports are paid for in US$. If a country like Pakistan experiences devaluation of the Pakistanni Ruppee against the US$, even a period of backwardation would not result in any benefits as the decline in fuel prices would be offset by a further depreciation in the value of the rupee. However, now to hedge against fuel prices, non-US flag airlines would have to match their fuel trades with their currency trades. US airlines do not have to worry about this issue as they earn their revenues in US$ and pay their expenses in US$ as well. Airlines of other countries such as the UAE, earn in dirhams and have to pay for oil in US$, so they must hedge their trades accordingly.

Shariah Rulings on Futures and Forwards

The futures markets rely on 2 basic principles, a buyer is able to enjoy ownership of an asset by only paying a margin amount, and secondly a buyer is able to sell the asset before actually owning the asset or taking possession of it. Both these principles are contrary to basic fundamentals of the *shariah* with regard to contracts of sale. The *shariah* recognizes a sale contract as executed when either the purchase price is transferred from the ownership of the Buyer to the Seller, or, the ownership of the subject matter is transferred from the Seller to the Buyer.

In a futures contract neither of these conditions are met. In a contract of *salaam* or deferred delivery, purchase price is transferred from the Buyer to the Seller. In a contract of *murabahah, or bai bithman ajil,* where payment is deferred but delivery is on spot, the ownership of the subject matter is transferred to the Buyer. In a futures arrangement, a Buyer makes partial payment into a margin account more as a form of collateral than a purchase price. This partial payment is not transferred to the ownership of the Seller, rights over this margin payment is only effected at the conclusion of the contract. Thus, this margin payment can be compared to *Hamish jiddiyah* and not to *urbun*. The asset or subject matter of the sale is to be delivered in the future and may not be in the ownership or possession of the Seller at the time of entering the contract. It is debatable as to whether the Buyer has a right over the subject matter such that the Buyer can sell the asset prior to taking delivery as this violates the ruling expressed in the hadith of the Prophet (pbuh), "sell not what is not with you".[10]

The general consensus amongst the *shariah* community is that given the prohibition on selling an asset prior to obtaining ownership of it, the futures industry is a no go area for Islamic Finance. Professor Muhammad Hisham Kamali, in his work, Islamic Commercial Law feels otherwise and writes extensively in favour of the product citing some basic perspectives. Professor Hisham, cites that certain scholars feel that the above mentioned *hadith,* is not a *sahih hadith,* as there is doubt with regards to its chain of transmission, and therefore should not be a source for devising any laws. Secondly, he points out that the language of the *hadith* does not clearly indicate whether a prohibition is implied or a recommendation is implied. Mr. Kamali also proposes that as there is no punishment or warning that accompanies this *hadith,* one may interpret the language to be one of recommendation rather than prohibition.

---

[10]   Kamali, Muhamamd Hashim, Islamic Commercial Law, 2002, Ilham Publishers.

Mr. Kamali also points to the interpretation of certain scholars, which suggests that although the *hadith* has a prohibitive tone, the prohibition applies to only certain goods. Certain scholars have limited the prohibition to the sale of wheat, whereas others have extended it to include food stuffs whereas others have granted permissibility for fungible goods. The *illah* or cause behind the prohibition is to prevent uncertainty and protect the buyer in a forward sale from the risk of non-delivery from a seller. A group of scholars feel however, that in the case of futures contracts for commodities such as copper, aluminium, gold, zinc, wheat and other goods, there are readily available brokers, exchanges, inventories and transparent pricing mechanisms that in fact exist to mitigate all such risks, and in an environment of exchange traded futures, the risk of non delivery is mitigated by the markets themselves and the customary trading practices. As the cause of the prohibition is removed, the prohibition itself can be removed. Where the cause exists, the prohibition remains. Thus, forward sales contracts can be deemed permissible if they are transacted on an exchange and may be deemed impermissible in a OTC setting. A final defense offered by Mr. Kamali, that taking delivery is not the intent or motivation behind futures contracts, and therefore the risk of non-delivery is again not a major concern as more than 98% of futures contracts are cash settled.

Certain proponents of the futures industry have also distinguished between "ownership or *milkiyat*" and "possession *qabd*.. An individual may possess an asset that he or she does not own, and has to assume the risks associated with possession, and others may own assets they may not possess. Ownership has its own set of rights, obligations and risks attached to it and possession has its own set of rights, risks and obligations attached to it. Thus, certain scholars, have claimed, that by making a partial payment in the form of a margin payment, extends rights of ownership to a buyer, whereas rights of possession remain with the seller. The buyer can thus sell the asset to a third party prior to taking possession as he or she already enjoys ownership.

Futures and *wa'd*

The final verdict of forward sales under the contract of *bai* seems to be a distant event. It is possible however, for 2 parties to actually promise to sell/buy a particular asset in the future. If forward sales come under the ambit of *wa'd* many of the controversial issues surrounding futures can be circumvented.

This is made all the more easier in Malaysia where a promise is deemed legally binding. A buyer in a futures contract can also therefore promise to sell the asset to a 3ʳᵈ party prior to receiving possession of the underlying asset.

Forward Sales of Foreign Currency

The sale of currency in the forwards market is made more complicated with the Islamic stipulation that requires the sale of currency to be in the spot market. The contract of *bai al sarf,* is the fundamental contract used in this arrangement. However, merchants, traders, manufacturers and buyers all require to lock in a rate for payments or receivables that need to be settled at a future date in a foreign currency. *Shariah* scholars have encouraged the industry to adopt the practice of purchasing foreign currency upfront and stock up for any future expected payments. However, this may be an expensive option, especially if profit rates on bank deposits in that particular currency are low. This option may also prove to be rather expensive and would not allow the customer of the bank to benefit from any changes in exchange rates. Foreign currency options offer a considerable amount of flexibility to purchase currencies at specific exchange rates or to choose not to. Currency futures allow for parties to lock in a rate in today's market for a future transaction.

However, given the restrictions imposed by the *shariah,* forward sales in currencies can be executed under the concept of *wa'd* and that too in a legal environment where *wa'd* is considered to be enforceable. In Malaysia however, an elegant option has been used to develop foreign exchange future sales contracts using the contracts of *bai al inah, commodity murabahah* and *tawarruq.* These transactions are basically sequences of sale and buy agreements, where one sale is made for spot delivery and a spot price and a buy back is executed for spot delivery but a deferred credit price.

Conclusion

Although Mr. Kamali has some elegant defences in favour of futures contracts, the only prickling point is that if there is no restriction on an individual to sell something that is not in his or her ownership, trade contracts can be floating between various parties for amounts of goods far in excess of readily available supply. For instance without this restriction, given a supply of say 5,000 tons of gold in the world, there can and in fact do exist futures contracts for amounts far in excess of 5,000 tons of gold. Interestingly enough, all these transactions are guaranteed by their respective exchanges such as the London Metals Exchange. In fact a sure way to cause the LME to default would be for any one party to demand delivery on all the futures sale contracts on gold at any given time. The total transactions may be for instance for 10,000 tons of gold, whereas there is only 5,000 tons available on the planet at any given time. In this regard, futures markets can easily become paper markets, trading in assets that may only exist on paper.

An offer to sell in the future may look something like this:-

"I _____ offer to sell to _____ 100 tons of gold in 30 days for a price of $1,000 / ton".

The specifications of the gold are such and such.

A buyer may enter into this contract, but if the 2 parties settle the contract in cash, there would never be any need for the gold to ever come into existence, or be delivered. In this case, both parties are technically not trading in gold but prices of gold.

However, the futures markets play an essential role in commodities trading and we shall address this issue in a later chapter.

CHAPTER 16

REAL ASSET VS SYNTHETIC ASSET

What is the best way to invest in an asset? The answer to this question emanates from what is perceived as the "best" way. Does "best" way imply cost effective way, in a way in which the investor is exposed to the minimum risks with the possibility of earning the most returns? Does the "best" way imply any level of commitment or "skin in the game" on the part of the investor?

The Capital Asset Pricing Model where $E(R) = Rf + \beta(Rm - Rf)$, suggests that investors seek the maximum return with the minimum risk. Return is seen as a premium for risk taking. One of the ways of investing in an economic activity is to merely undertake it lot stock and barrel. If an investor feels that coffee bean farming is a lucrative venture, an investor can buy or lease land and participate in the economic activity of farming coffee beans. This would include leasing or buying land, hiring workers, purchasing seeds, planting seeds, protecting the crop from pesticides, purchasing fertilizer, purchasing harvesting machinery, ware houses for storage and finally seeking out buyers. A coffee bean investor may secure a distribution channel for the product by entering into the retail business of actually selling coffee to end users as a finished product or the wholesale business of selling beans to other retailers. This mechanism of investing carries with it all kinds of risks, with everything affecting the coffee crop, to coffee prices in the commodities market. Factors ranging from rainfall to interest rates will affect the profitability of selling coffee beans. If the investor wishes to sell globally, then foreign currency exchange rates, international weather patterns, and even things like levels of tourism may all play a small role in the actual profitability of the business venture. Each factor or variable can be assigned a weightage to the extent that it affects the final price of a coffee bean.

Such an investor may be referred to as a Private Equity Investor, a Venture Capitalist or by any other name. From an Islamic point of view this is the most beneficial approach, of having an equity stake. There is a downside to this approach. When the company makes profits the investor is the first one to enjoy the returns, if the enterprise makes losses, equity holders have "residual claims" over assets, in that if losses are borne, or the company is liquidated, the owner must settle all claims, expenses, salaries, payables, interest payments and debt payments and what is left over belongs to the equity holder.

Unfortunately, fund managers that manage private savings of millions of citizens, insurance companies, banks, investment banks cannot invest in this economic activity directly. The commercial lending department of a bank may actually be able to take a hands on approach by lending money to a coffee bean enterprise, but that is the fullest extent of the exposure. Financial institutions can only invest in financial instruments whose "pay outs are linked to the performance of" the coffee bean farm or the industry as a whole. One such financial instrument would be shares issued by a large coffee bean enterprise that may be listed on a stock exchange. An enterprising investor may also purchase shares in industries linked to the coffee industry, such as logistics, distribution, retailers etc. Ultimately the investor is long on the demand for coffee and makes judicious investments in those companies that bring the product to market effectively.

Investors can purchase bonds issued by companies that are involved in the coffee business. Both shares and bonds issued by coffee bean companies will appreciate in value and offer higher yields as the basic underlying economic activity of producing and selling coffee continues to be more profitable. However, the price of shares or bonds is also affected by other variables such as interest rates, and currency levels especially if international investors have exposure on a locally owned coffee manufacturing company. It is rather difficult to gauge how much of a companies' share price is a component of the actual value of the underlying business the company is involved in and how much of the share price is a function of external matters. Certain shares may be very sensitive to changes in interest rates, where a drop in borrowing costs may see a spike in buying, whereas other share prices may be inelastic in their relationship to external factors.

Nevertheless, investing directly in a coffee producing farm and or plant is the most robust way of investing in the coffee business. Lending money to a coffee manufacturer is a mechanism by virtue of which a bank can take exposure on the coffee business. Buying shares in the company is another option. The first 2 options are rather illiquid, direct business owners, and direct lenders cannot easily exit from the business in case things go wrong. Direct investors would have to sell all or part of their assets in a coffee business to recover funds, banks would have to call in loans to reduce their exposure. Shareholders on the other hand can simply sell their shares in the secondary markets with relative ease, provided a counterparty is willing to buy. Bonds too can be sold on capital markets with ease. Such investors, invest in the business but at "an arms length", they wish to benefit from the upside but want to be able to liquidate positions quickly in the event of a downside. One can in fact even argue that capital markets have encouraged, developed and nourished "fair weather investors" who invest funds in good times and pull out in bad times. This may be a subject of study from the perspective of Islamic principles of equity and commitment.

Financial engineering has developed products that offer pay outs linked to an underlying economic activity in layers. For instance, options are financial instruments that offer the rights to buy shares in a company. If coffee farmers are expected to have a good season, coffee producing and selling companies are also expecting increased demand, the sector will enjoy good profits and shares of companies engaged in this sector will increase in value. Consequently, the value of options that entitle investors to buy these shares also increases. However, a course on options pricing rarely looks at the impact of the actual underlying economic activity and its impact on options prices, but looks at mathematical models that see prices as a function of volatility in prices whether that volatility is created by actual perceptions of what is to happen in the coffee sector or is a result of speculative activity in the capital markets is a separate concern. Options are priced separately from the shares to which they are linked and eventually volatility in options prices itself can become an investable asset class. Products like futures contracts allow investors to enter into buy and sale contracts for coffee without actually intending to take delivery and benefitting from price movements and earning spreads from fluctuations in prices. Investors can net off positions via cash settlements depending on whether they are long or short on coffee over a given period of time.

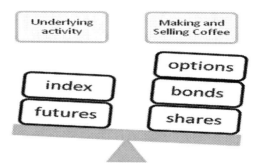

Figure 16.1 Financial Instruments

Such investment tools allow investors to benefit from changes in the demand and supply for coffee by not investing in the product or the companies that manufacture or sell the product. Such investors make gains from movements in prices of the underlying product. With banks, investment banks, mutual funds and hedge having access to huge surplus funds they become "arms length" stakeholders in the coffee business, impacting prices without having any exposure to the real underlying activity.

Such investors have now begun to play a crucial role in the economy, becoming market makers for the financial products that are linked to real assets and even affecting prices, and supply of the underlying as well. One can refer to options, calls, puts, futures contracts as synthetic products as they offer pay outs similar to those offered by investing in a real underlying asset. So the real asset would be coffee beans, and synthetics begin from shares in a coffee company, to options in shares in a coffee company, to options in the commodity itself and coffee futures contracts. A second layer of synthetics can be developed from the way the paper asset behaves, by making volatility in prices a product itself, or premiums paid for options in coffee an asset class of its own. We have seen real assets, paper assets that are linked to real assets, and then another layer of paper assets that are linked to paper assets linked to real assets. Ultimately, the layering is so intense, that an investor can lose the link to the real asset itself.

A question to ask is why investors invest in such products? One answer is that they are developed by investment banks, who are able to draw capital away from investing in real assets to investing in financial products as that is their bread and butter. Secondly, under various rules, fund managers, pension fund managers especially are not allowed to invest directly in such economic activity and can only invest in A-rated financial instruments. Financial instruments linked to an A rated share or an A rated bond also acquire an A rating, thereby allowing investment banks to develop financial products that are A-rated but not necessarily linked directly to any meaningful underlying activity. For a pension fund to invest directly in an economic activity may also require transferring funds to the country where such economic activity originates. Much of the supply side activity in commodities originates in countries outside the developed world where financial markets dominate. Yet banks benefit from market movements in commodities prices and demand patterns by bringing them into the fold of financial products.

The purpose behind this discussion is to distinguish between real assets and financial products that derive benefit from the way prices of the real asset "behave" in markets for the real assets. These movements affect how synthetic financial products "behave" in financial markets. The products are developed in a manner to mirror the behaviour of real assets, or the prices of real assets. Trading income comes from the basic difference between buying price and selling price, but buying and selling real assets is expensive as it requires cash outlays, storage costs and such, but if one could somehow, benefit from the same spreads without actually buying the asset, synthetic financial assets offer a viable alternative. However, whether such investments offer any real benefit to the economy is a matter of debate.

We shall aim to explain the complexity of synthetic financial products in our subsequent chapters.

"Synthetic" a financial instrument that is created artificially by simulating another instrument with the combined features of a collection of other assets.

An options trade

Example:-

Real Asset	= Stock in IBM
Price of stock	= $100 (at t = 0).
Price of call option	= $10. Each contract entitles you to purchase 100 shares of IBM.
Price of put option	= $9. Each contract entitles you to sell 100 shares of IBM.
Trade:-	Purchase a call option with an Exercise Price of $102. Sell a put option with an Exercise Price of $98.

Scenario A:

If an investor purchases 10,000 shares in IBM, the cash outlay would be $1,000,000. If the Risk free return is 3%, and the investor holds the stock for 90 days, the opportunity cost of the investment is $7,500. The stock price appreciates by 2% in 90 days, and the investor earns a net profit of $20,000. Adjusting for the risk free rate, the risk adjusted monetary benefit is only $20,000 - $7,500 = $12,500 or a 1.25% return on an annualized basis. In effect the investor had to forego $7,500 to earn $20,000.

One could rewrite the trade as involving a cost of $1,075,000 instead of just $1,000,000 for a return of $1,020,000 over 90 days. In doing so one builds in the opportunity cost of the investment into the purchase price of the stock. A more accurate measure would be to build in the present value of the risk free return.

Scenario B

A similar return could be configured by using options. The investor purchase 10 call options contracts for $10 each with a cash outlay of $10 * 100 = $1,000. The investor also buys put options for 10,000 shares at a cost of $9 * $100 = $900. The cash outlay for the investor is $1,900.

The opportunity cost of this investment is $1,900 * 3% * 90/360 = $14.25.

If the prices of the share crosses to $104, the investor exercises the call and purchases the shares for $102 and sells them for $104. After deducting the opportunity cost of the position of $14.25, the investor makes a return of $19,985.75 on an investment of $1,900. The Return on Equity is however, 1,052% as the investor can short sell at $104 and cover the position with the call, financing the purchase of 10,000 shares with the proceeds of the short sale. Calls and put options offer an investor an opportunity to hold synthetic long or short positions in an underlying asset, without having to make the cash outlay for acquiring the asset.

Real Sale and Synthetic Sale

We shall illustrate a real sale using 2 parties A and B. A is a wholesaler who sources certain goods from a manufacturer hoping to sell them for a profit to B. The asset is bought for $10,000 and sold for $12,000 with actual cash outlays expected from both parties. Asset ownership is first acquired by A and then transferred to B and delivery is also made from A to B. The asset is also in existence at the time of the trade.

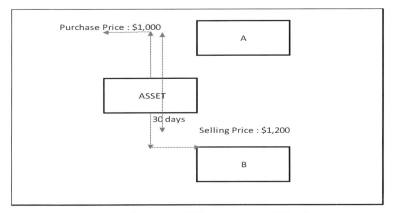

Figure 16.2 A Real Transaction of Trade

This is an actual trade transaction with the following cash flows. The motivation for A to enter this trade is based on expectations to sell the asset for a profit of 20% within 30 days.

CASH FLOWS SEQUENCE	
A TO B	
BUY	10,000
SELL	12,000
TENOR	30 DAYS
PROFIT	2,000
HPR	20%
PER ANNUM	240%

Figure 16.3 Returns from the Trade

B may be an end user of the asset or may want to resell the asset to a third party C for an additional profit of say $1,000. In the latter case, both parties A and B are not end users of the asset and wish to benefit from mere price increase over a given period of time.

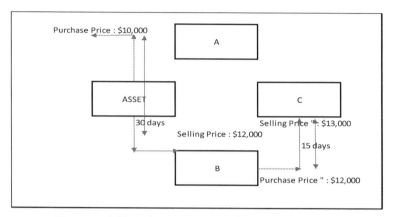

Figure 16.4 Trade Transaction for Intermediaries

The sequence of 2 consecutive sales at varying prices are represented in the figure above. The cash flows and the returns generated are expressed in the table below to compare the 2 trades.

CASH FLOWS SEQUENCE		CASH FLOWS SEQUENCE	
A TO B		B TO C	
BUY	10,000	BUY	12,000
SELL	12,000	SELL	13,000
TENOR	30 DAYS	TENOR	15
PROFIT	2,000	PROFIT	1,000
HPR	20.00%	HPR	8.33%
PER ANNUM	240.00%	PER ANNUM	200.00%

Figure 16.5 Returns Comparisons

Both the transactions require full payment of the price for the asset at each leg of the transaction. A expects prices for the asset to increase by 20% in 30 days and B expects asset prices to increase by 8.33% in a further 15 days.

What if a counterparty offers an investment opportunity where returns are linked to appreciation in the price of the asset over a total period of 45 days, without actually purchasing the underlying asset but rather a synthetic paper asset, that has no value in and of its own but is a contract that merely promises to pay a return of 20% if the asset prices behave as disclosed above.

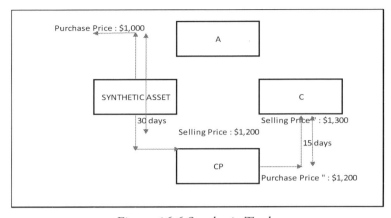

Figure 16.6 Synthetic Trade

In a synthetic trade A does not purchase the asset for $10,000 from a vendor but purchases a synthetic asset from a CP for 10% of the value of the asset at the time of the trade. If in 30 days the value of the asset appreciates by 20%, the CP would pay A $1,200 to replicate the 20% appreciation in the price of the underlying asset. A does not have any exposure on owning the asset A and enjoys the benefits and risks of how the price of A behaves in the market. Similarly, C approaches the CP for a similar arrangement where C only makes a cash outlay of $1,200 and if the asset prices appreciate by 8% in 15 days, the CP will pay C $1,300.

In the first transaction the CP would raise $1,000 and would end up paying $1,200 back to A. One may well ask what is the motivation for CP to enter into this transaction. The CP may have opposing views on what may happen to the prices of the asset in question over a period of 30 days. The CP may be expecting the prices of the asset to drop by 20% to $8,000. In that event, the CP would return only $800 to A. Subsequently, in the trade with C, the CP may expect prices to fall by 8.33%, in which case the CP would only return $1,100 to C.

CASH FLOWS SEQUENCE		CASH FLOWS SEQUENCE	
A TO CP		B TO CP	
BUY	1,000	BUY	1,200
SELL	1,200	SELL	1,300
TENOR	30 DAYS	TENOR	15
PROFIT	200	PROFIT	100
HPR	20.00%	HPR	8.33%
PER ANNUM	240.00%	PER ANNUM	200.00%

Figure 16.7 Returns on Synthetic Trades

The synthetic trade resembles a sequence of cash settled futures contracts, which offer a very generic basis for a synthetic trade transaction.

Options trading also offer opportunities of a synthetic investment where an investor is able to benefit from movements in the prices of an asset without having any exposure in the underlying asset itself. Investors can trade in options and benefit in movements in prices of options which are linked to movements in prices of an underlying asset.

"In derivatives contracts, the security that must be delivered when a derivative contract, such as a put or call option is exercised. In equities, the common stock that must be delivered when a warrant is exercised, or when a convertible bond or convertible preferred share is converted to common stock.

The price of the underlying is the main factor that determines prices of derivative securities, warrants and convertibles. Thus, a change in an underlying results in a simultaneous change in the price of the derivative asset that is linked to it. In most cases, the underlying is a security such as a stock (in the case of options) or a commodity (in the case of futures).[11]" Investopedia

Synthetic credit instruments

A loan is another contract whereby 2 parties exchange monies for a consideration. The lender parts with a loan amount for a specific period to be repaid by the borrower with a certain premium known as interest. Loans can be packaged into financial instruments and sold at a discount, par or a premium like a bond. The interest rate on these loans in part reflects the creditworthiness of the borrowers. Investors can develop products that replicate the changes in interest rates paid by borrowers based upon changes in their credit ratings and credibility over the term of the loan or bond issue.

A borrower may experience various downgrades and upgrades during the life of a loan as reflected in the figure below:-

---

[11]   Investopedia.com/Derivatives Site Visited on October 20th, 2014.

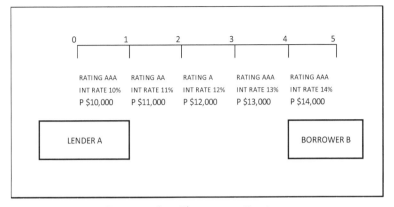

Figure 16.8 Changes in Ratings

With each downgrade for instance, the borrower will pay higher financing charges to lenders, alternatively, with any upgrade, the borrower will pay lower financing charges. Financial products can be engineered to offer pay outs linked to the changes in the creditworthiness of a borrower. For instance Party C and D may enter into an arrangement, whereby, if B's rating goes down from AAA to AA, C will pay B $5,000. Alternatively, if the B experiences upgrades from A to AAA, D will pay C, $4,000. These products resemble bets in their form, yet in essence, these products carry value linked to the credit worthiness of the borrower. The credit rating is a barometer of the health of the companies' cash flows, and its ability to pay its debts, just as share price is meant to be a barometer of the expected earnings of a company. Such a product "derived" from the credit worthiness of the borrower, or a credit derivative is a valid financial instrument. Other instruments can derive value from a credit event like a default, such an instrument is known as a credit default swap. Financial instruments that derive value from credit events are known as credit derivatives. The events can be positive or negative and will affect the value of the credit derivative accordingly.

Certain instruments are such that a negative credit event will increase the value of a credit derivative. Certainly, a product designed to provide credit default cover, like a credit insurance policy, will increase in value, the worse a loan portfolio becomes and the more the defaults occur.

Other instruments may be engineered such that they appreciate in value as the creditworthiness of borrowers in an underlying loan portfolio improves.

We shall examine the concepts of stripping and securitization in the next chapter to see how loan portfolios are developed en masse.

CHAPTER 17

STRIPPING AND SECURITIZATION

Stripping

As impolite as the word sounds the concept of stripping principal payments from interest payments has an important role to play in modern finance. We can illustrate the concept using an example of a 3 year car loan with total repayment of $1500 per month. This payment is comprised of a principal amount of $1,000 and an interest amount of $500. The total loan to be repaid is thus of $54,000, with total principal being at $36,000 and total interest of $18,000.

This is illustrated in the figure below.

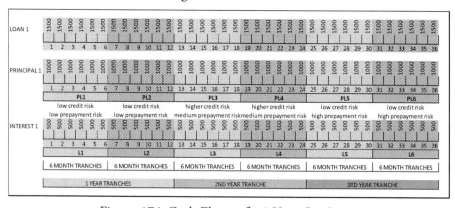

Figure 17.1 Cash Flows of a 3 Year Car Loan

Loan 1 presents cash flows for 36 instalments to be paid by the borrower. The same loan, and the same borrower represents different levels of credit risk during the life of the loan. The loan is relatively secure at the initial year of origination as it is likely that the borrowers circumstances will not change drastically, (given the due diligence conducted by the credit officer), and there will be a low risk of default. Possibly after 1.0 year, there is an increased risk of default as it is likely the borrower may lose his or her job and default on the payments. One can also assume that in the 3rd year, the borrower has reached stable financial conditions and instead of presenting credit risk, the borrower may present prepayment risk. Banks neither want their customers to default and not make payments, nor do they want borrowers to pay early, and deny the bank income.

The 36 months or 3 years payments can be divided into categories of risk, as shown in the figure above. The cash flows can also be stripped from each other and sold. In this regard, a $1,500 loan is broken up into a $1,000 payment and a $500 payment. Each payment can be bundled with other payments and discounted and sold to a third party. We have "sliced up" the cash flows above into tranches of 6 months each. Principal payments tranches are named PL1, PL2, PL3, PL4, PL5 and PL6. Interest payment tranches are named L1, L2, L3, L4, L5 and L6 respectively. Each tranche is a sequence of 6 consecutive instalments. A 3rd party can "buy" PL2 and L2, or PL4 and L2, different sequences of payments for the same loan or for 2 or more loans, or both.

We add another car loan to the scenario with different tranches of payments.

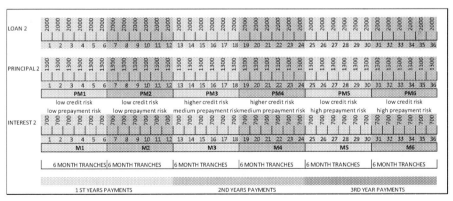

Figure 17.2 Figures for another 3 year car loan

If both these loans along with their 72 instalments are on the balance sheet of one bank, they can be sold to another bank in various combinations such as PM3 + PL3 + M5 + L3 for instance. The cash flows in each tranche will be discounted to the date of purchasing the loans, from a *shariah* perspective, these would be a sequence of *murabaha* payments and they would be discounted using the contract of *bai ul dayn*.

This process of stripping cash flows, bundling them with other cash flows is the essence of securitizing loans on a bank's balance sheet and then selling them. This process has given birth to the concept of originate and dispose for the lending business, where one institution develops a portfolio of term loans, either house loans or car loans, and then sells these loans to another party.

In the practical world, thousands of loans are put together by a financial institution or a bank. Each loan is assigned a credit rating based on the creditworthiness of a borrower. In fact each tranche is also treated as a separate cash flow and assigned a credit rating as well. Different tranches of varying risk profiles are then bundled together into a package which carries its own credit rating. So for instance if both borrowers in the above example have AAA rating, it is likely that a package including different tranches of these receivables will also be assigned a AAA rating. However, in practice this is not always the case. Various loans with ratings of AAA, AA, A, BBB or B are bundled together, and rating agencies assign the bundle a unique rating, which is theoretically a weighted average rating of all the loans that make up the bundle. Another important factor to note is that the bank that buys these loans does not typically conduct any due diligence on the origination process and wholeheartedly trusts the ratings assigned by credit rating agencies. The purchasing bank may also end up buying various tranches of the same loans without even knowing it. (This occurred when RBS bought Abn Amro). It is very likely that an originator may have bundled up various tranches of its portfolio to other banks and sold them. Market participants may end up buying different tranches of the same loan from different banks and thus end up enhancing their exposure on the same borrowers instead of diversifying their risks.

For a detailed exposition on securitization of conventional assets, we refer the reader to Moorad Choudry's, The Mechanics of Securitization: A Practical Guide to Structuring and Closing Asset-Backed Security Transaction.

Conclusion

An essential element of the securitization process is to remove assets from a bank's balance sheet to that of a third party. If the assets are sold all risk is absorbed by the purchasing bank. A bank can also however sell such assets to a Special Purpose Vehicle. The assets are bought by the SPV in a true sale, the SPV in turn to fund the purchase of the assets issues notes or bonds. The pay outs on these notes are engineered to match the inflows from the underlying assets. What is crucial for the SPV is to ensure that the interest paid on these notes is less than the interest earned from the financial assets. We have discussed in Contracts and Deals in Islamic Finance: A User's Guide to Cash Flows, Balance Sheets, and Capital Structures by Hussain Kureshi and Mohsin Hayat, the importance of funding assets with liabilities and associated capital charges with various assets.

In the normal business of banking, banks mobilise deposits at a certain cost of fund and use these deposits to fund assets such as bank financing contracts. The process of securitization removes certain assets from the balance sheet and parks them onto the balance sheet of a SPV. Typically, the cost of issueing notes for funding these assets should theoretically be cheaper than issueing bonds or raising deposits. One must recall that deposits are short term in nature, whereas bonds offer the comfort of providing long term funding at a specified cost. Banks do not have to worry about rolling over deposits at maturity dates to continually fund assets. Thus, securitization offers banks a cheaper option for funding assets as opposed to the bank issueing bonds to fund a portfolio of loans. If for instance, a bank sells its home mortgage portfolio to its own SPV, the cost of funding this particular pool of assets would be cheaper than issueing a bond by the bank as the SPV has separated credit risk on its books from market risk and liquidity risk which is still a headache for the bank at large. The only cause of worry in such a structure is that in the event the asset portfolio defaults, note holders do not have any recourse to the bank's capital. Note bearers may have recourse to the SPVs capital, but this is typically less than the 8% required by Basel for banks.

Chapter 18

COMMODITIES

The study of commodities in the domain of banking or finance is not a recent phenomenon. Commodities can be divided into several categories, agricultural commodities such as sugar, wheat, corn, grain, rice and cereals have been in existence since time immemorial. Other commodities are inputs or raw materials that have become part of the production cycle for many finished goods. These include such commodities that produce energy like coal, natural gas or oil. Other commodities are direct inputs into the production cycles and include base metals such as zinc, copper, aluminium, steel, and iron ore. Commodities can also include sand, rock, marble, silica, inputs essential to the construction industry. Electricity is an essential input of all production processes, needless to say no factory in the world runs without electricity. Electricity is also treated as a commodity, and financial products have been developed linked to the prices of electricity as well. Plastics although a bi-product of the petroleum industry are now an essential component of almost any finished good in the world. Some inputs use other inputs to be manufactured. Electricity for instance may require oil and gas to be generated, or the process of refining copper or aluminium for industrial use requires the process of electrolyses, so the price of copper is linked to the price of electricity which in turn may be linked to the price of oil or gas depending on what process is used to generate electricity in a certain region.

Other goods can also be categorized as commodities such as coffee, cocoa beans, chocolate or chicken, pork bellies, beef, chicken feed and really any other good under the sun. Carbon emissions have developed into a commodity or asset class of its own as well. Even timber, oak, teak, can be treated as a commodity as varying qualities of wood serve as a valuable input in the production of many finished goods. Rubber and tin are again essential inputs.

Those commodities which are demanded in standardised measure, with certain standardised qualities and features attract the attention of not just end users but also speculators and bankers. Oil is sold in standardised measure and with 3 or 4 major standardised quality, the same applies to gas, coal, zinc, copper, aluminium and electricity. Aluminium is as essential to the automobile industry, as copper is to the construction industry, where the latter is employed in developing copper wires. Copper is also essential to the electronics reasons for developing circuit boards, wiring etc.

What is crucial to understand that these goods are required by factories all over the world. In many cases, raw materials are typically located in one part of the world, and are demanded for processing in another part of the world. Extraction processes are expensive, risky, and require intensive commitment of labour, and capital and have long lead times. A certain quantity of tin or rubber may take several months to extract. Any such commodity which is found in nature exists as either

i)   Still undiscovered reserves
ii)   Discovered reserves but un extractable with current technology
iii) Discovered reserves in conflict areas and therefore un extractable
iv)   Discovered reserve in non conflict areas and under extraction
v)   Extracted commodities undergoing processing
vi)   Extracted commodities in transit to refinery point
vii) Extracted commodities in refined state in inventory
viii) Commodities being utilised in production process

At any given point in time any particular commodity is in one of these 8 stages. Each stage carries its own costs, at times costs in one stage are incurred in one currency and in other stages incurred in another currency. The commodity may ultimately be sold in yet another currency. For instance oil is extracted in Malaysia, where costs are incurred in Ringgitts, it is sent to Singapore for refinement, where costs are borne in Singapore dollars, and then the refined oil is sold back to Malaysia for Singaporean dollars where it is onward sold to citizens for Malaysian Ringitts. Without foreign exchange hedging tools that allow Malaysia to lock in a price at which it would buy the oil from the refineries for a pre-agreed exchange rate between the 2 countries, Malaysia could not come up with a price for selling oil to its citizens. Needless to say he process of extraction to transportation to refinery and then final delivery may take several months during which all fluctuations in currency rates need to be covered.

Companies engaged in the extraction process may be government owned companies of the country where the natural resource is found, as the resource is seen as a natural asset. Alternatively, the land on, under, within, which the resource is found may be leased to a domestic private company and the resource may be extracted by a private company and a royalty may be paid to the government. Finally the private company may also be of foreign origin, may have a joint venture with the local government or a joint venture between a foreign firm and a local firm.

Extraction processes are full of risks, the earth's surface is studied up to certain depths and the mineral content may be studied and expected reserves are calculated. Needless to say natural resources are extracted or mined in large quantities to justify costs. Yet all buyers may not require large quantities of a specific commodity, others may like to lock in a country's entire output for the next so many years. Between the extracting company and the final end user a host of intermediaries exist that serve as brokers between buyers and sellers. A broker at any one time may negotiate deals for several buyers and sellers at the same time or may work exclusively for 1 buyer or 1 seller.

We may well add that in the universe of commodities extraction costs, refining costs, transportation costs play a major role in bringing the raw material to its final state where it is can be referred to as an asset ready for sale. At this juncture storage costs and insurance costs play a vital role for traders and intermediaries alike. (Transportation costs are borne typically by buyers). A cost we have not addressed is the cost of research and development. Companies that first braved the challenges of extracting oil invested in the necessary technology that later became a standardised process. Companies that came later in the game did not have to invest in R&D and simply bought extracting tools off the shelf from other companies. However, we ignore this cost for our discussion.

A company that is engaged in extracting oil or copper for instance incurs cost of operations and incurs certain risks. Price risk is a major risk for a company involved in extraction. If a company like Rio Tinto for instance plans to excavate 100,000 tons of copper from a certain mine in Brazil, it factors its costs to be at $1,800 per ton. If prices of copper at this time are at $2,000 per ton, the venture offers a profit margin of 11.11%. Yet Rio Tinto will take 6 months to extract 100,000 tons of copper, and as in normal circumstances the company may make the raw material ready for sale in 6 months, it becomes vulnerable to price movements.

If in 6 months the prices of copper have dropped for whatever reasons (and there can be many) by 5%, from $2,000 to $1,900 per ton, this affects Rio Tinto's margins by 5.55% as the new profit margin is only 5.55%. Rio Tinto may well have earned more by investing their capital in some other business. To hedge against this risk, the company can lock in a price for its product with end buyers or brokers. Let's assume that Rio Tinto locks in an average price of $1,998 for 100,000 tons of copper with 5 brokers using futures contracts. Rio Tinto is hedged for a decrease in prices, but what if prices increase to $2,100 per ton of copper. In this case, Rio Tinto would like to exit the arrangement made with the 5 brokers. The brokers would be eager to buy from Rio Tinto for $1,998 and sell in the market for $2,100. In this stage Rio Tinto may wish it had bought a hedging instrument to hedge its hedge.

Another alternative for Rio Tinto is to buy put options that give them the right to sell 100,000 tons of copper at prices of $2,000 or above. Although options don't come cheap they offer Rio Tinto the luxury of either exercising these options or not and therefore they are not locked into their promises or positions.

A valid question to ask here is who out there would be willing to be the counterparty for these trades? If the market was full of only end users, it is unlikely that they would enter into such contracts which involve contingent liabilities. End users are interested in actual deliveries of said goods, and are not interested in entering into contracts to buy or have available for sale certain assets in case prices reach a certain threshold or not. Remember, the seller of put options too has to have capital on hand to buy the underlying asset and the counterparty of a forwards contract also must have the necessary capital to purchase. End users do not leave capital lying around to trigger off purchases if certain events happen or they do not.

Brokers also may be a counterparty to such trades, but typically their business model is different. They do not typically make decisions to buy inventory and hold till prices increase for sale. They buy and sell on behalf of original sellers and buyers and therefore earn commissions. Commissions are a main source of income not buy and sell spreads or entering into derivatives structures.

Speculators or investment banks are necessary to be on the other side of these trades and we shall explain why. Rio Tinto projects costs to be at $1,800 per ton and prices its' end product to be at $2,000 per ton when the copper is ready for sale. If prices fall to $1,900 per ton Rio Tinto would make losses of $100 per ton. If Rio Tinto purchased put options to sell at $2,000 per ton, it would likely exercise these options instead of selling the copper in the open markets. If the option issuer is unable to come up with the required $200M (100,000 * 2,000) to buy the copper inventory, the issuer can also settle his (or her obligations) by just paying $10,000,000 to Rio Tinto(100,000 *100). This amount reflects the profit component for Rio Tinto from the trade. Rio Tinto would still hold its own inventory of 100,000 tons of copper and would sell it to the open market for $1,900 for another profit of $10,000,000. In this manner however, Rio Tinto would lock in $20,000,000 of profit as it had originally calculated. The option issuer although offered a "cash settlement" to Rio Tinto without purchasing their inventory and without coughing up $200M to purchase it either.

If the counterparty to the trade, the issuer of the put option is the Commodities trading desk of an Investment Bank, the general sentiment of post 2008, views the motives of the Investment bank to be market manipulation or betting. This may be slightly exaggerated. Certainly if copper prices rise, and Rio Tinto does not exercise its put options, the Investment bank, be it a JP Morgan or a Barclays Capital walks away with the sale price of the put option. But if the option is exercised the investment bank has to incur a cash outflow. How does this resemble a bet? Changes in copper prices are not a function of random events such as the swing of a wheel or the flipping of a card, but is a function of changes in demand and supply for copper. By the way Rio Tinto can also sell call options giving other parties the right to buy their copper at a certain price, to finance the purchase of put options, and can thus become a player itself in the options market and not just a buyer.

What is important to understand here is that in contracts simple sale and purchase have reached such a scale, that the seller needs to have some control on what price the underlying asset can be sold at once ready for the market, thus making hedging tools a necessity. Rio Tinto may be incurring extraction costs in Brazilian reals for extracting copper, and for refining it. Yet its revenues may be in US$, as that is the currency in which the company will sell the inventory. This requires Rio Tinto to also lock in an exchange rate for its costs and for its sales.

Forward Sale/ Margin Sale between Miner and an End User.

A typical order for a large quantity of commodity may be as follows. The seller is Rio Tinto and the buyer is an end user Emaar for instance. Both parties are interested in locking their sale price for RT and their purchase price for Emaar.

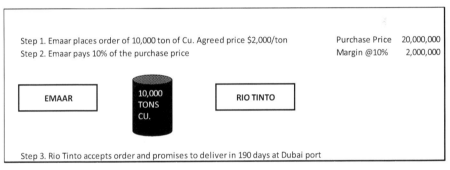

Figure 18.1 Sale of Copper

Margins sales and sales where delivery is deferred and only a partial down payment is am grey area in Islamic Finance and needs to be resolved.. Here Emaar however has contracted to receive the goods upon delivery and does not hold the option to renegade from the contract. If Rio Tinto delivers the copper as per specification and on time, Emaar must make the remaining payment of $18,000,000 to Rio Tinto and take delivery of the underlying commodity. *Bai al urbun* therefore does not perfectly match this contract as in *urbun,* the buyer can opt not to purchase the asset at delivery date. Were full purchase price made, the contract would be a contract of *salaam*.

Rio Tinto can demand that Emaar maintain 10% margin at all times in a margin account, to show their commitment to purchase the copper once it is ready for sale. Emaar may also demand of Rio Tinto to maintain 10% margin in the margin account. The reasons for these are two fold. If market prices increase to $2,003 per ton, Rio Tinto may be tempted to default on their sales contract with Emaar, and choose to find another buyer at the higher price. If this happen, Emaar requires Rio Tinto to beef up their margin payment to $2,300,000 and thereby placing any amount they would earn as additional profit (by defaulting) in the margin account.

Similarly, if prices for copper fall to $1,990 in the markets, Emaar may be tempted to default on their purchase arrangement with Rio Tinto and look to buy the copper from other companies that may have the copper ready for sale at the new price. Emaar would be required to maintain an additional $10 per ton in their margin account.

Neither, Emaar or Rio Tinto can avail the funds kept in the margin account. The balance in the margin account is used to settle the final payments made between RT and Emaar. RT may if Emaar permits use the balance in the margin account to acquire banking facilities to finance part of the production process. The contract of margin buying resembles the concept of *Hamish jiddiyah,* but even this contract does not fully recognize the rights and liabilities of parties involved in a margin purchase.

The above trade contract, is described in the financial world as a forward or futures contract. One can easily google the differences between the two. Standardised quality, quantity, (10,000 tons is a purchase of 400 lots of 25 tons of copper), where 25 tons is the lot size for each forward contract. However, in the financial world the parties to a futures contract may have nothing whatsoever to do with the copper business as such, in that a seller of a futures contract may not be a mining company and a buyer may not have any interest in using the copper whatsoever.

An important feature of this contract is that it is privately negotiated. Only Emaar and Rio Tinto know at what price the deal has been made. In our example we assume that both parties look at market prices, but if we consider for an instance that there is no exchange or mechanism at which to determine a market price, RT will accept a price which is well above its costs to earn a profit, and Emaar will accept a price which it can incorporate into its end product and earn a profit. If the figure of $2,000 is mutually agreeable to both parties that would be a private arrangement. Further, even if market prices are available, which are quoted as $2,000 per ton, these are average prices which a market exchange develops after keeping records of thousands of buy and sell orders that are transacted over a commodity exchange. But all these orders are for various quantities. Even Rio Tinto, may have a different price for selling 5,000 tons of copper as it may have for selling 10,000 tons of copper. At what price a buyer can purchase say 4,000 lots of copper may involve a detailed search of the market for seller, and offers to various sellers either over exchanges or through private communications which allow the buyer to "discover" a price for 3,000 tons. It may be a few percentage points above the standard $2,000 quoted on an exchange.

Many of the buy and sale transactions are confidential, where buyers seek out sellers who can offer a particular quantity of a good at a particular price by a specific time at a specific location.

Forward Sale/ Margin Sale between Miner and a Broker.

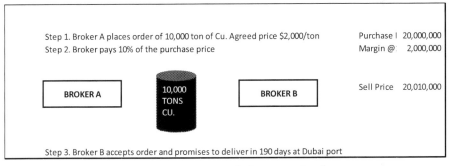

Figure 18.2 Margin Sale between Brokers

Here we stick to the same contract, but alter the parties to the contract. Instead of Emaar, we have an end user who wishes to purchase 10,000 tons of Copper. All terms remain the same. The Broker will be looking for buyers for this 10,000 tons of Copper even before delivery. The Broker may find 10 buyers of 1,000 tons of Copper who are willing to purchase at $2,001 per ton, therefore according the broker a tidy profit of $1 per ton or $10,000. If the Broker is able to find buyers for his copper before Rio Tinto makes delivery and demands full payment, the Broker would have only invested $2,000,000 in the margin account and earned a profit of $10,000 even before the copper is delivered, a ROE of 0.5%. (If the Broker borrows the money to put up margin, his ROE is higher, but earnings have to account for interest expense).

In 90 days, Rio Tinto delivers the copper to Dubai. The Broker informs his customers where to collect the Copper from and receives payment from the 10 deals made, which earn a total proceed of $20,010,000. The Broker then pays $20,000,000 to Rio Tinto and the deals are done.

This arrangement is deemed questionable from a *shariah* perspective as scholars would not allow the broker to sell the copper without first having possession of the inventory. Actual possession would delay the copper reaching its end users, would expose the Broker to fluctuations in market prices by delivery date and therefore reduce the margins and increase the risks for the broker. Certain scholars have worked around this controversy by suggesting that if the Broker has made arrangements to get delivery, or has intent to own the goods before the subsequent sale is executed, this makes brokerage business permissible. The jury is still out on this one.

The contract we have described above resembles a futures contract. The contract between Rio Tinto and Emaar cannot happen on a spot basis unless RT has 10,000 tons of copper in their inventory. Thus the price at which the two parties agree upon, i.e. $2,000 per ton can be interpreted as the 3 month futures price for copper. Can one conclude that were a spot purchase of 10,000 tons of copper 3 months from now were to be transacted it would be at $2,000 per ton? A transaction (even if it were to be between RT and Emaar again) 3 months from now should be a function of costs of inputs and levels of demand 3 months from now, at best the 3 months futures price may just provide certain benchmark for pricing the future spot contract.

Conclusion

We wish to conclude this chapter by merely raising the point that the nature of industry in the 21st century requires buyers and sellers to lock in prices for goods that are traded in the future. Manufacturers need to lock in prices for their end product well before they begin to incur costs to in the manufacturing process. Conventional finance has developed sufficient financial tools and the markets for these tools to help companies in this regard. Islamic Finance must develop financial products that learn to embrace uncertainty, price it and engineer solutions for forward sales. Islamic Finance can and will not grow if this aspect of trade is not recognized and accepted.

CHAPTER 19

HEDGING THE PRICE OF GOLD USING *IJARA*

Investment bankers have taken a lot of heat in the past few years being blamed for the financial crises and for giving out bonuses at a time when employees were being laid off. The perception that investment bankers are evil sells books like tabloids, with the general populace looking to blame someone. Although investment banks have put many of us through much misery we must not forget that banks, and investment banks do for our society what many of us are unable to do, and that is take risk from those who cannot bear it, break it up into smaller lots, and pass it on to those who can.

We shall look at how some risks are traded by investment banks. We live in an exceedingly volatile world with consumers all over the world expressing their likes and dislikes through their purchasing power. Corporations spend billions of dollars to influence our tastes and get us to buy their products. We as consumers are faced with unprecedented choices from toothpaste flavours to the colour of car interiors. With changing tastes also come changing prices at which goods can be sold. For a company to market their goods in the coming fall, purchasing departments get to work a year in advance. Product teams make sophisticated estimates of what the distribution price should be for the end product keeping margins in mind. However, manufacturers must ensure that they are able to sell their goods in the markets 1 year from now at a price greater than the cost of getting those goods to the market.

Investment banks are not in the business of ensuring prices, they do not buy out Georgio Armani's fall men's line but they can help lock in a price for the cotton they purchase. India is famous for its wedding season when globally gold prices are affected by the demand generated in India. Yet few consider the toil, effort and risk that goes into extracting gold from the earth. Gold extraction rates are around 1 gram per 1 ton of earth extracted, with many of the mines being far below the earth's surface. Gold mining companies must ensure that the cost of extraction is below the price at which the commodity will go to market. This applies to any commodity be it precious metals, base metals, any raw material extracted from the ground and any agricultural good that is bought to market. For raw material or commodities that have intricate, elaborate, lengthy and expensive extraction processes, producers need to hedge the future sale prices of their end product to ensure that they are not doing negative business. In fact producers that require funding from commercial banks are not able to secure financing unless they do not hedge the prices at which they will sell their products.

Forward Sales

Thus, to lock in prices of inputs, and the currencies at which these inputs are purchased, corporations enter into forward sales of commodities and currency. The subject of forward sales especially of currency are an anathema to *shariah* scholars at large. The conventional industry uses such instruments as forwards, futures and options to enter into transactions that are negotiated in the present but transacted in the future.

The contract of *salaam* has been incorrectly applied to futures and forward sales as in *salaam,* a buyer is required to pay the full purchase price to a seller for future delivery, whereas in a futures or a forwards contract buyers purchase on margin. A buyer in a *salaam* contract is exposed to performance risk on the seller and to market risk, in that when the goods are actually delivered to the buyer they can be sold at a price higher than the cost price. The market risk can be mitigated by entering into another *salaam* contract with a 3rd party with the resale price locked in. The *salaam* contract offers a funding mechanism for the seller as the seller is required to pay the full purchase price on spot.

Forward sales allow for the seller and buyer to both lock in a price for a good that is to be delivered in the future. However, as the buyer pays a margin amount, there is no feature of funding the seller in this contract. The particular good in question however is trading in the market place at any given time at a spot price as well.

Hedging Trade

We will illustrate our trade using a simple example. Party A is a producer of a rare metal, say gold. On January 1st 2013, the price of gold in the market is around $300 per ounce for example. Party A has been awarded a contract to mine a certain area in Latin America where it is expected that 50 tons of gold are to be found. At current prices, 50 tons of gold would be worth 32,000 * 50 * 300 = $480 M, given that there are 32,000 ounces in one metric ton.

Party A must ensure that if they are to mine the gold, that they must be able to do so at a cost lower than $480M to earn a decent profit. However, these costs can only be estimated and cannot be locked in. Party A however, can find a counter party willing to take the risk to agree to a sale price for the 50 tons of gold which is to be extracted within a 1 year.

Party B may take up the risk if B is an end user of gold and requires 50 tons of gold. This could be a Central Bank or a very large jewellery manufacturer, or it could be a hedge fund or an investment bank that feels money can be made. As an investment bank is not interested in holding inventory of 50 tons it may look into several options.

The investment bank may lock in a resale price with various other end users or even intermediaries for different lot sizes of gold, where the average resale price is above the current $300 price. Counterparties may not be willing to enter into deals to buy gold in 1 year at prices higher than $300. The 1 year future price would be based upon expectations that the counterparties have with regards to movements in prices of gold.

A second alternative is for the investment bank is to buy put options for prices above $300. The investment bank may buy put options for exercises prices of $303, $304, and $305. However, if the price of these put options is $3, $4, and $5 respectively the trade will not benefit the investment bank.

A third alternative is a hedge trade which involves short selling gold at market prices to lock in a resale price and then leasing gold from a Central Bank or any other counterparty that holds inventory of gold for a lease rate which is lower than the rate on deposits for 1 year. This hedge trade would work as follows:-

STEP 0: Gold producer approaches investment bank to offer a forward price for gold in 1 year.

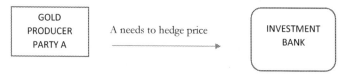

Figure 19.1 Step 0 of trade

STEP 1: Investment Bank leases 50 tons of gold for x% rental for 1 year.

Figure 19.2 Step 1 of trade

STEP 2: Investment Bank sells 50 tons of gold for SPOT price of $480M.

Figure 19.3 Step 3 of Trade

STEP 3: Investment Bank places proceeds of SPOT sale in a bank account for y%

Figure 19.4 Step 3 of Trade

STEP 4: At the end of the year, Producer delivers 50 tons of gold to the Investment Bank

Figure 19.5 Step 4 of Trade

STEP 5: Investment Bank returns gold leased from Central Bank

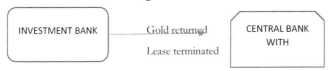

Figure 19.6 Step 5 of Trade

STEP 6: Investment Bank receives spot price + y% mark up from the commercial bank.

Figure 19.7 Step 6 of Trade

STEP 7: Investment bank secures a forward price for the 50 tons of gold sold by the Producer SPOT PRICE + y% - x% which is paid to the Producer from the hedging proceeds.

The forward price of gold thus becomes the spot price of gold plus the cost of covering the hedge for 1 year, which is Spot Price + y% - x%, where y is the interest rate and x the lease rate.

The gold is passed onto the Central Bank who is the ultimate buyer. The Central Bank receives the gold without actually selling it but by having the gold leased out returned. 2 gold trades occur, one between the

Figure 19.8 Price of Gold in Future

The Investment bank will short sell 50 tons of gold at the spot price of $300/ounce for $480M. The bank will borrow the gold for the transaction from a Central Bank for a Lease Rate of 1% for 1 year. The cost of this borrowing will be $4,800,000. The Investment Bank takes the proceeds of the short sale of $480M and invests it in a fixed deposit for 1 year at 3%, earning $14,400,000. The Investment Bank earns a spread of $14,400,000 - $4,800,000 up to this leg of the transaction = $9,600,000. In 1 year's time Party A will deliver 50 tons of gold and the Investment Bank will repay the Central Bank with the delivery.

The Investment Bank will quote a forward price which would reflect it's cost + profit or in industry terms, spot price + cost of carrying the hedge.

> Forward Rate = Spot Rate + Cost of carrying the hedge.
> = Spot Rate + Earnings on deposit – cost of leasing gold.
> = $480,000,000 + $14,400,000 - $4,800,000
> = $489,600,000.

This rate transfers to a price of $306 per ounce which is what the Investment Bank offers to Party A.

The hedge is a very simple trade where the investment bank basically finances the sale of gold by leasing gold from a Central Bank for a low rate of 1% and invests the proceeds of the sale at a higher rate of 3%. This spread is added as a premium to the spot price to compute the forward rate for 1 year. The forward price of gold is therefore affected by lease rates of gold and of interest rates in the banking markets.

End result

The gold miner may receive $300 per ounce as a quoted buy price from the Investment Bank. The Investment Bank may sell the gold to the Buyer for $300 or a price slightly higher than $300 to earn a profit. The Investment Bank will however make a net gain as if the sale price effectively was $306 plus a profit margin. Effectively the Investment bank makes certain profits from the differences between the prices at which it offers to buy the gold from the miner and the price it receives from the Buyer, plus the interest earned on depositing the sales proceeds less the cost of leasing gold from the Central Bank to cover the short sale.

The system overall receives another 50 tons of gold, effectively increasing the supply of gold in the system. The investment bank is however exposed to performance risk on the gold producer to deliver 50 tons of gold within 1 year as the bank would have to return the gold borrowed. In this manner however, the investment bank shares the performance risk faced by the gold producer yet mitigates the price risk at which the gold will eventually be sold. In essence, the gold to be extracted is bought and sold in the markets even before it makes it to market. This is only possible when goods are produced in standardized quantities and standardized quality. As long as the gold producer is able to mine and produce gold of the exact same quality as that held by the Central Bank the above trade can be executed.

Shariah Compliant Hedge
The trade above can be *shariah* compliant if a sequence of contracts is followed:-

Step 1. The Investment Bank issues Miner A, an enforceable '*wa'd*' to purchase gold from A in 1 year at $300 per ounce for 50 tons.

Step 2. Miner A enters into an enforceable *wa'd* to deliver 50 tons of gold to the Investment Bank in 1 year.

Step 3. Investment Bank leases under the contract of *ijara* 50 tons of gold from the Central Bank, for 1 year with its permission to sell the gold to a third party. Investment Bank sells 50 tons of leased gold to a 3rd party at the spot price of $480M under the contract of *bai*.

Step 4. The Investment Bank pays a rental rate for the leased gold of 1% to the Central Bank.

Step 5. The Investment Bank deposits the proceeds of the sale contract in a *commodity murabahah* account that pays 3% for 1 year.

Step 6. The Investment bank takes delivery of gold from Miner A in 1 year and returns the gold to the Central Bank to cover its short sale position.

Conclusion

The transaction above not only requires the necessary *shariah* contracts to execute but also the necessary markets to execute as well. The Investment Bank literally "borrows or leases" the required asset from a 3rd party, in this case the Central Bank, and there must be in existence a market for such transaction and a mechanism to price borrowing commodity or leasing commodity. This trade only works if the costs of leasing gold are less than the profit rates on *mudharabah* accounts for matching tenures.

CHAPTER 20

RISK REVERSAL STRATEGIES

Basic Version:- Selling (writing) an Out of the Money Put Option (OTM), and using the proceeds to purchase an OTM call option.

Share: IBM
Share Price: $100
Put Option Price: $10:   Exercise Price $90:   Contract size 1 option 1 share.
Call Option Price: $9:   Exercise Price $115:   Contract size 1 option 1 share.

Trade:-

Write OTM Put and Buy OTM Call

Sell 1,000 put options for $9,000 and buy 1,000 call options for $10,000. Net cash flow is a credit of $1,000. Put options are typically more expensive than call options as they have higher *implied volatility* than call options. They are typically more in demand as put options and behave like insurance policies for long positions on stocks. If share prices go to $116, the option is called and the investor makes profits of $1,000.

If prices go to $89, the counterparty will hold the issuer (investor) to buy the stock at $90 which would have a market value of only $89. The investor would make a loss of $1,000 in this scenario. This trade known as the bullish risk reversal offers high returns if market prices of the underlying increase drastically, so as an OTM option becomes In The Money. The structure is obviously loss making if prices for the underlying fall sharply making the investor or issuer of the put option liable to perform.

In the above scenario, the investor can offset the loss on falling prices by the difference in premiums for selling put options over the premium of buying call options. However, there may well be instances where there may be no difference in premiums, this would be a zero – cost trade. Call options may at times however be more expensive than puts, in which case the trade would have a negative cost.

The above position can be described as a synthetic long position.

Write OTM Call and Buy OTM Put

Investor writes/sells the OTM Call option and earns $9,000. The proceeds are used to buy OTM Put options for $10,000. A negative cost of $1,000 is associated with this trade. If share prices fall to $89, the investor will earn $1,000 on the trade, however, if share prices rise to $116, the investor would have to purchase shares of IBM at market prices of $116 and sell them for $115 to the counterparty at a loss of $1,000. This position known as a bearish risk reversal benefits investors when market prices fall and is unprofitable when market prices rise. The current position is described as a synthetic short.

The reader must bear in mind that Out of the Money options are typically cheaper the further the exercise price is from current market prices when the option is issued. Both the strategies above are useful in mitigating the risk associated with movements in prices that would counter the returns of a pre-existing exposure, be it a short position or a long position. Long positions are taken with an expectation of rising prices, whereas short positions are taken with the expectation of falling prices. These hedging trades allow the investor to benefit from either circumstance.

Therefore, Writing a Put and Buying a Call is a trade to counter a pre-existing short position as it allows investors to earn returns if unexpectedly prices increase. Similarly, Writing a Call and Buying a Put, also known as a collar allows an investor to make gains from a decline in prices and therefore hedging against a long position on a stock. Hedging is meaningless without taking into consideration the original trade and the exposure linked to that trade. A hedged position may end up offering returns of its own but that means an original trade ended up losing money.

Microsoft (MSFT) closes on June 10th, 2014 at $41.11

	Buy Price / Sell Price
MSFT October $42 calls quoted at	*$1.27 / $1.32*
Implied volatility of calls	*18.5%*
	Bid Price / Ask Price
MSFT October $40 puts quoted at	*$1.41/$1.46*
Implied volatility of puts	*18.8%*
Contract Size	*100 shares of MSFT*
Trade:	
Write MSFT October $40 Put for	$1.41 (counterparty buys at $40)
Buy MSFT October $42 Call for	$1.32
Net Cash flow	$.09

MSFT is being traded at $41.11 in market, therefore $40 put is $41.11 - $40.00 = $1.11 out of the money, and the $42 call is $42 - $41.11 = $.89 out of the money. ***The bid-ask spread has to be considered in all instances. When writing an option the seller gets the bid price, but when buying an option, the buyer has to shell out the ask price.***

Scenario A - MSFT trades at levels above $42.
Sell 5 October $40 Puts for $1.41 each - $7.05
Buy 5 October $42 Calls for $1.32 each - $6.60
At expiry   MSFT is trading above $42

Value of $42 puts would be worthless, while $42 calls would have a value of Stock Price – Exercise Price, or market price - $42. If by maturity date the price of MSFT shares have gone up to $45, the value of each $42 Call option would be at least $45 - $42 = $3. As each option entitles the holder to buy 100 shares of the stock, the net profit from exercising the Oct $42 call will be $3 per share. As the investor is holding 5 contracts the net proceeds are $3 * 5 * 100 = $1,500.

Scenario B - MSFT trades between $40 and $42.
MSFT is trading between $40 and $42. In this case the $40 put will likely expire worthless as only if prices fall below $40 would the put have any value.

The $42 call will also expire worthless, as this too would have value only if MSFT share prices rise above $42.

Scenario C – MSFT is trading below $40.

MSFT shares drop below $40. In this case the $42 Call will expire worthless. The $40 Put option will have a value of Market Price less Exercise Price, however, as in our trade we are short on the trade by selling Puts, any advantage to instrument holder will translate into losses for the issuer. If MSFT share prices fall to $35 per share, the issuer will bear a loss of $5 per put sold which will incur a net loss of $5 * 100 * 5 = $2,500. Fortunately, for the investor, both circumstances of rising and falling prices cannot happen simultaneously, therefore, either profits are made from falling prices or rising prices.

Hedging transaction

Original trade:-	Investor is long 500 MSFT shares.
Required Hedge:-	Hedge long position for downside risk.
Trade:-	Write 5 **MSFT October $42 Calls** at $1.27.
Buy 5 **MSFT October $40 Put** at	$1.46.
Net Cash Flow per pair of trades	-$0.19
Trade Name:	Covered Call + Protective Put

Scenario A MSFT trades above $42

Investor will call in the option, or the stock will be "called away".

Scenario B MSFT trades between $40 and $42

Put expires worthless and call expires worthless. Cash outflow is $0.19 * 5 * 100 = $95/-

Scenario C MSFT trades below $40

Call option expires worthless, but the $40 put has value of market price less exercise price

CHAPTER 21

REVERSE SALAAM

This concept has been covered in detail in a concept paper published in the June 2014 ISRA Journal. The authors of this work are Professor Yusaf Saleem, Ghaith Mahaini and myself. The idea for this product structure evolved during a lecture offered by Professor Saleem at the prestigious International Centre for Education in Islamic Finance.

I am indebted to Professor Saleem and to Ghaith for their contribution to this structure. Both Ghaith Mahaini and myself presented this structure to the products teams at CIMB Islamic, Standard Chartered Sadiq Malaysia, OCBC Al Amin and Hong Leong Islamic in various formal and informal settings. We also had extensive meetings at Bursa Malaysia's Suq A Sila and I wish to thank all the participants of these meetings for their feedback and perspectives.

The structure is rather simple and is illustrated in the 2 figures below.

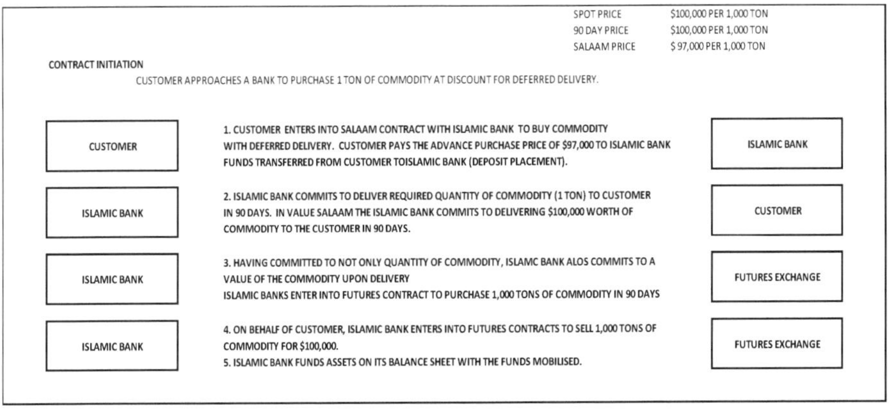

Figure 20.1 Reverse Salaam Contract Initiation

At contract conclusion the following steps are taken.

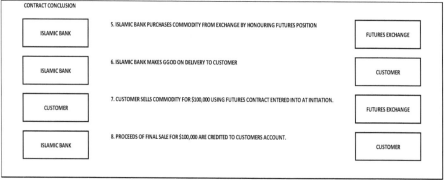

Figure 20.2 Reverse Salaam Contract Conclusion

The product structure relies on the concept of a deferred delivery sale. The purchaser of the asset is akin to an investor seeking to make returns on an investment of a certain amount of money. In our example, this amount is referred to as the discounted price for an asset or commodity which has a spot price of $100,000 for 1,000 tons. The reader may refer to our first publication Contracts and Deals in Islamic Finance to understand the process flow of a *salaam* contract.

A customer purchases 1,000 tons of commodity from an Islamic bank on deferred delivery basis. The Islamic bank commits to delivering not a quantity of commodity, but commodity with a value of $100,000. This contract is referred to as *value salaam*. We refer the reader to Michael Mahlknecht's work.

The Islamic bank uses the funds mobilised, which are the $97,000 to fund assets on its balance sheet. However, to guarantee its performance in the *salaam* arrangement, the bank goes long in futures contracts (or options contracts) to purchase 1,000 tons of commodity worth $100,000 to customer in 90 days. The Islamic bank guarantees the value of the commodity for the customer by being short on futures contracts for the commodity at a strike price of $100,000 per 1,000 tons of commodity.

The Islamic bank can earn an additional spread between the long and short prices of the commodity and this spread can be shared with the customer with a *mudharabah* contract. The cost of purchasing hedging instruments if options are used are borne by the Islamic bank, and in the event that futures contracts are used, the Islamic bank would have to put up margin on the contract.

Conclusion

The additional costs associated with the derivatives instruments make this structure rather expensive and somewhat impractical. However, the mechanism for locking in prices for commodities also allows theIslamic bank to earn additional income from the purchase and sale of the commodity. The Islamic Bank itself could offer the customer hedging opportunities and be the counterparty to some of the trades.

CHAPTER 22

FINANCIAL RIGHTS OR *HAQQ MALLI*

Hussain Kureshi
Mohammad Ghaith Mahaini

The word right (*haqq*) has a wide meaning in Islam. It covers the rights of Allah (swt), the rights of the own self (*nafs*), the rights of family such as parents, husband, wife, and children, political rights, and the rights of the physical nature and the environment. Rights could also be financial or non-financial, over a person or over a property. Some of the rights could be waived, inherited or transferred. Every right has a corresponding duty or obligation. Islamic law while entitles a person to a set of rights also imposes certain obligations on him. Moreover, rights in Islam are not absolute but should be exercised in a way that should not violate other person's rights. Islam has imposed certain limitations and restrictions so that individuals could not abuse the exercise of their rights.

Although the concept of rights is a fundamental theme of Islamic literature discussions on commercial and financial rights have not received its due attention. There is a considerable progress in the evolution and development of Islamic financial institutions and financial and banking products There are institutions dedicated solely to either research in Islamic Commercial Law or practicing financial intermediation under Shariah prescriptions. However, the domain of commercial rights is relatively untouched and the authors of this paper believe that unless the Islamic Financial Industry comes up with Shariah compliant products that cater to the needs of international trade practices, Islamic banking will not be able to serve the needs of companies in the Muslim world.

DEFINITION OF RIGHTS, OR *HAQQ*

Haqq literally means proper, right, true, authentic, valid, established, a just claim, confirmed as a truth, duty, or an obligation.[12] The jurists define *haqq* as a *Shari'ah* prescription that gives authority and assigns responsibility.[13] This definition includes both rights and obligations. The source that confers a right or imposes an obligation is *Shari'ah*. All our rights and obligations arise out of Allah's laws. Thus, there is no right or duty unless it is provided for by the *Shari'ah*.

In financial rights, the common Shariah basics regarding contracts (Akad) applies, this means that the contracting parties should express their consent the form of *Ijab* and *Kabul*. The contracting parties should also have the required legal capacity to conclude a contract. The Financial right is the subject matter which must be in existence and must be owned by the party granting right to the counterparty. There must be an underlying asset which must also have a value and must be permissible in Shariah.

HAQQ MALI, DEFINITIONS

Financial rights *(Huquq Mali)* are those that have financial value or relate to property or its usufruct or rights that may arise from commercial transactions. For instance, a tenant has a right to stay in a house which he has rented, and a wife has a right to maintenance. A creditor in a deferred sale contract has the right to claim his debt (the price) from the purchaser and a lender in a loan (*qardh*) contract has the right to claim the loan from the borrower. Similarly, intellectual properties such as copyrights, trade logos and franchises are included in the category of financial rights. Options (*khiyarat*) such as the option of defect, the option of condition and the option of inspection are also included in the financial rights. Modern derivatives and options are also examples of financial rights.

One of the important issues concerning financial rights is their tradability. For instance, can a creditor who has the right to claim his debt sell his right to others? Muslim jurists have agreed that such a right could be transferred

---

12   See Edward William Lane, *Arabic-English lexicon*, (Cambridge: The Islamic Text Society, 1984) pp. 606-6.

13   For a discussion on the definition of *Haqq* see Wahbah Zuhaili, *al-Fiqh al-Islami Wa Adillatuhu*, vol. iv (Damascus: Dar al-Fikr, 1989) pp. 8-10.

to others though *Hawalah* for its par value. However, the sale of right or debt (*bay' al-dayn*) to a third person is a contentious issue particularly when the debt arises from a loan (*qardh*) contract. The tradability of rights that do not arise from contracts such as copyrights, franchise and some customary financial rights, which will be discussed in next pages, is not the subject of disagreement among the jurists.

HAQQ MALI FEATURES

A financial right does not have an independent existence and is tied to a certain underlying asset. The asset should be in existence at the time when the right pertaining to the asset is sold. Similarly, the right which is sold should already be in existence. The sale of right that may come into existence in the future is not valid. For example, a heir cannot transfer or sell his right in the property of his father to another person while the father is still alive. Similarly, it is not valid when a person sells his right to claim the price for a thing that he will sell tomorrow.

CONCEPT OF HAQQ MALLI FROM THE QURAN.

Evidence of the recognition of financial rights can be inferred from Quran. Verse 178 of in Surah al Baqarah states:

(يَا أَيُّهَا الَّذِينَ آمَنُوا كُتِبَ عَلَيْكُمُ الْقِصَاصُ فِي الْقَتْلَى الْحُرُّ بِالْحُرِّ وَالْعَبْدُ بِالْعَبْدِ وَالْأُنثَى بِالْأُنثَى فَمَنْ عُفِيَ لَهُ مِنْ أَخِيهِ شَيْءٌ فَاتِّبَاعٌ بِالْمَعْرُوفِ وَأَدَاءٌ إِلَيْهِ بِإِحْسَانٍ ذَٰلِكَ تَخْفِيفٌ مِّن رَّبِّكُمْ وَرَحْمَةٌ فَمَنِ اعْتَدَى بَعْدَ ذَٰلِكَ فَلَهُ عَذَابٌ أَلِيمٌ)

(O you who believe! *Al-Qisas* (the Law of Equality in punishment) is prescribed for you in case of murder: the free for the free, the slave for the slave, and the female for the female. But if the killer is forgiven by the brother (or the relatives, etc.) of the killed against blood money, then adhering to it with fairness and payment of the blood money, to the heir should be made in fairness. This is an alleviation and a mercy from your Lord. So after this whoever transgresses the limits (i.e. kills the killer after taking the blood money), he shall have a painful torment). (please provide the source of this translation)

Surah Al Maʾidah verse 45 states:

(وَكَتَبْنَا عَلَيْهِمْ فِيهَا أَنَّ النَّفْسَ بِالنَّفْسِ وَالْعَيْنَ بِالْعَيْنِ وَالْأَنْفَ بِالْأَنْفِ وَالْأُذُنَ بِالْأُذُنِ وَالسِّنَّ بِالسِّنِّ وَالْجُرُوحَ قِصَاصٌ ۚ فَمَنْ تَصَدَّقَ بِهِ فَهُوَ كَفَّارَةٌ لَهُ ۚ وَمَنْ لَمْ يَحْكُمْ بِمَا أَنْزَلَ اللَّهُ فَأُولَٰئِكَ هُمُ الظَّالِمُونَ)

(And We ordained therein for them: "Life for life, eye for eye, nose for nose, ear for ear, tooth for tooth, and wounds equal for equal." But if anyone remits the retaliation by way of charity, it shall be for him an expiation. And whosoever does not judge by that which Allah has revealed, such are the *Zalimun* (polytheists and wrong-doers - of a lesser degree)).

It can be inferred from the previous two verses that the right to retaliate can be converted into a financial right, meaning that the original right has been replaced with the Diyyah, and it is still an option that the heirs of the victim can exercise. Diyyah was a pre-Islamic custom ('Urf) which was subsequently retained by Islam. In the following lines we will define ʿurf as a secondary source of Islamic law and discuss some customary practices in selects Muslim countries that involve the sale and purchase of financial rights.

URF AND ITS PLACE IN FIQH MUAMALAT

'Urf literally means known. Technically 'Urf is defined as recurring practices which are acceptable to people of sound nature. It refers to the known, familiar and customary practices as opposed to unknown, unfamiliar and strange ones. A custom must represent a common and recurrent phenomenon and should not contravene the principle of Shariah is valid and authoritative. (Kamali, 2011) Urf is recognised as one of the secondary sources of Islamic law. Islam does not exclude the customary practices of the societies provided such practices do not contravene the Quran and the Sunnah.

(please be consistent in using references either all footnotes or APA style like this one)

HAQQ MALI FROM URF PERSPECTIVE

The concept of financial rights "Haqq Mali" has been practiced by Muslims all over the world, in spite of it was not considered as a stand-alone kind of agreement. The customary practises in financial transactions is full of evidences.

A. Rights in *Urf tijari* as practiced worldwide

Looking into more details in customs, more examples of financial rights can be noticed, School Admission Fees is a concept most parent are familiar with especially if their children are reading at a private school or college. Private schools charge a tuition fee which is the actual purchase price for the services they offer, but they also charge an admission fee which entitles the child the right to study at the said school. This fee is non-refundable, no-transferable and is non-negotiable. School admission fees are being charged in Private Schools all over the Muslim world.

Franchise Fees is an excellent example of a fee for rights. A franchise fee involves payment by one party to a principal that entitles the first party the right to sell the products or offer the services of the principal. This is not similar to *Wakalah* as in that instance the *Wakeel* or the agent charges a fee to the principal, whereas in this case the principal charges the agent a fee as it is deemed a privilege that principal allows a certain party to act as an agent. Examples of these are numerous from McDonalds franchise fees to distributors of Sony, Panasonic, LG, Samsung Electronics, all who must pay a fee to the principal that gives them the right to become distributors of the Principal.

B. An example of rights in *Urf tijari* in Pakistan and Syria: *Pugree: Right to be a market participant and Faragh: Right to be the lessee*

Pugree is a custom in Pakistan which is employed in a commodities market called Nankari Bazaar in the city of Rawalpindi. The city has traditional markets like Raja Bazaar, Saraafa Bazaar, Gunj Mandi, and Nankari Bazaar. These markets are wholesale markets and deal in a wide array of spices and commodities. The turnover in Nankari Bazaar has never been calculated as most transactions are in cash but it has been estimated by the funds channelled through the banks to be close to PKR 40 billion a month.

Merchants of each bazaar had typically developed a union or committee, which would approve new entrants into the marketplace. New merchants were screened for credibility, integrity, capital and new entrants had to purchase the right to sit in Nankari bazaar. This right to be a member of the Traders Association of Nankari Bazaar was purchased by new applicants through a system of *Pugree*.

Any merchant that wanted to sell his goods in Nankari Bazaar had to first purchase the Right to be a member of the Traders Association. In current terms this *Pugree* can range anywhere from $500,00 to $ 5,000,000. Any merchant who was approved for membership would then have to purchase or rent his own lot and warehouses to carry out his normal course of business.

Pugree is an example of purchasing a right. The concept is used in other contexts as well and is still the custom of merchants, landlords and tenants in Pakistan. Another variant of *Pugree* is used in renting out commercial property in highly expensive locations. Landlords here converge their rents to a standard market rate which they cannot influence. What they can influence is the amount of *Pugree* they receive. Potential tenants purchase the right to rent highly expensive retail locations. This is an amount over and above the rental amount agreed to in a rental agreement. The lessee can in this case sell this right to a third party (with the consent of the lessor) for a premium, at cost, or at a discount.

Faragh is a customary practice in Syria regarding the transfer of usufruct of assets owned by the government but leased out to another party, as the owner of the asset, the government rents it out to an individual or corporation, the lessee can›t cancel the rental agreement with the government. Instead, the lessee can transfer his right to a third party for a premium payment. The new lessee will be substituted in the government documents through the *Faragh* contract, the premium paid can be as high as the market value of the asset. Basically, it is nothing but a price for transferring his right, since he doesn›t hold ownership to the asset.

Both *Pagree* and *Faragh* are of the same concept that is categorized under financial rights, both of them can serve as evidence of how rights can be traded when the subject matter is in existence.

COMMERCIAL RIGHTS

Commercial rights have existed in pre-Islamic times, in fact since the dawn of mankind. Rights can best be explained through practical examples. For instance, two farmers own grazing land and a watering hole adjacent to each other. The two farmers can exchange their rights over their respective assets by allowing each other to use their assets. This is an ancient example of exchange of rights, but what is fundamental is that rights carried value.

Both of the farmers can grant this right to a third party for other barter services or products or monetary fee as well,

However it may be, rights carried value. In pre-Islamic times and Islamic times, rights to watering holes, pastures, trade routes, right of passage all carried commercial and financial values. One Bedouin tribe may grant the right to another tribe for access to their wells in exchange for right of passage of their caravans through the latter's lands. In pre-modern times such rights were crucial assets at times upheld the status of a certain tribe or community. Certainly the pre-Islamic merchants of Mecca enjoyed the rights of granting other tribes the right to make the pilgrimage to the Ka'aba.

Rights have existed in other forms as well, where great armies were granted access to pass through certain lands belonging to an ally or neutral party. Certainly the granter of such rights could charge a fee or be secure in that the army would forego their right to invade them.

In modern days, rights to use a sovereign country's air space carries financial values. An aircraft of a particular national airline has to pay a fees for crossing the airspace of another country. Similarly rights of passage are granted for ships to enter or pass through a nation's seas to access ports for trade. As mentioned earlier there is scarcely any literature on rights and their commercial values in Islamic Jurisprudence. There is discussion on rights embedded in contracts but there is no discussion of rights as a standalone entity, there is even no discussion on the right to contract as in the case of future sales or options.

SALE, RENT AND SALE OF RIGHTS

In modern and pre-modern days there has existed a wide variety of commercial transactions of which so far 14 have caught the attention of scholars and authors alike. These 14 make up the building block of Islamic Finance and include, salam, istisna, musharikah mudharabah, murbahah, wadiah, ammanah, ibra, kafalah, hawala, wakalah, inah, ijara, hibah, ibra and qard.

We will just step aside and look at subtle differences between contracts of sale and purchase, contracts of ijara, and contracts involving rights. In a contract of sale, there must be an offer and acceptance, there must be a subject matter of the sale, a good or a service, the asset must be deliverable, must be in the possession of the seller and must be in existence (except in salam and istisna). A sale contract concludes with the transfer of ownership of an asset from seller to buyer, this transfer is perpetual and irrevocable. The consideration for a sale is price or *sa'r*. Durable and non-durable goods, both can be the subject of sale. Typically a sale involves one buyer and one seller for ach particular asset. In calculating the price of an asset, the cost of the asset plays a considerable role.

Contracts of ijara are considered as sale of usufruct, where there is no transfer of ownership of assets, just usufruct of an asset. It does not apply to non-durable goods, apples cannot be leased to be eaten. Ijara involves one asset, a lessor who owns the asset and a lessee who leases the asset in exchange for a rental payment or *ujr*. Lease contracts are not perpetual and are revocable. The asset that is leased may or may not be in existence at the time of entering a lease contract. The cost of an asset plays a considerable role in determining the rent charged for it's usufruct. The contract of ijara can be specified for hiring of services as well, and can be specified by duration and purpose. In an ijara contract a lessee can sub-lease the asset he has leased for rental income as well. Suitability of the asset is the charge of the lessor.

In cases that involve stand-alone rights, two parties are involved. One party must enjoy the risks and responsibilities of an asset before granting a counterparty the right to use the asset. it must be in existence. One person can grant several persons rights to the usage of their asset simultaneously. For example, an owner of a garden grants multiple rights to different people to walk through his garden and enjoy the nature charging a fee for that.

Rights can be granted for usage of durable and non-durable goods. There is no transfer of ownership in the granting of rights, they are not perpetual and are revocable. The compensation for granting a right to another party over one's asset is termed as *Rasm* or fee. Costs associated with an asset may not play a major portion in determining a fee, as at times no cost incurred by asset owner. Fee is linked to the importance of the usage if the asset to counterparty. It is the responsibility of the party granting the rights over an asset to maintain the suitability of the asset.

As can be seen the topic of rights justifies its own discourse. Rights are embedded in contracts and at times are independent contracts on their own. The acknowledgement of this can have considerable impact on the future of Islamic Financial Engineering as we explore the boundaries o financial rights.

FINANCIAL RIGHTS

The authors of this paper believe that the modern tool of financial derivatives need to be revisited in the light of Islamic financial engineering. This requires a shift in stance on how to interpret the rights offered by derivatives.

A. Stock Options:

Stock option provide the holder the right to enter into a *Musharikah* contract with other shareholders or exit from a *Musharikah*. An option represents a unit of co-ownership of a company's assets along with other shareholders. A stock call option is a right to purchase a stock, a right to become a shareholder or partner and a put option is a right to sell one's stake in a business.

It is easy to imagine that in pre-modern days merchants would reserve their rights in advance to buy shares in trade caravans. These rights could be purchased for a fee and subsequently be traded with other merchants. If a call option simply reserves the right of a potential buyer to purchase a share in a company, in our opinion this is permissible. A call option is similar to a right of first purchase. Call options are purchased when investors feel the price of a stock is expected to rise. A company's stock price typically rises on the back of good performance or expected performance. A call option holder will then have the first right to buy the company's shares as their prices rise. As with rights, the holder of the right is under no obligation to exercise the rights. He smay choose to exercise his right to buy a company's stock, if he does, he will make an offer to which the seller of the call is bound to accept. To make the structure shariah compliant, naked options can be deemed a impermissible as an option seller must own the asset he is selling an option in. This should limit speculative activity in options.

B. Commodity Options

Options on commodities offer the same rights to issuers and holders as do stock options. The underlying asset however would be a defined quantity of a specific commodity such as metals, steel, copper or gold, or agricultural produce like grain, coffee, rice and so on. Options would allow holders the right (call option) to purchase commodities in the future at a specific price. The seller of the call option must own the asset for which the option is to be sold in. This would greatly limit the potential for speculative activity. In the case of selling a put option, again the seller must own the asset in which he wishes to pay for the right to sell.

The tools of call and put options can be misused but this can be monitored by regulators in terms of limiting the number of daily trades for example.

C. Down Payment ("*Urbun*)

Down Payment or *Urbun* (Earnest Money) is one of the accepted transactions that can be looked at as a practice of a financial right. It's where a Buyer of goods makes a partial advance payment for goods he intends to purchase and will be delivered in the future to bound the seller not to sell the goods to others. In this case, *Urbun* payment grants the buyer a financial right. the cost of this Haqq Mali is losing the down payment if the buyer does not wish to exercise his right.

Would a prudent merchant factor the opportunity cost of tying up his capital in *Urbun* into his sale price. If the value for the right might be the profit rate on deposits for the same tenor or other suitable opportunity cost.

Additionally, if the Buyer subsequently changes his mind and decides not to purchase the goods at delivery, can the *Urbun* be traded and sold to a third party. The deposit can be sold in cost "the exact amount paid" or it can be traded with discount or premium according to market forces. This right is not a debt so rules of debt do not apply. *Urbun* is also not a claim to full or partial ownership, and possibly are not in existence as yet either, as per law of sale, the Buyer cannot sell the goods he does not own.

SHARIAH OPINIONS OF OTHER SCHOLARS ON RIGHTS

(Kamali, 1997) argues on whether compensation is allowed under Shariah by illustrating that the typical *khyiar* (option) that the Sunnah permits is an option of stipulation (*khyiar al shart*) which grants to the buyer the option, limited to a time frame, to either exercise the contract or to cancel it. Under such options, Kamali opined that the Sunnah entitles the parties the freedom to insert stipulations that will "Legitimate needs and what may be of benefit to them. Nevertheless, the liberty that is granted here is subject to the general condition that contractual stipulations may not overrule the clear injunctions of Shariah on halal and haram. Provided that this limitation is observed, in principle, there is no restriction on the nature and type of stipulation that the parties may wish to insert into a contract". (Kamali, 1997). (Please include this source in your Refernces in the last page.

Depending on the general rule of permissibility of financial transaction, Kamali opines that the freedom to insert conditions in contracts can even include the request for monetary compensation. Kamali concludes that the charging a fee for the right granted by options is valid under the Shariah.

Rights are intangible and have no external existence but are presumed by the Shariah to exist as they relate to underlying asset.

Muslim jurists have discussed the issue of inheriting right in the context of options (*Khiyarat*) in a sale contract. For instance, the *Maliki* and *Shafi'I* jurists argue that if the person who holds the option of condition dies, his heirs inherit the option and should be able to exercise it. could be inherited in case if the owner while argue for the heritability of the option of condition. (Zuhaili, pp. 245-160) All Schools of *Fiqh* agree that the option of defect could be inherited (Zuhaili, 261-264). The *Maliki* jurists also argue in favour of the heritability of the option of inspection. These arguments in favour of the heritability of these options imply that they view these options as a property (*mal*) that could be inherited by the heirs in the same way that they inherit other properties. It is therefore argued that the financial value of proprietary or financial rights and ownership over them should be recognised. Such rights should not be taken without the consent of their owner who should also be able to exchange it with mutual consent. In *Urbun*, for instance, the owner of *Urbun* should be able to sell his right to others in case if he does not want to purchase the asset.

CONCLUSION

This paper elaborates on the concept of financial rights (*Haqq Mali*)from *a* Shariah perspective., There are evidences from customary practices ('Urf Tijari) that recognise the financial value of certain rights and their sale and purchase. Sometimes, *Haqq Mali* is embedded in other contracts such as sale or Ijarah. These rights are also sold independently without affecting the status of the underlying asset as seen in customary practices. Haqq Mali can carry a financial value and can also be traded. However, measure should be taken that the sale and purchase of financial rights should not deteriorate into speculation.

The authors of this paper suggest the usage of the concept of financial rights in revisting the discussion on financial derivatives, provided that the underlying subject and the derived financial right are in existence and the ownership over financial right is obtained in a Shariah compliant way and the transaction fulfils the general the general Shariah principles that govern commercial contract. The authors also suggest that more research is needed to explore the various issues involving financial rights.

References

- Iqbal, Imran, Sherin Kunhibava, and Asyraf Wajdi Dusuki. "Application of options in Islamic Finance.", ISRA Research Paper, 2012 No.46
- Kamali, Mohammad Hashim. "Principles of Islamic jurisprudence.", British Library, U.K. (2011): p. 369.
- Zuhaili, Wahbah. *"al-Fiqh al-Islami Wa Adillatuhu"*, Vol. IV (Damascus: Dar al-Fikr, 1989) pp. 8-10.

Kamali, Mohammad Hashim, Islamic Commercial Law

CONCLUSION

We hope that we have walked the reader through the world of derivatives and markets in such a manner that the products make sense. We hope that a new generation of *shariah* scholars can look at the structures favourably and are innovative and progressive in their approach to these products. At the time of writing these books, many of these structures are found on the shelves of Islamic banks across the globe, however, controversy still surrounds many of the underlying principles.

Much of financial engineering in the world of Islamic Finance has been done in Malaysia, and we expect some interesting developments in this arena in Saudi Arabia, Pakistan and Indonesia as well. With more countries opening Islamic Banks, and centres of finance such as Luxembourg, Hong Kong and London making changes to their tax regulations to accommodate Islamic banking, it is likely that complex structures and hedging instruments in the Islamic Banking industry are going to become standard products.

ABOUT THE AUTHORS

Hussain Kureshi (Kuala Lumpur, Malaysia) obtained his degree in Business Administration at Stony Brook University in the US and a Master's degree in Islamic Finance in Malaysia. He has extensive experience in consumer banking, credit risk management, loan origination and monitoring for SME and Commercial clients. Hussein has a lucrative banking career spanning over 15 years specializing in Banking Operations and Management with organizations such as Barclays Bank Plc (Pakistan), Bank Al Habib (Pakistan), Union Bank (Islamabad), Emirates Bank International (Islamabad), Standard Chartered Bank, Commerce Bank (New Jersey, US), and Chase Manhattan Bank (New York, US).

Mohsin Hayat has over 20 years of institutional & international capital market experience. Simultaneously as an entrepreneur & investor, Mohsin Hayat has specialized in creating strategic alliances in over 45 countries and building businesses in New York, Hong Kong and across Asia-Pacific. His success is driven by a keen interest in combining business knowledge and investment management fundamentals. Managing Partner of Millennium Land as well as Senior Advisor & Director of Millennium Capital Management

Septya Iriani Mukhsia (Kuala Lumpur, Malaysia) is a Monash University graduate with a Bachelor's Degree in Business and Commerce, majored in Accounting, Banking and Finance; with a professional qualification specializing in Islamic Finance. Her experience extends in auditing and banking industry within Malaysia and Indonesia. Septya is also a contributor for *Contracts and Deals in Islamic Finance: A User's Guide to Cash Flows, Balance Sheets and Capital Structures* by Hussein Kureshi and Mohsin Hayat.